THE ALAN BOWN SET
BEFORE AND BEYOND

ALAN BOWN
MY STORY

BY
JEFF BANNISTER

First published in Great Britain by:

Banland Publishing Ltd.

Registered Address:-

5 Jupiter House, Calleva Park, Aldermaston, Reading, Berkshire,

RG7 8NN, UK.

Author - Jeff Bannister with Alan Bown

Cover Graphics - Design Smart, UK.
Typesetting and Layout - Design Smart, UK.
Book Design - Design Smart, UK.
www.designsmart.biz

The images in this book have all been sensitively restored to a printable standard, digitally enhanced and formatted by Design Smart. It has been the intention of the publishers to retain the original 'flavour' and atmosphere of all the historic material.

Printed in Singapore

www.banlandpublishing.com

ISBN: 978-0-9551513-2-3

To

My wife Jean, my sister Marion, my brother Ted, my children Nicole and Julian and my grandchildren Lauren and James, all of whom have enriched my life in so many ways.

Memories come flooding back. I first met Alan and the boys in the 60's when they played at my club, The King Mojo.

At the time The King Mojo was becoming one of the most famous clubs in the UK, even though it was nothing more than an old dance hall. I had created something special at the time – I was booking groups from England and America; Georgie Fame and the Blue Flames, Geno Washington and the Ram Jam Band, Graham Bond, Wilson Pickett, Little Stevie Wonder, Ike and Tina Turner and in the midst of all these bands The Alan Bown Set did more than hold their own. They were a big star attraction.

In Sheffield we had never seen anything like The Alan Bown Set. Alan's trumpet was bent at the end, and when I first saw this I thought he had stood on it and broken it but it was one of the things that helps us to remember how talented the band was during this period.

I booked the boys so regularly they became personal friends. Alan Bown, Jeff Bannister, Jess Roden, Stan Haldane, John Anthony, Vic Sweeney and Tony Catchpole, all actually came to my wedding in 1967. The local press called it 'The Wedding of the Flower Children'. There we were, Alan Bown included, in flower-print jackets and flowers in the hair - the lot!

I met the boys when they were a soul band, then they moved into flower power, and before long they would become a progressive band along the same lines as Yes. One thing about the 60's, the bands such as The Alan Bown Set were not only brilliant but loved their time on stage and loved to party.

I do not want to sound like an old fart, but we will never see the like of them again. Madonna miming on MTV will never ever be as good as The Alan Bown Set live on stage at The King Mojo Club in 1967.

PETER J. STRINGFELLOW

ACKNOWLEDGEMENTS

Jeff and I would to thank the following people who have made valuable contributions to the contents of this book;

Julian and Jean Bown, Jenny and Hank Shaw, Randy Jones, Bob Downes, Tony Holly, Roger Sutton, Geoff Leonard, Terry Childs, Stan Haldane, Vic Sweeney, John Anthony Helliwell, Hugh Attwooll, Peter Stringfellow, Paul Stringfellow, Keith Mansfield, John Mansfield, Dave Lawson, Derek Griffiths, Richard 'Plug' Thomas, Trevor Jones, John Jones, Jimmy Kaleth, Mac Poole, Jack Lancaster, Jill Sinclair and Jeff Walden (BBC Archives).

My special thanks go to Jeff Bannister for foraging through reams of press cuttings, diaries, photographs et al, making all the necessary enquiries and leaving no stone unturned to research all the material for this book (and for typing out every word!). Without Jeff's inspired commitment, the book would not have been possible.

Also my thanks to Peter Rutland of Design Smart for his expertise with the graphics, formatting and all design aspects, which has helped to make the publication of this book a reality.

Alan Bown

NB: For authenticity, all press articles and reviews in this book have been reproduced as they originally appeared in the press. Therefore, any spelling or grammatical errors contained therein have not been amended.

FOREWARD

Jeff Bannister and I go back a long way, to October 1964 when I first met him prior to his debut gig with The John Barry Seven. I was leading The Seven at the time and it was the beginning of a long friendship that has continued since our years together in that band and The Alan Bown Set.

As can be seen from the tributes on the back cover of this book, The Alan Bown Set did not go unnoticed. My gratitude goes to Sir Elton John, Phil Collins, and Francis Rossi for their generous quotes.

I also want to thank all of the people who came to see the band and the many journalists and record company executives that supported our cause. The 60's have gone but the great thing is that our music survived and just by playing the album, 'London Swings Live at The Marquee Club', those years come back to life. It's crazy but it doesn't seem that long ago!

The book is not solely about the 60's. It is also the story of my musical career and what inspired me to become a musician. It has been my great privilege to work alongside musicians of the highest calibre and share stages with name bands and artists, many of whom are still around today.

Some say that it is not the 'destination' but the 'journey' through life that enriches us most. The journey I have made is now revealed for the first time in this book, The Alan Bown Set – Before and Beyond.

Alan Bown!

CONTENTS

XB 405448

211615

1 & 2 ELIZ. 2 CH. 20

CERTIFICATE OF BIRTH

Name and Surname Alan James Bown

Sex Boy

Date of Birth Twenty first July 1942

Place of Birth
- Registration District Eton
- Sub-district Slough

Certified to have been compiled from records in the custody of the Registrar General. Given at the General Register Office, Somerset House, London, under the Seal of the said Office, the 22nd day of March 19 63

CAUTION :—*Any person who (1) falsifies any of the particulars on this certificate, or (2) uses a falsified certificate as true, knowing it to be false, is liable to prosecution.*

3a/2343/464

PROLOGUE

In 1942 the world was a much different place.

The Second World War was into its third year and the German Combined Forces had conquered and occupied half of Europe.
The Japanese attack on Pearl Harbour in late 1941 was followed in the New Year with the conquest of Burma and, in swift succession, the capture of the British outpost, Singapore.
In Russia, the battle of Stalingrad began in desperation to repel Hitler's advancing armies.
The Allies were united in their campaign to halt the Nazi war machine with combat on many fronts on land, sea and in the air.
Few major British cities escaped the frequent bombing raids by the German Luftwaffe and London was still reeling from the Blitz of 1941.

At the time, no one knew what the outcome of this war would be and three more years of bitter conflict would have to be endured before its conclusion.

In the war years, radio was the only medium for mass entertainment and the British music scene was dominated by big bands such as, Glenn Miller, Benny Goodman, Geraldo, Victor Sylvester, Joe Loss, Henry Hall, Oscar Rabin and Billy Cotton.
The war also bought certain artists to the fore, namely Arthur Askey, George Formby, Donald Peers, Bud Flanagan and Chesney Allen but particularly Vera Lynn 'the forces sweetheart' whose record 'We'll Meet Again' became an anthem for the troops serving abroad.

It's hard to imagine now, that in those days, there was no television, no home computers, no Internet, no mobile phones and no DVD's or I-Pods. They were all yet to come, as indeed was the music that would be the platform for future bands like The Alan Bown Set.

It was against this backdrop that Edwin and Marion Bown gave birth to their second son, Alan, who relates this story.

Back row: Edwin and Marion Bown (Father and Mother)
Front row: Marion, Alan (me) and Ted

1

INTRO

I was born at home, in the front room of my parent's house in Slough, on the 21st July 1942.

In those days, there was nothing unusual about home births. Hospitals were devoting more time and space to injured servicemen who had returned from the war.

My father was an engineer at a machine factory called G. D. Peters. My mother was a housewife and already had two children, Marion and Ted. Marion was seven years old and Ted was two. Our family lived in a semi-detached house, at 7 Sydney Grove, Slough.

The only significant memory I have of primary school is when I was about four years old and it was there that I met Randy Jones, who would become my best friend. Randy claims that my first words to him were, 'Do you wanna fight?'

When I was eleven years old, my secondary education began at William Penn Secondary Modern School in Slough. It was a boys only school and some of the pupils were hard-cases. You either had to be able to run fast or take care of yourself. Fortunately, I inherited a survival instinct from my father who, it turned out, had a reputation for liking a scrap. Ted, my older brother, went to Slough Grammar School and my sister Marion went to Slough High School for Girls so I faced my schooling without the protection of an older sibling. However, one big bonus for me was that Randy Jones also went to this school.

I became interested in boxing and was schoolboy boxing champion in the flyweight class for about three years. I was also a member of The Slough Centre Boxing Club, during which time I collected several medals. However, I met my match when fighting Johnny Pritchard who later became lightweight champion of the region. The fight was stopped in the second round after my opponent gave me a severe beating and knocked me down. Although he was an aggressive fighter, Johnny was actually a really nice guy and afterwards gave me a lift home. He apologised for the defeat but it heralded the end of my boxing aspirations.

Before enrolling at William Penn, I had started playing the cornet with The Slough Town Military Band, which was based at the Slough Centre Boys Club and rehearsed once a week. The clubhouse was part of The Slough Centre Stadium, the local football ground and was literally only five minutes walk from my house. At ten years old, I was actually too young to join the band but they let me sit in because I was so keen! The band was lead by Sid Brown, a volatile ex-army band leader. He could sometimes be scary and throw his baton at the musicians when they faltered over an arrangement. I was the youngest in the band and the older members were very kind and encouraging towards me so I stayed on until long after I had left school. It was Sid Brown who encouraged me to renounce the cornet and play trumpet. There was a collection of brass instruments that had been left behind by Polish military personnel, who had been posted in Slough during the war, so he as able to loan me a trumpet. It was a Besson silver trumpet that had seen better days but I soon got used to it. The mouthpiece was filthy but my dad took it to his place of work and had it dipped in acid to clean it up. After that it was like a brand new mouthpiece, which I used for years afterwards.

(Photo by courtesy of the Windsor and Slough Express)

The Slough Town Military Band 1956
Back row, second from left, Alan Bown, Keith Mansfield, Tony Holly
Front row centre, The Mayor of Slough and far right, bandleader, Sid Brown

The Windsor, Slough and Eton Express published an article on the 30th November 1956, which was about The Slough Town Military Band. A photo of the band, taken at The Slough Centre Boys Club, accompanied the article and the bold caption above it read, 'Mayor Visits Town Band.'

The original caption under the photo read, 'Mr. Sidney Brown of the new Slough Town Military Band shows the Mayor of Slough (Alderman R. Taylor) how a double bass works when the Mayor called in to hear one of their practice sessions at the Centre Stadium on Sunday.'
No wonder the Mayor looks puzzled. He would have had great difficulty grasping 'how a double bass works' while holding a tuba!

The photo represents only a small proportion of the band, which had around twenty members. Sid Brown would organise marches around the local streets and proudly walk in front with his baton. We would then stop at certain locations and play a couple of tunes from musicals. Sid realised that these would be more popular than military numbers and we would often attract a crowd. He also arranged for us to play at works functions, the proceeds of which went to financing overheads at the club. These appearances introduced me to the concept of playing in public and in effect were my very first live gigs!

It was at The Boys Club that I met the young talented sax player/trombonist, Keith Mansfield, who is still a good friend today. Keith was thirteen at the time and would later emerge as one of Britain's top arrangers and composers. Everyone is familiar with the BBC 'Grandstand' theme, which Keith wrote. I met several other musicians at the club who also became friends of mine like Johnny Butts, the drummer, who went on to play in Ronnie Scott's house band. Among other notable musicians, Johnny worked and recorded with were Tubby Hayes, Ian Carr and Blossom Dearie and he also became a member of The Johnny Dankworth Orchestra. I met Dave Ballinger there, the drummer, who eventually joined The Barron Knights and Cliff Hall the pianist who went on to do session work with Cliff Richard, The Shadows and The Tremeloes. Tony Holly, sax player and close friend of Dave Ballinger, was also a keen member of the club. He first joined local band The Flintstones and then the chart-topping Migil Five. (It was Tony who introduced Dave Ballinger to The Barron Knights). Randy Jones started playing drums when he was about eleven and would sometimes come along to The Boys Club to hear the older kids play, particularly Johnny Butts. Randy would join me for a blow now and again but didn't become a member of The Slough Town Military Band. Years later he went on to join The Maynard Ferguson Orchestra. He also worked with many other luminaries including Gerry Mulligan and Dave Brubeck. Ernie Cox was also a regular at The Boys Club and he later became the drummer in The John Barry Seven when I took over the leadership.

**Slough Centre Boys Club
circa 1958
Dave Ballinger, left and
Alan Bown, watching
Johnny Butts**

2

PAYING MY DUES

After leaving school at 15, I became an apprentice for a firm called Hazel Offset Printing Company on The Slough Trading Estate. I stayed at the printers for a year then went to The Standard Box Company, also on the Trading Estate, making wooden boxes for assorted products like lemonade bottles and items of machinery for home and abroad. It wasn't my idea of a vocation so I was still keenly rehearsing in the evenings with the band at The Boys Club.

During this period, I went along one night to The Dolphin Hotel in Slough with my brother Ted to see the Joe Harriott Quintet. Because of the licensing laws, I was too young to be allowed in but my brother knew the doorman very well and consequently I was spirited in, on the understanding that I didn't have an alcoholic drink.

It was here that I met Henry Shaw (known to everyone as 'Hank') who was playing trumpet with the Quintet and I went up to him in the break to compliment him on his playing. Hank's hero was Dizzy Gillespie and the band played a favourite number of mine, 'Night in Tunisia' during their second set. The drummer in the Quintet was Bobby Orr who also became a good friend of mine.

Soon after that memorable night at The Dolphin Hotel, I started having lessons from Hank who lived in The Archway, near Highgate. I was still working full time at the Standard Box Company so I went to Highgate by train on Saturdays, which took me half a day to get there!

I was heavily influenced by modern jazz players, particularly trumpet players like Miles Davis, Clifford Brown, Dizzy Gillespie and Jimmy Dukas, to name a few so Hank encouraged me to make regular trips to The Marquee Club in London, which was in Oxford Street at the time, to see various bands like, The Harry South Quintet, The Tubby Hayes Quintet and Phil Seamen's Band. I also went to various venues around London to see other bands on the jazz scene.

Hank also played in The South London Jazz Orchestra, which he introduced me to and I sat in on several gigs, playing venues like the Bull's Head in Barnes.

In May 1960 Hank was offered a residency with the Danny Mitchell Orchestra in Redcar, Yorkshire. The sax player with the orchestra, Johnny Rogers had recommended him. Hank and his wife, Jenny moved up to Redcar and, after a month I had a letter from Jenny, saying that the house they were renting had a spare room and I was welcome to stay at any time.

I decided that I had had enough of my day job and after I had worked my notice, I went up to Redcar. Jenny recalls; 'Alan came up by train, originally for a music lesson from Hank. He ended up staying with us for seven months!'

Hank had already settled into the residency at The Pier Ballroom, Redcar. He used to bring home his music scores of the Danny Mitchell tunes and also the parts for the 2nd and 3rd trumpet. This gave me the opportunity to blow through the tunes and familiarise myself with them. I used to go along to the ballroom most nights for a listen and soon got to know the members of the band. Danny Mitchell was the bandleader and keyboard player, Hank Shaw was playing lead trumpet and John Rogers/alto sax.

Back row: Alan Bown (centre) with Hank Shaw on his left
Redcar 1960

Hank suggested to Danny that I sat in one night and I became an unpaid part-time member, playing 2nd or 3rd trumpet. It was hard work for the resident horn players to blow three hours a night, six nights a week, so they welcomed the opportunity to have a break and let me sit in.
Danny was impressed with my playing, not realising that I had been practising the parts at Hank's! The band member playing 3rd trumpet then decided to leave and, after negotiating a fee with Danny Mitchell, I took his place for the remainder of my stay.

During this period, Jenny and I went to Newcastle to see visiting jazz legend, Miles Davis. It was the first time I had seen Miles 'live' and it was a fantastic experience. He was a one off and a great influence, although Hank was my original inspiration.

I came back to London in January 1961 and briefly moved into my parent's house. At this point, I signed on the dole or National Assistance as it was called in those days. My father wasn't happy with this. He thought I should get a job and regard music only as a hobby but, after the experience in the Danny Mitchell Orchestra, I knew that I wanted a career in music.

When Hank and Jenny returned from Redcar, they moved into a flat in Linden Gardens, Notting Hill, London. Hank was soon offered work in Germany and while he and Jenny were there, I occupied a room in their flat. Jenny still reminds me of the time I emerged from my room in a slick double-breasted suit, with a tab collar shirt and she said, 'It's Steve McQueen!'

Hank Shaw went on to play with bands led by Tubby Hayes, Johnny Dankworth, Harry South, Stan Tracey and a host of others but it would be The Bebop Preservation Society that maintained a thread through his long and illustrious career.

Although I was now living in Notting Hill Gate, I still made trips to The Slough Centre Boys Club to have a blow with the band. One Saturday, the RAF Band played at the local football ground, which was adjacent to the clubhouse and after the match I got talking to the musicians. They encouraged me to apply for an audition at the RAF School of Music in Uxbridge and the next day I wrote off for the forms. Without realising all the implications of this decision, I was committing myself to being a full time musician. My father was disappointed when I told him that I had applied to join the RAF as a bandsman. He thought I had taken a soft option. As a young man, he had been a corporal in the Army and was posted to India. Although he didn't see any combat he thought that being a soldier in the Army was more 'manly' than being in the RAF. There was always a rivalry between the services and he disdainfully referred to RAF servicemen as 'Brylcreem boys'!

3

THE RAF AND THE EMBERS

I passed the audition and joined the RAF when I was eighteen as a full time bandsman in The Central Band at the Uxbridge RAF Base. There, I met some great talented players. I became friends with Bob Downes who played all the saxes and flute. He was a great player and his style of blowing reminded me of Archie Shepp. Bob was older than me and had actually been 'called up', which meant compulsory military service. I also met John Stevens, the drummer who eventually became a legend on the avant-garde jazz scene in London. He crossed paths with trombonist Paul Rutherford and saxophonist Trevor Watts in The Central Band and they later went on to form The Spontaneous Music Ensemble. Another memorable member of The Central Band was bass player Herbie Flowers who also played amazing tuba! He later became a notable session musician, recording with, among others, David Bowie and Elton John. I also met Ray Edmonds there who would become the sax player in The Embers, my first professional band.

In the summer of 1961, during my period at RAF Uxbridge, I spent one Saturday evening in a dance hall that was situated over the Essoldo Cinema in Slough. I often went there with Randy Jones because the resident band sometimes encouraged musicians to sit in with them for a blow. At the end of the evening, after everyone had made their way out of the building, Randy and I noticed two girls walking down the road and one of them caught my eye. I took the initiative and spoke to one of the girls who told me her name was Jean Blackman. She agreed to meet me for a date the next day and has never let me forget that I was late! Jean was 17 and I was 19. Three years later we would be married.

Meeting other musicians was the up-side of being in the RAF. The down-side was that I then had to go through a rigorous six week training programme at Henlow RAF Camp, which involved mostly marching up and down the parade ground in all weathers.

As a musician, I hadn't anticipated these spates of square bashing and the weeks of purgatory made me want to quit. To add to my misery certain non-musicians who had signed up merely as combatants took their wrath out on me, the slight-framed, blonde haired recruit and called me names like, 'pansy' and made other intimidating sexual remarks. Bob Downes, seeing my vulnerability, frequently came to my rescue and made it his business to look after me. It wasn't that I couldn't look after myself but bullies rarely come alone and the last thing I wanted was a split lip.

Jazz was looked down upon by our mentors in the RAF and some of the musicians became so fed up with the routine that they deliberately pretended to be crazy. At Henlow all kinds of bizarre antics were going on. Sometimes the marching on the parade ground would become chaotic with musicians deliberately tripping over or turning at the wrong time. Bob Downes was one of the main culprits and he had us all creased up. He and I would sometimes be put on a charge and we had to report to the guardroom three times a day, where we were constantly reminded to get our haircut!

Henlow Training Camp was not far from Hitchin and, on weekends when the opportunity presented itself, Bob and I would play there in a pub with a band, which included other RAF musicians. It was a great chance to blow a few jazz standards and some original tunes that Bob had written. The landlord was very keen on music and welcomed us anytime, even at short notice.

Bob has since managed to find a photo of us appearing at the pub, which is reproduced here.

Hitchin circa 1962
Alan Bown, left and Bob Downes

I hated the cold and damp living quarters at Henlow Camp and I still hold the belief that these conditions contributed to me getting fluid on the lungs. I was diagnosed with this complaint and, although I had treatment for it, the medical staff decided that I was unfit to continue my career in the RAF and I was eventually discharged. It got me out of the RAF but it took a long while to restore my lungs back into good working order. My recovery was aided by my old friend Hank Shaw, who introduced me to a term of extensive breathing exercises.

The RAF may not have been the most satisfactory of musical experiences but it paid my way and more importantly introduced me to some great players, some of whom I would cross paths with in the future.

 I next began gigging on and off with The South London Jazz Orchestra and Gary Boyle sometimes sat in as a dep guitarist. At the time, he was also in a band called The Embers and although they didn't have a trumpet player he mentioned me to the leader Roger Sutton, who invited me along to one their rehearsals. It went very well and after a couple of rehearsals Roger offered me the gig, which I gladly accepted.
The line up of the band was Roger Sutton/leader/bass guitar, Gary Boyle/guitar, Ray 'Spud' Deville/keyboards, Ray Edmonds/tenor sax, whom I first met in the RAF, Randy Jones/drums and myself on trumpet.
The Embers played a regular three-night residency at The Café des Artistes, situated on the corner of Redcliffe Gardens and the Fulham Road, London.

On 22nd March 1963, my first passport was issued.

I went abroad for the first time with The Embers on the 28th March. We travelled by ferry to Ostende then drove to Germany. We took a girl singer with us called Tania Stevens and played residencies in clubs for two weeks in Brunswick, two weeks in Hannover and four weeks in Bremen. The Hannover club in which we played was called The Savoy and it was just across the road from the Top Ten Club.

When we returned from Germany, Roger Sutton learned that our agent had started booking other bands into The Café des Artistes and had consequently jeopardised our residency.

At this juncture, The Embers went their separate ways. Roger Sutton later reformed the band but, before then, my career took a significant turn.

The Embers (part of) circa 1963
From left to right: Ray Edmonds, Alan Bown and Ray 'Spud' Deville

The John Barry Seven circa 1963
Back row left to right: Ray Russell, Dave Richmond, Bobby Graham,
Ron Edgeworth and Terry Childs
Front row left to right: Bob Downes and Alan Bown

4

THE JOHN BARRY SEVEN

I was playing a gig with The South London Jazz Orchestra during The 1963 Richmond Jazz Festival when Len Black, a member of John Barry's Agency, approached me with a proposition. He arranged a meeting for me with John Barry whom I subsequently met at his London office in Soho. There, I first met John's secretary and personal assistant, Miss Ackers, who was very kind to me and made me feel welcome. John and I hit it off straight away. He explained that he needed a trumpet player for The John Barry Seven and, on Len Black's recommendation, offered me the position.

The John Barry Seven was a popular band long before I joined. John Barry had already had major chart success with Adam Faith and the now legendary James Bond Theme. Back in 1961, because of growing commitments, he had decided that he could no longer tour with The Seven but, rather than break up the band, he let it continue under the leadership of guitarist Vic Flick with Bobby Carr on trumpet. Vic Flick eventually left The Seven in 1963, Bobby Carr also moved on and John Barry, who had been using drummer Bobby Graham for session work, persuaded him to take over the leadership.

I joined The John Barry Seven in September 1963 when Bobby Graham was still the leader. I was 21 years old and played my first gig with The Seven at The Locarno Ballroom in Coventry in October 1963. Apart from Bobby Graham/leader/drums, already in the band were, Ray Russell/guitar, Terry Childs/baritone sax, Ron Edgeworth/keyboards, (later replaced by Tony Ashton), Ray Styles/bass, (later replaced by Dave Richmond) and Bob Downes/tenor & alto sax, whom I had originally met in the RAF.

It was great to work with Bob again and as usual he had some daft routines, which amused the band. When we played out in the sticks, he would sometimes tell everyone there was a great new dance in London called The Windmill. He would demonstrate this by flailing his arms in time with the music and encourage the audience to copy him. Inevitably, some of them were gullible enough to do this but it was such a ridiculous spectacle that I had to look away or risk blowing out tune. Even though John Barry was now no longer in The Seven, audiences were none the wiser and people would sometimes approach the band to ask which one of us was John Barry.

Bob and I would take it in turns to say that he was, or that I was. As far as I know, no one disputed this and fortunately we were never caught out but I'm afraid it means that there is a few forged John Barry autographs out there!

When Bobby Graham left the band, John Barry appointed me as leader. I then offered the vacant drum position to Ernie Cox who was a friend of mine from my schooldays and at the time in a local band. There were a number of other personnel changes in The Seven, which eventually led to this penultimate line-up; Alan Bown, leader/trumpet, Mike O'Neil/lead vocals/keyboards, Ron Menicos/lead guitar, Stan Haldane/bass, Dave Green/tenor sax/flute and Ernie Cox/drums. Bob Downes left to pursue other ventures but Terry Childs stayed on playing baritone and alto sax.

It was Terry who introduced Stan Haldane to The Seven. Terry had been depping at The Café des Artistes in Fulham and had met Stan there playing bass in a band called The Counts, a name which Stan says was sometimes deliberately mispronounced (as you can imagine). He also recalls The Counts alternating sets with Chico Arnaz, who had quite a following. Stan's first gig with The Seven was at The Floral Hall in Scarborough.

Our stage repertoire at the time included; 'Sack of Woe', 'Cutty Sark', 'Image', 'Honky Tonk', 'Let There Be Drums', 'Walk Don't Run', 'Peter Gunn', 'Gurney Slade', 'Hit and Miss', 'The Magnificent Seven', 'From Russia with Love', 'Coming Home Baby', 'The Human Jungle', 'Night Train', 'Water Melon Man', a dramatic version of 'I Who Have Nothing' and of course, 'The James Bond Theme'.

In November 1963 The Windsor, Slough and Eton Express interviewed me and an article appeared on the 29th November, in their 'Showbiz' column. It was entitled; 'Alan, 21, Now Plays With Top Pop Group.'

The agency for The John Barry Seven was the Harold Davidson Organisation and Dick Katz booked out the band, which continued to tour the UK, playing mostly one-nighters. We all travelled together in a Bedford van with our equipment and a driver called Len. On stage the band wore collarless shiny maroon mohair suits (visible in the early photographs) and I wore a light grey suit of the same style. We also used pancake make up on our faces to prevent the stage spotlights making us look anaemic but there was a price to pay for this 'tanned' image. Firstly, the collars on our white shirts soon bore witness to an orange/brown discolouration at the point of contact with the neck and secondly, we would get some very strange looks from people in the local pub or café, ten minutes before the show was due to start. Seven guys in shiny suits wearing make-up entering a pub in somewhere like Kings Lynn on a Wednesday night, certainly turned heads!

The John Barry Seven circa 1963
Back row left to right: Bobby Graham, Alan Bown, Bob Downes and Terry Childs
Front row left to right: Dave Richmond (in shades), Ron Edgeworth and Ray Russell

A Corporation of Weston-super-Mare Entertainment

General Manager: B. H. Flavell

WINTER GARDENS PAVILION
"SATURDAY DANCE DATE"

MEET THE COUNTRY'S TOP
BANDS, GROUPS, and PERSONALITIES
WINE and DINE IN THE GRILL ROOM

8 to 11.45 p.m.

6th February
THE JOHN BARRY SEVEN

13th February
THE JACK DORSEY BIG BAND

20th February
BILLY J. KRAMER & THE DAKOTAS

27th February
THE APPLEJACKS

6th March
THE ANIMALS

13th March
JOE BROWN and THE BRUVVERS

20th March
KENNY BALL with his JAZZMEN

27th March
BOB MILLER and his MILLERMEN

(Subject to alteration — see weekly advertisements for full details)

Tickets & Table Reservations obtainable in advance at the Winter Gardens Pavilion Booking Office — open daily 10 a.m. to 1 p.m. & 2.30 p.m. to 9 p.m. (Sunday from 2.30 p.m.) Tel. Weston-super-Mare 512

G. & M. Organ, Wrington, Bristol.

WINTER GARDENS - BOURNEMOUTH
Manager: SAMUEL J. BELL

Programme

Sunday, 23rd August, 1964 at 6.00 and 8.30 p.m.

1
2
3   The John Barry Seven
4   Ray Fell introduces
5   STEVE PERRY
    Ray Fell introduces
6   interval   THE SEEKERS
7
8   The John Barry Seven
9   The Barry Sisters
    Ray Fell
    THE BACHELORS

General Manager (for George Black Ltd.) ... ... Harold Boyes
Manager (for George and Alfred Black) ... ... Peter Panario
Stage Manager (for George and Alfred Black) ... ... Anthony Beeston
Stage Manager (for Bournemouth Corporation) ... Barrington Kemble

NEXT SUNDAY at 6.00 and 8.30 p.m.
George and Alfred Black present
The Fabulous
SHIRLEY BASSEY
KENNY BALL
and his JAZZMEN
12/6   10/6   9/6   7/6   NOW BOOKING

Early in 1964 I urged John Barry to let the band record a single and we went into the studio to record a track called '24 Hours Ago'. The song had a bluesy feel about it, which suited Mike O'Neil's voice and his style of organ playing. On the B-side (remember those?) was an instrumental co-written by myself and Keith Mansfield, called 'Seven Faces'. Keith also played trombone on the track. Shortly after we recorded the single '24 Hours Ago', keyboard player Mike O' Neil decided to leave The John Barry Seven. He agreed to stay on until I could find a suitable replacement.

Jean, Alan, Terry Childs, Ray Russell and Ron Edgeworth
March 1964

The Slough Observer on 21st February 1964 printed a picture of Jean and me. I was shown blowing the trumpet and the caption read;
'Jazz trumpeter, Alan Bown, who plays with the John Barry Seven, strikes a romantic note for 20 year old Jean Blackman, the fan he fell in love with while appearing at The Essoldo. They are marrying at St Paul's Church next month.'

Jean and I were married in St Paul's Church, Stoke Road, Slough at 1.30 on Saturday the 7th March 1964. The best man was my brother, Ted. Terry Childs, Ray Russell, Dave Richmond and Ron Edgeworth of The John Barry Seven also attended the wedding. Hank Shaw and Ernie Cox were also guests. Some of the guys had to rush off to a gig before the reception ended. Typical of musician's life styles then and now. We had a week's honeymoon in Weston Super Mare and when we returned from our honeymoon, we moved into Jean's mother's house in Maple Crescent, Slough.

The John Barry Seven circa 1964
Left to right: Ernie Cox, Jeff Bannister, Dave Green, Ron Menicos,
Stan Haldane and Terry Childs
Centre front: Alan Bown

5

A NEW FACE

In the autumn of 1964, I was invited to be a judge on the panel of a talent contest in The Slough Community Centre. Also on the panel was music agent Sidney Rose. Being concerned about finding a replacement for Mike O'Neil, I asked him if he knew any keyboard players who could sing. He recommended a musician who had his own band that Sidney's agency booked out on a regular basis. He said he would contact the guy and see if he was interested.

The following day he rang Jeff Bannister. The band that Jeff had originally put together was called The Five Statesmen (because of their regular appearances at The Empire State ballroom in Kilburn) and it had since merged with Rey Anton to become the latest incarnation of Rey Anton and The Peppermint Men. There were a few gigs in the book but Jeff found Rey Anton's repertoire unchallenging, being mostly R&B 12 bars, so he was ready for a change.

Jeff rang me that same day and I told him we had two days of rehearsal booked for the following week. He agreed to come down to Slough then and meet the other musicians for a blow but, three days later, I had an unexpected call from Mike O'Neil to tell me that he'd decided to quit the band and wouldn't be doing the two scheduled JB7 gigs over the weekend!

The John Barry Seven could hardly go out as a six-piece so I made a frantic phone call to Jeff and asked him if he could do the gigs, Saturday and Sunday. It meant, of course, that there would be no time for him to rehearse or get acquainted with the repertoire. He agreed and I arranged to meet him at midday Saturday, on the way to the gig.

We were still travelling to gigs in the Bedford van with our driver/road manager Len and the band had just taken a new consignment of WEM equipment from Charlie Watkins. The two PA columns were long and narrow and doubled as seats in the back of the van, which incidentally had no side windows. Anyone looking through the windows of the back doors at the two rows of musicians seated facing each other, would have thought the scene to be reminiscent of a World War Two Anderson shelter! However, for Jeff Bannister, the bombshell hadn't yet dropped.

I met Jeff, as planned, outside Paddington Station on Saturday the 3rd of October 1964. He was 21 years old, six months younger than me. Jeff was the last 'pick-up' on the route so the other musicians were already in the van. He piled in the back and was introduced to everyone.

We travelled out of London and then on the A11 to Norwich. (There was no M11 motorway in those days. In fact there were only two motorways in England; the M4, which ended at Maidenhead and the MI, which ended at Northampton where the Blue Boar motorway services was and still is).

During the journey I showed Jeff the dots of the tunes in the set. Numbers like, 'The James Bond Theme', 'Magnificent Seven', 'From Russia with Love' etc. The other guys enthusiastically sang some of the top lines to help out. Half way up the A11, someone said, 'I wonder what numbers Marty will do tonight.'

Now Jeff, having been introduced to everyone, none of whom were named Marty, wondered who they were talking about, so he said to me, 'Who's Marty?'

The casual reply from one of the guys was, 'Marty Wilde, we're backing him tonight.' For Jeff, it was a bombshell. Not only had he to cope with music parts he'd never seen before but he had to back Marty Wilde as well and Marty was still a big name in those days!

We arrived at The Samson and Hercules Ballroom in Norwich in good time to set up the gear with the help of Len our driver. Some of the new WEM equipment was in cases and, after everyone had decided what was what, we were left with one curious box which when unfolded revealed itself to be a Farfisa organ. Jeff had never played one of these before and it had a variety of buttons along the top that were supposed to reproduce the classic sounds of a pipe organ. It certainly wasn't Rock 'n' Roll!

Synthesisers hadn't yet been invented so, for keyboard players, there was little choice of portable electric instruments on the market. Some still favoured mic-ing up upright pianos but then you were at the mercy of the venue's piano, often noticeably out of tune. However, Jeff got stuck in and not only had to negotiate the bank of sounds but also had to balance the sheet music on the top of the organ.

The John Barry Seven played the opening set, which went down well. Jeff handled the keyboards well and I was pleasantly surprised with his vocal ability on the two or three songs in the set. He settled in quickly and gave the impression of being confident. Marty Wilde joined The Seven for the second set. He had worked with the band before so he was quite happy with our backing. The ballroom was packed and his performance went down a storm.

We drove back to London that night and met up again the following day for the next gig, which was at Sussex University. This time we weren't backing anyone but the pressure was still on for Jeff, coping with more tricky arrangements.

That night, also on the bill, was Pink Floyd. It was one of their early gigs and we stood and watched them in fascination as, to us seasoned musicians, it appeared that none of them were accomplished players or singers. Our verdict was quite damning but what did we know?
Their star was about to rise. Ours was about to fade.

One thing that was positive about the night was that Jeff Bannister proved himself to be the right choice of keyboard player.

The general consensus from the other musicians was that he could deliver, he looked the part and the suit fitted him perfectly! Although I'd already made up my mind before asking the other guys for their opinion, I approached Jeff and offered him the position on keys and vocals. He was delighted.

We got into rehearsals, as scheduled, the following week in Slough at The Dolphin Hotel. We had always included at least four vocal numbers in the set and now introduced some new songs, which suited Jeff's voice and had strong brass riffs. Stan Haldane and Dave Green added some useful harmonies.

Some of the songs were from the catalogues of popular American recording artists at the time like, The Impressions, featuring Curtis Mayfield and also Major Lance. For example, 'It's Alright', 'I Need You' 'Little Boy Blue' and 'Um Um Um Um Um Um', later recorded by Wayne Fontana and The Mindbenders who had a hit with it (after hearing us perform it!).
We used to open our set with the old classic, 'Let the Good times Roll', which became a sort of signature tune for the rest of The Seven's career.

Almost immediately, we made several appearances at The Adelphi Cinema in Slough. We contrived a dramatic moment when I would move to the side of the stage during The James Bond Theme. At the climax of the chorus, with the spotlight on me, I would pull out a starting pistol and fire two or three shots into the air. One night I took the pose at the appropriate moment, took out the gun and pulled the trigger but to my dismay the blanks didn't fire. Just a few pathetic clicks could be heard! The band all looked at me with crinkly smiles. I abandoned the idea after that.

Today of course, I would be carted off by the Anti-Terrorist Squad for brandishing a firearm in a public place.

We then played a two-week residency in The J.M. Ballroom in Dundee. This was run by a promoter, who at first thought we were a dance band that played Victor Sylvester-type tunes.

On the first gig we had a bad argument over this and the promoter said if we didn't play what he wanted to hear he would throw us out. He made it clear he had thrown Emile Ford down the steps of the ballroom and would take no nonsense from us. However, after our first night's performance it was clear that the crowd loved our music.

The following night, the audience returned for more of the same and the promoter's fears were forgotten. After that, he became much friendlier and we had a good laugh with him.

The single '24 Hours Ago / Seven Faces' was released by EMI around this time but was given little promotion and failed to attract much attention. Although Jeff had personalised the song for our stage show, it rapidly became past tense as we moved on and introduced new songs.

6

ON TOUR WITH BRENDA LEE

The George Cooper Organisation engaged The John Barry Seven for The Brenda Lee Tour, which was scheduled to commence in the UK on 14th November1964.

The itinerary appeared in the music press and is reproduced here;

November 1964

14th	Hammersmith Odeon
16th	Finsbury Park Astoria
17th	Chelmsford Odeon
20th	Handsworth & Oldhill Plazas*
21st	Dunstable California*
22nd	Tooting
23rd	Maidstone
26th	Dublin Adelphi
27th	Belfast ABC
28th	Boston Gliderdrome*

December 1964

1st	Sheffield
4th	Bristol Colston Hall
5th	Norwich
6th	Wakefield
8th	Bedford
9th	Kettering
10th	Walthamstow
11th	Slough
12th	Blackpool

* These venues were ballrooms, the others were mostly cinemas.

Brenda Lee had come over from the USA with her husband and manager especially for the tour and it was the first time I had met her. I thought she was a sweetheart and her husband was fine, but her manager Dub Albritten, was a slick American with an intimidating persona,

THE

George Cooper Organisation Ltd.

Presents

The John Barry Seven

Bob Bain

The Tornados

Heinz and the Wild Boys

Marty Wilde

BRENDA LEE

God Save the Queen

This programme is subject to alteration at the discretion of the management.

TOUR MANAGEMENT AND ADMINISTRATION: HARRY DAWSON & MARK FORSTER

In accordance with the requirements of the L.C.C. and the various Watch Committees of the cities and towns of this tour :
1 The public may leave at the end of the performance by all exit doors and such doors must at that time be open. 2 All gangways, passages and staircases must be kept entirely free from chairs or any other obstructions 3 Persons shall not in any circumstances be permitted to stand or sit in any of the gangways intersecting the seating or to sit in any of the other gangways. If standing be permitted in the gangways at the sides and rear of the seating, it shall be strictly limited to the number indicated in the notices exhibited in those positions. 4 The safety curtain (where applicable) must be lowered and raised in the presence of each audience. 5 No smoking shall be allowed to take place on the stage except as part of a performance or entertainment.

★ Get your favourites to autograph their pictures ★

so the atmosphere wasn't exactly one of bonhomie with him around.
At the beginning of November, we rehearsed with Brenda Lee in the foyer of The Granada Cinema, Walthamstow. An earlier incarnation of The John Barry Seven had backed Brenda on her previous visit to England but her repertoire was new to the current members and it produced some head scratching on the first day. We were also engaged to back Marty Wilde on the tour and, having worked with him before, we had no problems with his songs.

Before the UK dates, Brenda had a series of gigs booked in Europe opening at the Paris Olympia then making appearances at USA air bases in Germany. It was arranged for The John Barry Seven to back her at these venues.

We flew to Le Bourget airport in France on the 3rd November 1964 with Brenda Lee, her husband Ronnie and manager, Dub Albritten, whom we had now secretly nicknamed 'Rub-a-dub-dub'. Brenda was only 19 at the time and her husband, was not much older. Ronnie was about six foot two and towered over his wife who was just under five feet tall. He was a fresh faced chap and in contrast to Brenda's manager, very friendly towards us. On our arrival at the airport he faced a dilemma. The aerosol spray containers in Brenda's make-up case had ruptured in the un-pressurised compartment of the plane and had covered all the contents with foam. While he was cleaning this up in the gent's washroom he said to Jeff and Ernie, 'Brenda will go crazy if she sees this.' Then, trying to illustrate to us that Brenda was less worldly than he was, he added, 'You know, Brenda's so naïve, she didn't even know what a queer was, until she married me.' Everyone laughed, but not all for the same reason.

We were booked with Brenda Lee to play two shows at The Paris Olympia, a theatre with a vast auditorium. When we drove up to the venue, to our astonishment, a large poster adorning the front of the building proclaimed, 'Brenda Lee avec Le Jamboree Seven'. Something had been drastically lost in translation!

We played the first set of the first show and there was little response until we began 'The James Bond Theme'. It was almost comical to see the transformation of the sedate audience. They suddenly changed into raving dervishes, leaping out of their seats as they realised we were, The John Barry Seven and not The Jamboree Seven. The audience reaction to us unnerved Brenda's manager so much that he cut down our set from 45 minutes to 20 for the second show. We were angry at this decision but had no choice in the matter. This was also a sign of things to come.
Jeff recalls, 'When Brenda made her entrance on to the stage to The Seven playing the intro of 'Tell Me What I Say', she strode past the organ, took off her cloak and unthinkingly draped it over the keyboard! I was horrified to see the keyboard and the music on top of it suddenly disappear, but rather than disrespectfully throw the garment on to the floor in front of an adoring full house, I completed the opening number by holding up the cloak with one hand and playing the keys with other! After the song ended, I folded up the cloak and quickly gave it to someone in the wings.'

We stayed in a hotel in Paris that night and, when we were about to leave in the morning, the hotel manager stopped us in the foyer and discreetly informed us that the bill had not been paid. It had been previously agreed that Brenda Lee's management would pay this in advance. After a frantic phone call to Dub Albritten is was clear we would have to stump up the hotel bill or re-enact scenes from the French Revolution. Rather than face the guillotine we paid the bill and left under a dark cloud, unimpressed with this fait accompli.

We next appeared at the Star Club, Hamburg where the Beatles had last played in 1962 and it had now become a legendary venue. This gig had been slotted into our itinerary and as Brenda Lee did not appear at this venue we were billed as the main attraction.

Unlike most clubs, the stage had curtains and The John Barry Seven was poised behind them awaiting the cue to begin playing. As we began with the intro of 'Let the Good Times Roll', the curtains opened and swirled across the stage, taking Jeff's boom-stand and microphone with them!

The band got to the part of the song where the vocals come in and turned to face Jeff but then realised to their astonishment that his mic had disappeared! He had to shout the words to bring the band back in. Fortunately, the audience realised what had happened and found it very amusing. The mic was quickly re set-up and the gig went perfectly well from then on. We were told beforehand that, if the club liked the band, the spotlights would flash and swing in approval. After our performance they did so, prompting a well received encore.

The next tour date was at an American Air Base in Bielefeld, Germany. Here we had a showdown in the office with Dub Albritten, over the money that we were still owed. I said that if we didn't get the cash we would not go on stage and the gig would have to be abandoned. There was a full house of USA army personnel in the mess hall and the whole affair could have turned very ugly. Dub picked up a heavy object from the desk and made a threatening gesture with it towards us. Ernie Cox, the drummer said, 'Oh that's capital, capital!' suggesting that the primitive behaviour of this uncouth American fell well beneath acceptable English standards.

Brenda Lee was seated at the office desk on a high swivel-chair and had taken this all in without comment. She suddenly stood up and, bizarrely, it occurred to everyone that she looked shorter standing up than when she was sitting down! However, she was clearly distressed by the whole scenario and said to everyone including Dub, 'Boy's, you make me feel so small'. (This is absolutely true - Alan).

We got paid in cash and played the gig. However, it was the beginning of the end of our association with Brenda, which was sad because we all liked her as a person but felt that her manager was a shyster.

Before our return to England, I made it clear to Dick Katz at the Harold Davidson Agency that The John Barry Seven would not work with Brenda Lee again under the management of Dub Albritten. For the second part of the tour it was therefore arranged for Brenda to be backed by The Bobby Patrick Big Six, who were added to the tour for that specific reason.

Bern Elliot & The Klan opened the show and were followed by Heinz & The Wild Boys. Johnny Kidd & The Pirates closed the first half. As before, The John Barry Seven opened the second half with 'Let the Good Times Roll'. We had a fifteen-minute set then stayed in position while Marty Wilde was introduced and then joined us on stage. Marty was always easy going with us, confident that he had experienced musicians behind him. In fact, at one point, he asked me if The Seven could become his backing band. I was not opposed to the idea but told him he would have to contact John Barry's office, as I didn't have the authority to make such a decision. I thought the idea had merit and discussed it with John Barry, pointing out that Marty would only be doing a moderate amount of gigs and we could fit The John Barry Seven around his schedule. Although the band had previously backed artists on many tours, John felt that the uniqueness of The John Barry Seven would be compromised by a regular commitment to one artist and therefore he vetoed the idea.

On some of the shows the tour was joined by The Tornados and on others, Wayne Fontana & The Mindbenders. The compere of the show was Bob Bain.

The opening night was a great success and Brenda's nickname; 'Little Miss Dynamite' was well deserved. She had a tremendous voice and was a great performer. She was a true professional.

The tour dates were mostly in cinemas and all artists had to use the Tannoy House PA, which wasn't really designed for much more than announcements so the quality of amplification left much to be desired. There was no out-front mixing desk with a sound engineer and the sort of on-stage monitor system you see today at music concerts was non-existent in 1964. As for backing tracks and lip-syncing, it was still science fiction. How many artists of today would have survived in such an environment, I wonder?

The show at Chelmsford Odeon was reviewed in the 24th November edition of The Braintree, Witham and Dunmow Herald. It was a full-page review, featuring photos of The John Barry Seven; Marty Wilde and Brenda Lee together, (autographing a pound note for a fan!);

Heinz and Johnny Kidd & The Pirates.

The review had the headline, 'The Brenda Lee Show – at the Odeon' and is reproduced here;

'Chelmsford Odeon has witnessed many 'On Stage' shows in recent years and Monday's Brenda Lee Show was in all probability the best of the lot. The supporting acts were solid and professional without raising the roof but in half-an-hour of sheer magic Brenda Lee, so aptly dubbed 'Miss Dynamite' had a near capacity crowd screaming for more. The diminutive 19-year-old spellbinder from America is surely one of the most versatile and remarkable performers in the world and this visit will have confirmed that fact for the patrons whose first sight this was of Brenda. Bern Elliott and The Klan opened the show in strong fashion. Elliott, a dark eligible Londoner, who not so long ago broke away from his old backing group, 'The Fenmen', performed two of the numbers which have carried him into the charts, 'New Orleans' and 'Money' and in more subdued vein gave a first public airing to the ballad 'Guess Who', which will be his next record release. Next came Heinz, just back from a tour of Australia. But his spot was marred by such massive backing from his group, The Wild Boys, that his own voice was often barely audible. He impressed the female audience with a series of agile, sinuous movements around the stage, sang several familiar numbers including 'My Baby Left Me' 'Please Little Girl' a tumultuous rendering of 'Hound Dog' and finally 'You Keep A Knocking' which brought the shrill of teenage screams to a crescendo. Johnny Kidd, complete with traditional eye patch, and The Pirates, also impressed with several of the numbers which have brought him hit parade honours – 'I'll Never Get Over You', 'Hungry For Love' and 'Shakin' All Over' - plus 'Ecstasy' and his latest recording, a revival of the thumping 'Whole Lotta Woman'.

After the interval the John Barry Seven were, as expected smooth and polished as they breezed through several numbers, among them, 'Let the Good Times Roll' and, of course, 'The James Bond Theme'. One-time idol Marty Wilde, regarded as something as a back number in the entertainment world these days at least in so far as commercial recordings are concerned, followed up well and in between his calculated goonery sang, 'Any Way You Want It' followed by his own composition 'Mexican Boy' and wound up with a popular version of 'Twist and Shout'. The promising Bobby Patrick Six, after rendering their own version of 'Monkey Time' provided the backing for the long-awaited and enthusiastically-received Brenda Lee. The elfin-like figure with the fantastic voice and personality plus, got everyone going with 'Dynamite' followed with the appealing 'Aint It Funny How Time Slips Away' and then surged into 'Sweet Nothings' the great hit which established her as an international star some four years ago. The punchy 'Let's Jump the Broomstick' contrasted with the poignant 'As Usual', which she followed with 'Is It True' 'Anybody but Me' and 'All Alone Am I'. Then Brenda really cut loose with a belting raucous performance of 'Tutti Frutti' an enthralling 'What I Say' and after making one exit, was recalled for a final electric rendering of 'When The Saints Go Marching In'. It was grand foot-stomping, hand-clapping fare and yet another triumph for the world's greatest little girl.'

On one night of the tour, the appearance of Johnny Kidd and The Pirates was subject to a hilarious incident, which Jeff recalls; 'Johnny Kidd was closing the first half of the show this night and I went into the backstage toilet minutes before they were due on. Johnny Kidd's guitarist was in the washroom frantically trying to undo a knot in the elastic of Johnny Kidd's 'pirate' eye patch. In desperation he asked me if I could undo the knot, as he had no prominent fingernails. I managed to achieve this without great difficulty, much to the relief of the guitarist. When we got into the wings of the stage, Johnny Kidd took the patch and said jokingly, 'Which eye shall I put it on tonight?' It was then that I realised that he had a caste in one eye and had therefore cleverly invented this 'pirate' persona to conceal this from the public. The curtains were closed and the band took their place on the stage awaiting the announcement. Most theatres used to have a stagehand who walked with the curtains as they open, to prevent them swirling and crashing into the wings. Tonight, it appeared that there was no one doing the honours so someone stepped forward to remedy the apparent oversight. The identity of this person was not clear but he may have been Johnny Kidd's tour manager. However, whoever he was, it would soon be revealed that he was not a stagehand familiar with the foibles of this particular theatre. He took position, centre stage and stood at the ready, holding on to the curtain with an ear cocked for the announcement. I was still standing in the wings with some other members of the cast looking forward to hearing the band. We then heard the announcement from the compere out front, which was something like, "Please welcome, Johnny Kidd and The Pirates" Instead of the curtains dividing and opening across the stage, they went up! The 'stagehand' looked startled as his feet left the floor. He had been holding on to the curtain so tightly that he was at least four feet in the air before he let go! He landed with a crash in the middle of the stage in front of Johnny Kidd and looked like a rabbit caught in the headlights. The band had already begun to play and as the hapless man got to his feet, it was clear that he had sprained his ankle. The audience, not quite sure what was going on, stared at this apparition of a group of pirates, fronted by a middle-aged man in a suit who had just dropped onto the stage from nowhere. He hobbled to the sanctuary of the wings in full view of the entire auditorium and I'm sure the band had great difficulty in holding it together. I know we were in stitches.'

Heinz had a much less amusing time. His image frequently stirred up a frenzy with the female members of the audience. This in turn, made certain males, hostile. In fact after one show, he had to be smuggled out of the theatre under a blanket due to receiving threats of violence from local Teddy Boys who hated him.

One of the tour dates was at The Adelphi Theatre in Dublin and the trip across the Irish Sea was horrendous. It was a night crossing and snowing when we set off, then a storm developed and tossed the boat around mercilessly. Unlike today, the ferries were very basic then and you were lucky if it wasn't a converted ex-tugboat! Jeff and Stan shared a cabin and recall looking through the porthole, seeing the sky one minute and a deep chasm between waves the next! Jeff actually rolled out of his bunk several times and gave up trying to sleep.

The next day, before the concert, we went for a meal at a Chinese restaurant in Dublin city centre. To our surprise, the entire waiting staff consisted of Irish women in dark matching outfits with white aprons. Not a Chinese person in sight! It was weird to be asked, in a Southern Irish accent, if you wanted 'Sweet and Sour' or 'Chicken Chow Mein'. However, the food was authentic, cooked it seemed, by the only Chinaman in Dublin.

One night, returning to London from a tour venue, we stopped at a roadside café. It was around 1am. These places were the only watering holes in those days, prior to the motorway network services and were universally known by musicians as 'greasy spoons', which gives you an indication of the quality of the cuisine. In one place we used to stop at, they had a huge tea pot, which had two spouts welded on to it so that the demand for cups of tea could be met in half the time! It was a masterpiece in chrome but if you returned to the counter and asked for one cup of tea, a smaller pot with one spout was produced with less enthusiasm. There were always a number of long distance lorry drivers in these places and although we never had any trouble from them, you had a healthy respect for their presence, which could sometimes be intimidating.

On this particular night, Brenda and her husband, Ronnie, had also pulled in for a meal, accompanied by Dub Albritten. We were still on reasonable terms with Brenda and Ronnie but Dub preferred to ignore us. The feeling was mutual so we weren't bothered when they chose to sit at a separate table. After they had finished their meal, Dub pulled out his wallet, which was visibly stuffed with banknotes and paid the bill. He then went off to the gent's toilet, situated behind the main building of the café. Fifteen minutes later, Brenda was concerned that Dub had not returned so Ronnie went out to see if everything was ok. He found Dub in a semi-conscious heap on the toilet floor. Two heavy guys had followed him into the toilet and robbed him of the entire night's takings! In the process, they had punched his lights out. Of course, they were long gone by the time Dub came round. It was a kind of poetic justice and, for the rest of the tour, Dub had a black eye, which in my opinion, was a testament to the bad karma he had generated. It gave us pleasure to see him on each gig and, without reference to the obvious 'shiner', making a point of saying something like, 'Alright Dub?'

The last night of the Brenda Lee tour was at The Opera House, Blackpool on the 12th December 1964. Our paths never crossed again.

After the Brenda Lee tour we went back to a series of one-nighters, playing places like the California Ballroom Dunstable and the Winter Gardens, Weston Super Mare.

On the 24th February, The John Barry Seven recorded Saturday Club, a popular radio show hosted by Brian Matthew at The BBC Playhouse Theatre. London.

We also made several appearances at Quaintways in Chester. This was an old Tudor style building with four floors. On the ground floor there was a busy restaurant and on certain nights, bands were booked to play on the upper floors. The most popular bands would play on the first floor, a disco would be on the second floor and the top floor would host the support band. Being more of a name band at the time we were always allotted the first floor and during our breaks we would usually go up to the top floor to see who was playing and what they were like. On one gig we stood and watched a very young band that was playing to a couple of roadies, no more than three refugees from the lower floors and two or three of our band. It was hard to tell if they had any great potential but I did remember their name. It was Davy Jones and the Lower Third. The singer was yet to emerge into the limelight as David Bowie!

Staying in guesthouses in those days was like playing Russian roulette. Most of them were grim and the cleanliness of the rooms could be (and often was) suspect. One night after a gig in South Wales, we stayed in a guesthouse located in the Mumbles area near Swansea. It was known to all visiting bands as 'Mrs Soboluska's' and run by a Polish woman of that name. Also staying there that night were The Merseybeats and in the morning, Tony Crane had written a note and pinned it to the door of his room. Jeff recalls; 'The note said, 'This room is already occupied.' You had to get close to the note to read it and I then saw that Tony had impaled some sort of bug with the shaft of the pin securing the note to the door. It was a cockroach or something similar. After that event I nicknamed the guesthouse, Mrs Bedobugska's.'

Towards the end of February we had an engagement at Birmingham Town Hall. It was for Birmingham University's Rag Ball and by the time we went on, the crowd were very rowdy.

We were followed by the Spencer Davis Group, which featured a very young Steve Winwood.

He was only about seventeen at the time and even then, clearly a very talented musician/singer. They'd had recent chart success with their single, 'Every Little Bit Hurts' but the crowd, having consumed too much drink, were not responding favourably to anyone.

All the artists had to use the same dressing room, which was a typical changing room with lockers and benches, located behind the auditorium. Tom Jones sat in the corner of this room with his manager and was visibly unhappy about the drunks in the crowd. He had signed the contract for this gig long before releasing a record but since then, his single, 'It's Not Unusual' had reached the top of the charts. His fee (inclusive of payment for his band) for this appearance was reported to be £35 and this, undoubtedly, added to his chagrin.

After hints of legal action from the Secretary of the Student's Union, and much gentle persuasion from his manager, Tom Jones agreed to go on and do his act. Later, as we stood on the side of the stage to watch, the Secretary walked out on stage and was greeted with loud booing and catcalling. He attempted to calm the audience down and Tom's backing band, The Squires, stood apprehensively behind him as the din gradually subsided. Finally, Tom Jones was announced and the band played him on. He strode onto the stage, ignoring more boos, towards the mic-stand, a man with a mission. Half way there, someone threw a toilet roll at him in 'football-match' style and it went straight over Tom's head with sheets of tissue trailing behind, accompanied by a loud cheer.

Tom's composure was shaken but, as a true professional, he launched into the first song. We couldn't help laughing at the sheer irony of it all. Here was Tom Jones, top of the charts, not happy with the crowd or his paltry fee, persuaded against his better judgement to go on and, lo and behold, some idiot out there had to put the last nail in his coffin. That's showbiz!

7

ON TOUR WITH BILLY FURY

On March the 1st 1965, we rehearsed the programme for The Billy Fury Tour and the opening night was on March the 2nd, at the ABC Cinema, Romford. We were billed as The John Barry Orchestra, augmented by four other horn players, Ray Hutchinson/trumpet, Derek Wadsworth/trombone, Don Faye/alto sax, plus Roger Waghorn/tenor sax.

The tour was organised by the legendary Larry Parnes and included The Kestrels, The Gamblers, The Zephyrs, Brian Poole & the Tremeloes, Dave Berry & The Cruisers and The Pretty Things. We were engaged to back The Kestrels and Billy Fury. The compere of the show was Bobby Pattinson from Gateshead. It was a typical 'package show' of its time.

This tour was a lot more fun. The bands and artists got on so well that it was like a large family outing on every gig. I can't recall anyone having a cross word or feeling any bad atmospheres on this tour (apart from the last night which was a victim of high spirits).

All the London based artists and musicians met by the Planetarium, north of Baker Street and we travelled by coach to every venue. The driver of the coach was named Alf and his company was called Thompsons.

Just prior to the tour we had been measured up for new band suits. Rather unwisely, someone had chosen classic Ivy League woollen cloth. This looked great but in reality was far too warm for stage gear. One night on the tour, we put our bags and suits in the dressing room and sat around waiting for curtain up. Jeff recalls; 'The dressing room was typical with bare light bulbs around all the mirrors. As usual there was a shortage of hooks so I hung my suit up on a nail protruding from the wall. After 20 minutes or so we could all smell something burning, like fabric smouldering. We looked around the room and to my horror we discovered that my suit had been hanging against a bare light bulb and the heat had burnt a hole right through the back of the jacket and through the knee of a trouser leg! When we walked on stage that night, I had to walk sideways to prevent my white shirt being visible through the hole in the back of the jacket and also twist my leg so that my knee couldn't be seen either. From the front row of the audience, my body language must have suggested that I wasn't the full ticket!'

Get Ready Steady Go-go-go!!

presented by **LARRY PARNES**

The John Barry Seven & Orchestra

Bobby Pattinson

The Kestrels

The Gamblers

THE ZEPHYRS

BRIAN POOLE & the Tremeloes

DAVE BERRY & the Cruisers

NOT APPEARING AT GLOUCESTER

THE PRETTY THINGS

BILLY FURY

This programme is subject to alteration at the discretion of the management

Tour Management and Administration — MARK FORSTER

Company and Stage Manager — SCOTT ROBERTSON

In accordance with the requirements of the local authority: 1. All gangways, passages and staircases must be kept entirely free from chairs or any other obstruction. 2. The public shall be permitted to leave by all exit and entrance doors after each performance or entertainment. 3. No smoking shall be permitted to take place on the stage except as part of a performance or entertainment. 4. The safety curtain must be lowered and raised at least once during every performance or entertainment, to ensure its being kept in proper working order.

I particularly remember Roger Cook, Roger Greenaway and Tony Burrows of the Kestrels having a laugh with us on the long coach journeys.

During one of them, half way through the tour, Roger Cook played us the song 'You've Got Your Troubles', which he and Roger Greenaway had just written. He sang it to us while accompanying himself on ukulele then asked us if we would like to record it but we didn't think it was suitable for The John Barry Seven and the matter was forgotten. However, I remembered it vividly some time later when it crashed into the charts by The Fortunes. It's easy to say in hindsight that we should have recorded it but in reality The John Barry Seven may not have been given the kind of exposure that The Fortunes had. They were a new up and coming band and the John Barry organisation had no plans to record any more singles. In fact, as we later discovered, there were no plans at all.

Our tour itinerary covered about 30 dates, spread over three months and were mostly ABC cinemas, which was quite usual for 'package tours'. We played a few John Barry Seven gigs between the tour dates and the full itinerary is reproduced here:

March 1965

1st	Rehearsals
2nd	Romford - ABC
4th	Dublin – Adelphi
5th	Belfast – ABC
7th	Blackpool – ABC
9th	Chesterfield – ABC
10th	Chester – ABC
11th	Wigan – ABC
13th	Manchester – Ardwick
14th	Wakefield – ABC
15th	Cleethorpes – Ritz
17th	Lincoln – ABC
18th	Cambridge – Regal
19th	Bexleyheath – ABC
20th	Ipswich – ABC
21st	Leicester – De Montfort Hall
25th	Birmingham (JB7)
27th	Barnes (JB7)

April 1965

1st	Southend (JB7)
3rd	Felixstowe (JB7)
24th	Gloucester – Regal
25th	Northampton – ABC
27th	Plymouth – ABC
28th	Exeter – Savoy
29th	Southampton – ABC
30th	Croydon – ABC

May 1965

1st	Dover – ABC
2nd	Harrow ABC
4th	Kingston-Upon-Hull – ABC
5th	Stockton – Globe
6th	Edinburgh
7th	Carlisle – ABC
8th	Norwich – Theatre Royal
9th	Bristol – Colston Hall (last night of tour)

On board the tour coach was a twenty-foot long electric sign. It had the appearance of a hollowed out iron girder and was about as heavy. This was carried into each venue every night and suspended, rather precariously, above the stage. It took at least six volunteers to carry it and as the tour progressed, most musicians managed to deliberately avoid being press-ganged into lifting this monstrosity. Alf could be heard cursing all the absent artful dodgers. The funniest part of this was that the sign, although quite sophisticated for its time, was really not robust enough to be manhandled in this way. It was often being dropped or banged into various walls. Once plugged in, it functioned with words created by large dots moving across its long screen from left to right and, at the beginning of the tour the words said; 'Welcome to the Billy Fury Tour - We hope you have a great night!' (words to that effect). Towards the end of the tour after all the wear and tear, it read something like, 'We com to he illy Fu To r. W op ou hav a reat ight!'

As it would have taken a week or so to return it to the manufacturers and have it repaired, nothing was done to rectify the garbled words. It was a great source of amusement to everyone in the show, if only to see the puzzled faces in the audience.

The John Barry Orchestra sat in a row on stage, with old style big-band music stands. During one show the horn players were passing photos along the line and when I glanced at them I could see they were explicit to say the least! They were more to do with 'private parts' than 'music parts'.

Bobby Pattinson, the compere, used to tell a few jokes while an act was getting ready behind the curtains. One of his jokes was, 'I went to the doctor and he told me I had water on the brain. So I said, what shall I do doctor and he said, you need a tap on the head!' With that punch-line, Bobby would produce a kitchen tap and stick it onto his forehead, using an attached suction disc. This always went down well and, after striding up and down the stage for maximum laughs, he would remove it and go on to the next joke. One night before the show, Stan, our bass player, discreetly went into Bobby's empty dressing room and put boot polish all over the suction disc of the 'prop' tap. By the time Bobby had reached the part of his routine that involved the tap, the rumour of the boot polish had gone round and many of the acts were standing the wings. Bobby got to the punch-line, stuck the tap on his head and the audience laughed. However, when he removed it, they laughed even louder, seeing a large black circular mark on his forehead! When he came off stage he said, 'Blimey that joke never went down that well before.' It wasn't until he saw himself in the mirror that he realised that the joke was on him. He took it well but double-checked all his props after that.

Viv Prince, the drummer with the Pretty Things turned out to be the wild man of the tour. On one occasion, during their act, he crawled across the stage on all four fours holding a lighted newspaper with the look of an obsessed pyromaniac. The audience had a clear view of this but Phil May, the singer, carried on obliviously until he suddenly realised there was no drums. He turned round and for a brief moment the performance ground to an embarrassing halt. On another occasion, we were sitting in our dressing room, which had the traditional mirrors with bare light bulbs around them and the door dramatically burst open. Standing in the doorway was Viv Prince, pointing a gun at us! He said just one word, 'Duck!' and started firing the gun at the light bulbs. Considering his glazed eyes and vacant expression, his aim was quite accurate and he took out about ten bulbs before disappearing down the corridor.

There were a lot of practical jokes going on throughout the tour and the last night at Colston Hall, Bristol, turned into a riot on stage. Billy Fury's act was invaded by other members of the cast and the bouncers leapt on stage attempting to throw them off! During the interval, backstage, Viv Prince had already soaked some of us with a fire-hose and by the finale he appeared to be totally out of control, trying to demolish the drum kit, in full view of the audience. It was a prank too far and, as the music ground to a halt, he was wrestled off the stage, knocking over mic stands and people on the way. I felt sorry for the audience who hadn't paid to see this sort of scrum and it wasn't the kind of finale I would have wished for at the end of the tour.

In contrast, Billy Fury was the consummate professional; always polite and quite laid-back offstage. He was a great performer and a real star of his era. I was so sorry to hear the news when he died. To my mind, no one has followed in his footsteps.

After the Billy Fury Tour, The John Barry Seven went back on the circuit playing one-nighters around the country.

It was now becoming increasingly obvious that our drummer in The Seven, Ernie Cox, was drinking more heavily than was good for him or the band. Ernie and I had known each other from our schooldays and we had also rehearsed together at The Slough Boys Club so the personal connection between us made it difficult for me to come on strong to Ernie as the bandleader. However, something had to be done so I went to Ernie's house and spoke to his parents about the drinking problem. I asked them to talk to Ernie about this and hoped they could make him see sense. It was a classic case of a musician not realising how destructive alcohol can be in a professional situation. It was affecting Ernie's timekeeping and although I brought this to his attention many times in a sensitive way, he was convinced that a few drinks helped him to play better.

One night John Barry came along to see the band without warning or making contact with me so I didn't even know he was there. Unfortunately, it was one of Ernie's off-nights. The next day, Miss Ackers, John Barry's secretary rang me up and asked me to come up to the office for a meeting with John. During that meeting, he told me that he had seen the band the night before and was very dissatisfied with the drummer's playing. He said that on some numbers Ernie was coming in late and during others speeding up. He was disappointed that I had let this situation develop and if he (John) had been bandleader, he would have replaced Ernie without hesitation. I explained that Ernie was an old friend and I had given him a warning but John didn't really want to know the personal side of the issue. He emphasised that The John Barry Seven had a high reputation to maintain and a drummer with suspect timekeeping was not acceptable. So that was it, the writing was on the wall for Ernie. I had a really serious talk with him, saying that if he didn't shape up he would have to go.

A week or two after my meeting with John Barry, we played a gig at Burtons Uxbridge. This was a dance hall situated over a Burtons menswear shop and was quite a prestigious venue.

Our first set had gone ok. Ernie played well but during the break he had a few drinks and the second set was a disaster. He was all over the place and I had to shout at him, on stage, to pull himself together but he seemed to be in another world. In the dressing room, after the gig, I had to tell him I could no longer have him in the band. It was quite distressing and Ernie responded angrily towards me and the other musicians, suggesting that there had been a conspiracy to get rid of him. He singled out certain members of the band, accusing each one in turn of betraying him. He said, 'You, you and you' and pointing at Jeff added, 'and you, a possible 4th…'

I recruited Clive Thacker, who had been in The Embers after me, to replace Ernie. He was more of a jazz drummer and found it difficult to provide the volume we needed for the seven-piece band. There was no mic-ing up the drum kits in those days so the drummer really had to be prominent. I kept asking Clive to play louder and after one or two gigs, he had large blood blisters on all of his fingers. During one set they burst, covering the snare drum and tom- toms with blood. It was an awful sight and the audience must have thought it was some bizarre part of the act. A vampire on the drums! Sadly, Clive had to admit the gig was not his scene and gave me his notice.

While I was still looking for a drummer, I had a phone call from John Barry's office to come in to see him. I thought it would be a routine meeting to view future engagements but what he told me was an unexpected blow. He said that he thought The John Barry Seven had run its course and he had therefore decided to phase the band out. He gave me three month's notice. I can't deny that his decision was probably influenced by what he had witnessed at the band's recent gig. However, I asked him to reconsider, pointing out that the drummer had been replaced and the band was still in demand plus, in my opinion, the line up was now probably the best it had ever been. My plea fell on deaf ears and it was with a heavy heart that I had to tell the other musicians that The John Barry Seven was to be disbanded. The news was received with great disappointment.

I put it to the musicians that, if they were prepared to give it a try, I would form a new band and look for management under a new name. I felt that we were entitled to use the suffix, 'ex-John Barry Seven' for future gigs, which would generate some interest and even boost our fee.

From this point on there were no future formations of The John Barry Seven.

8

THE ALAN BOWN SET

It was around May in 1965 that I formed The Alan Bown Set.

I had considered many versions of names for the band. One that came to mind was ABC, which would have been an acronym for Alan Bown Community. My agent dissuaded me from using this in the belief that no band with the name ABC would be taken seriously or get anywhere. Thanks to the later successful 80's band, ABC, this proved to be a fallacy.

I then decided to follow John Barry's example and incorporate my name into the band's name. However, I didn't want The Alan Bown Six! I chose the tag 'Set' long before ex-Animals keyboard player Alan Price, who later formed his band The Alan Price Set. If he had been on the scene before me, I would have used some other tag to avoid the similarity. It was infuriating and showed very little imagination from Alan Price who was fully aware of the existence of my band. If U2 had been around at the time, he may have conceivably used the name ME2!

Terry Childs, and Ron Menicos of The Seven had decided to go their own way, so the new band had a new line-up; Alan Bown/leader/trumpet, Dave Green/sax & flute, Jeff Bannister/lead vocals/keyboards, Pete Burgess/ guitar, Stan Haldane/bass and Vic Sweeney/drums.

It was Pete Burgess who introduced us to Bobby Pridden, who from day one became our road manager. Bobby was a happy go-lucky sort of guy and sometimes his good nature led him to be set up for practical jokes. Pete in particular could not resist sending Bobby up.

In the early days we travelled to gigs in an Austin J4 box van with side windows (luxury). Somehow we managed to squeeze in six band members, a roadie and all the equipment into the van but, because of the restricted space inside, the drum-kit had to go on the roof-rack. Vic, the drummer, insisted that Bobby cover the exposed drum cases with a tarpaulin on every trip in case it rained. However, Bobby always protested that, if it wasn't raining already, it was unlikely to do so.

One day, we set off for a gig and Bobby hadn't bothered to apply the tarpaulin. Almost inevitably, it began to rain. Vic was furious and we stopped the van in a lay-by then Bobby was unceremoniously ejected with much shouting and shoving to get on the roof and cover the drum kit. While he was up there, Pete, who was in the driving seat, decided to drive down the road to give Bobby a scare and teach him a lesson. We heard much thumping and shouting from above and, to other motorists passing, it must have looked like something out of a Wild West show. Like a cowboy on top of a stage-coach, Bobby hung on to the ropes and tarpaulin for dear life.

As the speedometer reached about 30 miles an hour we stopped laughing and asked Pete to slow down. Fortunately, he slowed down gradually to prevent Bobby being propelled over the top onto the road. Almost immediately, a red faced, wet and severely dishevelled roadie got back into the van with a long list of expletives. To add to his misery, because he was wet, no one wanted Bobby to sit beside them so he had to stand up for most of the journey!

The Alan Bown Set.

A BIG SOUND FROM THE ALAN BOWN SET

NO gimmicks of long hair and unwashed clothes—just a big sound produced by a group of professional entertainers. That's the aim of the Alan Bown set, recently signed up by one of the top A and R men in the business, Tony Hatch, for Pye records—before their first public appearance.

Such is the boys' musical ability that Tony hopes to produce their first single in the very near future.

For the past two and a half years, Alan Bown has been leading the John Barry Seven, appearing all over the country and taking the group to the Continent, but always remaining anonymous.

The line-up is: Alan Bown on trumpet; Dave Green on tenor sax; Pete Burgess on lead guitar; Stan Haldane on bass guitar; Geoff Bannister on organ and lead vocals; and Vic Sweeney on drums.

The first photo of The Alan Bown Set
Beat Instrumental July 1965
(Featuring The John Barry Seven shiny mohair suits!)

The seating arrangements in the old J4 were such that someone had to sit on the engine cover, between the driver and passenger seat (totally illegal these days). This became known as the hot seat, which was a bonus in the winter but purgatory in the summer. The words 'chestnuts roasting on an open fire' from the classic Christmas song, still come to mind. Not being a properly designated seat, the engine cover had no back to it, turning the occupant's spine into a banana after 50 miles. Also, vehicles had no seat belts in those days and the impact of a collision would have propelled the occupant through the windscreen, like a human cannonball! These thoughts had to be put aside through necessity but an incident revived them when, one morning, I was negotiating a three point turn in a narrow road and my foot slipped off the clutch. The van lurched forward into a telegraph pole and the impact toppled the pole onto a garden fence, which was promptly flattened! My pride was dented but not as much as the front of the van, which had a round cleft in it, half the circumference of the telegraph pole! Fortunately, few members of the band were in the van at the time and luckily, no human cannonball.

We started playing gigs on the circuit at venues I had cultivated in the old John Barry Seven days and on the 24th July 1965 at the Shoreline Club, Bognor Regis, Cathy McGowan, the presenter of Ready Steady Go, known as RSG, came down to the club to see the band. (see pages 56 / 57). Cathy was suitably impressed and thanks to her we later appeared on RSG.

Someone who used to come and see us regularly then was Richard Cowley who worked for the Malcolm Rose Agency. He was very enthusiastic about the band and offered to put us on the agency's roster. It was a gift at the time and good to have someone on board who was genuinely keen to promote us.

In August, we went into Pye Recording Studios, Marble Arch, London. This followed a chain of events, which had begun as far back as my days in the RAF. Pete Burgess, the new guitarist in The Set, used to be my hairdresser in those days and he had often told me that he also played guitar. Among the clients at the salon where Pete worked was Robin Blanchflower, who was A&R man at Pye Records. Pete mentioned The Alan Bown Set to Robin, who gave me a call soon after. He arranged for me to meet Pye executive Peter Prince and Robin also sat in on the meeting. Before anything was signed, we auditioned for Tony Hatch who was Pye's producer at the time and Tony Reeves, who was a talent scout for the label. They were very impressed with the band and this led to our first single as The Alan Bown Set on the Pye label. We recorded a song entitled, 'Cant Let Her Go', written by Eric Leese, a non-member of the band. The producer was Tony Hatch. It was an atmospheric track and had a haunting melody. Jeff sang lead vocals and Stan and Pete did some high backing vocals.

The Alan Bown Set
1965
Left to right:
Jeff Bannister,
Dave Green
(Cathy McGowan)
Alan Bown
Vic Sweeney
Stan Haldane
and
Pete Burgess

On the B-side of our single, was a Curtis Mayfield song entitled, 'I'm the One Who Loves You.' We had been doing this song on stage since The John Barry Seven days and consequently the arrangement was very polished. 'I'm the One', as we entitled it for brevity, was a great song and really suited Jeff's voice. In hindsight, this should really have been the A-side. Tony Hatch thought so but was outvoted in favour of the more mysterious and unique option.

Our first single, 'Can't Let Her Go', was released on the Pye label in early September 1965.

As can be seen in the photograph (see page 56 and 57), we were now wearing new white jackets with black trousers. Like the man in the detergent advert who wore a white suit on the London tube network, our jackets soon proved susceptible to attracting marks of all description. You knew which jackets belonged to the guitarists by the grubby diagonal stripe across the front and down the back!

On the 4th September, in The Record Mirror, a review was accompanied by a photo of the band. The review is reproduced here; 'The Alan Bown Set - Can't Let Her Go. – I'm the One. Marvellous sounds here, fully instrumental with organ, highly effective vocal harmonies. An American song of curiously jerky phrasing but a solid beat. Tenor sax also adds fullness. Deserves to do very well.'

The Daily Sketch, on the 14th of September, published this review; 'Alan Bown, erstwhile leader of The John Barry Seven, tells me that launching a pop group is an expensive business. He said, 'I have just had to sell my car – after financing the group for five months. Now he's hoping for a quick royalty return from his first disc from The Alan Bown Set, entitled, Can't Let Her Go.'

Radio plays of the single were limited due to our very recent emergence onto the scene. However, there was a lot of interest and it was a promising start.

Just after the Christmas of 1965, on the 27th December, we appeared at an old community hall in Camberley, Surrey. The hall was packed with post Christmas revellers and, being not far from home, many of the band's friends and family were also there. Jean, my wife, came along. After a couple of opening numbers, Stan our bass player realised that the mic-stand was too low for comfort and he attempted to adjust it. As he touched the metal stand with both hands, his bass guitar swung round and made contact with the stand. This immediately completed an electrical circuit, which violently surged through Stan's body. Unfortunately, the circuit was D.C. (direct current) and not A.C. (alternating current), and, although the shock threw him to the floor, Stan could not let go of the mic-stand. He rolled around, screaming in uncontrollable spasms, as the audience watched in horror fascination.

Bobby Pridden, our roadie, leapt from amongst them onto the stage and, realising that if he touched Stan he too would be locked into the circuit, he attempted to separate Stan from the stand by kicking him. As if Stan wasn't suffering enough! Meanwhile, someone had the presence of mind to pull all the plugs out of the wall-socket and stop the current. Like the other members of the band, I was completely traumatised so I don't know who called an ambulance (there were no mobile phones in those days).

The gig was then aborted, despite the protests of the promoter, Bob Potter, who urged us to continue without Stan. It was crass of him when, due to the faulty electrics in the hall, one of the band members had almost been electrocuted. There had been recent reports in the press of two fatalities in other bands for the same reason and Stan was lucky to survive. Fortunately, the girl friend of Dave Green our sax player, was a nurse and she was able to put Stan into a recovery position until the ambulance arrived. Stan recalls, 'I was put on a stretcher and the ambulance man (they were not called 'paramedics' then) asked my girlfriend, Monica, to remove my boots. Because the stretcher was on a trolley, as she pulled one of my boots, the stretcher followed her round in a semi-circle!' It was one of those silly moments in an otherwise desperate situation.

Stan was incapacitated for nearly three weeks, during which I had to cancel all forthcoming gigs. He eventually re-joined us on the 14th January 1966 for a gig at The N.C.O. Club on the USAF base in Ruislip. Stan's PS, 'I didn't go near a light switch or anything remotely electrical for months after that. Mic-stands were definitely off limits! The doctors told me I had a lucky escape but the electric shock had damaged a heart valve, which has led to problems and heart attacks later in life.'

The hall was shut down after that incident until the electrical wiring had been investigated by the Fire Brigade but by the time the investigation took place it was discovered that the building had 'recently' been re-wired. As it couldn't be established when this had occured, no further action could be taken by the Fire Brigade or us. However, we never returned to that venue.

The travelling and late nights were taking their toll on Jeff's throat. For some time he had suffered with recurring tonsillitis and now and again we had to get through a gig playing instrumentals only. Because of the motorway system being almost non-existent in those days, there were long arduous journeys to contend with, which could wear you down if you were not on top form.

THE PLAZA

DANCE & SOCIAL CLUB
ROOKERY ROAD, HANDSWORTH

****
**** Keep this Leaflet —This *
**** may be your Lucky No. *
****   Nº   6482   *
****   *
****   *
**** Listen for Announcements *

NEW YEAR'S EVE . . . Friday, 31st December

CELEBRATION DANCE
THE ALAN BOWN SET

(Ex John Barrie Seven)   Dancing from 1965 to 1966   By Ticket 9/-   At Door 12/6

Saturday, 1st January

MORGAN FAYNE SOUL BAND
THE MYSTERIANS AND TOP MIDLAND GROUPS

Sunday, 2nd January

SPENCER DAVIS
GROUP
THE SOUL SHOW

Monday, 3rd January UNDER 18 NIGHT

***************** COMING *********************
7th   THE CAESARS   8th   LULU and the LUVVERS   9th   DUSTY SPRINGFIELD
THE EXCITERS, from U.S.A   10th   DAVE DEE, DOZEY, BEAKY, MICK and TICH

Jeff went to see a throat specialist in Harley Street. The specialist said they were the worst tonsils he had ever seen and offered to take them out within two weeks. Unfortunately, the fee for the private operation would have been over £200. In those days that was a considerable amount of money so, reluctantly, Jeff went on the NHS waiting list and eventually had the operation 18 months later. It was then performed by the same Harley Street specialist that Jeff had originally consulted!

The New Year yielded a change of line-up. On 24th January 1966, Dave Green left the band. He had decided that the constant touring wasn't for him anymore. It was a blow to me as I had the highest regard for Dave. He was not only a really nice guy but a naturally gifted musician and I knew it would be difficult to find a replacement of such a high calibre. Jeff and Stan were particularly sad to see him go.

I placed an advert in the Melody Maker and we held auditions for a saxophonist. One of the guys who responded was John Helliwell who came to the rehearsal room for a blow. He was obviously an accomplished musician. However, he had a few issues to resolve. John's home was in Todmorden, Yorkshire and his girlfriend lived in Manchester where he was considering doing a day job in computing or something. John was also playing in a band called Jugs O'Henry but he was most concerned that if he joined our band he would have to move to London. His hesitation irritated me and I said to the others if he didn't make up his mind soon, we'd find someone else. I think the deciding factor was my suggestion for John to stay at my mother's house until he found other accommodation in London. She still lived at the house in Sydney Grove, Slough, where I grew up and she was quite happy with the idea. John turned out to be the perfect tenant at my mother's and I thought she treated him more like a son than me!

John Helliwell joined the band and used his middle name for stage thus becoming John Anthony for the duration of his time with us. He played his first gig with the band at The Royal Forest Hotel in Chingford. He fitted in well and eventually developed an on-stage personality, which the audience warmed to.

The next shift in personnel was the most dramatic of all. On Feb 11th 1966, we played at The Civic Hall in Birmingham. There were two stages in the hall, facing one another across the dance floor, which gave bands more room to set up and it also provided for a smooth changeover.

On the bill tonight, on the stage opposite to us, was a support band called The Shakedown Sound. They were booked to back Jimmy Cliff. Their appearance was about to change everything.

9

JESS RODEN JOINS THE SET

The Shakedown Sound was on before us and we listened out of curiosity, as we did on most gigs that included other bands. When their singer began, it was clear that there was a major talent at work and I thought that he was the best white soul singer I had ever heard. None of us knew who he was but after their performance, I made a point of asking him if he would like to sit in with us for a couple of numbers.

This was the first time that Jess Roden sang with us and we were all so impressed that, afterwards, I thought right there and then that he would be a great asset to The Alan Bown Set. The other guys were equally keen but before I made a decision to offer the gig to Jess, I spoke to Jeff to check that he was ok with the idea. It was a bit rough on him having been the lead singer with The John Barry Seven for nine months and with The Alan Bown Set for six months. Not forgetting that it was his voice on the first ABS single. Jeff recalls, 'I was a bit fazed by this sudden turn of events but I had to agree that Jess's voice was exciting and would be the icing on the cake for the band. It was almost as though fate had made the decision for us and we would have been foolish not to run with it.'

Having decided to go ahead with this plan, I invited Jess to come down to my house on the following Tuesday. He lived in Kidderminster and was only 17 years old at the time so I was aware that he might still have had plans that could conflict with mine. However, Jess was excited by the prospect of joining the band and he agreed to come down for the next gig.

On the 15th February 1966 at Blaises Club in London, Jess Roden made his first appearance with The Alan Bown Set and proved he was ideal for the band although, he put so much into the gig, that he lost his voice! However, it was an exciting night and we all felt that we had found a winning formula.

We already had a session booked for our next single and two days later, Jess was thrown in the deep end to sing the lead vocal. On February the 17th we went into Pye Recording studios and recorded 'Baby Don't Push Me' with 'Everything's Gonna be Alright' on the B-side. Tony Reeves produced both tracks. There was another session on Tuesday the

22nd for overdubs and mixing.

Jess soon moved to London permanently and stayed in Ruislip with our roadie, Bobby Pridden, at Bobby's mother's house.

Jess proved to be a nice guy and respectful of Jeff's vocal contribution. Between them they worked out a way of sharing the honours. Although weighted in Jess's favour, being a front-man and having the most dynamic voice, it resulted in a healthy mixture of songs in the repertoire. The set list at the time looked like this:

Jess	Jeff
My Girl	It's Alright
Driving Beat	Talking 'bout my Baby
Everything's Gonna Be Alright	I Love You Yeah
Shotgun	Let the Good Times Roll
Who's Cheatin' Who	Mama Didn't Know
You Don't know Like I Know	Meeting Over Yonder
Shake	I'm the One
Mr Pitiful	Little Boy Blue
Down in The Valley	I Need You
Baby Don't Push me	
Dance to the Boomerang	

Up until this point, we hadn't been regarded as a soul band. The genre of music was very popular at the time and all the clubs were playing records by The Temptations, Otis Redding, The Four Tops, Smokey Robinson, Aretha Franklin…the list goes on. With Jess's natural soul voice it was inevitable that we would go down that path.

To give some indication of the workload around the time when Jess joined, Jeff has reproduced some of the dates from his 1966 diary.

February 1966

1st	London - rehearsal
3rd	London - rehearsal
4th	London - recording studio
5th	London - Hounslow - Club Zambezi
7th	Basingstoke
8th	Rehearsal
9th	Nottingham
10th	Stockport - Manor Lounge
11th	Birmingham - Civic Hall

12th	Manchester - Twisted Wheel
13th	Farnborough - Carousel
15th	London - Blaises Club. (Jess Roden's first gig)
16th	Southend - Hawkwell
17th	London - Pye Studio
18th	Birmingham - Cavern
19th	Cheltenham
20th	Bournemouth
21st	Basingstoke
22nd	London - Pye Studio
24th	Cardiff*
25th	Penzance - Winter Gardens
26th	Cornwall – Redruth Flamingo Club
27th	Cornwall – Redruth Flamingo Club

*The prospect of the journey from Cardiff to Penzance in the Austin J4 van was so horrendous that we decided to drive through the night (there was no M5 in those days). Vic drove the last leg and became so exhausted that he pulled over into a lay-by, switched of the engine and fell asleep. Not long after, he woke us all up shouting and wrestling with the steering wheel. The headlights of a passing truck had woken him and he thought he was still driving and about to have a head-on collision!

As can be appreciated from the itinerary, our two consecutive dates in Redruth meant that we had to stay over. At the rear of the Flamingo Club ballroom there was chalet style accommodation provided for bands and bed & breakfast was included in the deal. We became a regular attraction at this venue and consequently we got to know the manager and staff quite well. The young rather plain waitress, who always seemed to be on duty here, was embarrassed by having to serve breakfast to seven musicians in the morning but after our more frequent visits she overcame the blushes. On one of our stopovers, the manager told us that it was the waitress's birthday and he dropped a hint that she would be delighted if we acknowledged it in some way. There was an air of anticipation when she first walked into the breakfast room and we gave her our orders. However, no comments were made from us about the birthday. She returned several times with plates of food etc but still no word was mentioned about her birthday. By the time it got to teas and coffees, it was obvious from her expression that she was annoyed that her birthday was being ignored and, as she was carrying a tray of crockery to the kitchen door, she looked round with a detectable frown.

We all looked back in silence in one of those 'snapshot' moments. Then, just before she disappeared through the door, Stan let out an enormous belch and 'through it' spoke the words 'happy birthday'. It not only broke the silence, it broke the waitress's composure and after a momentary

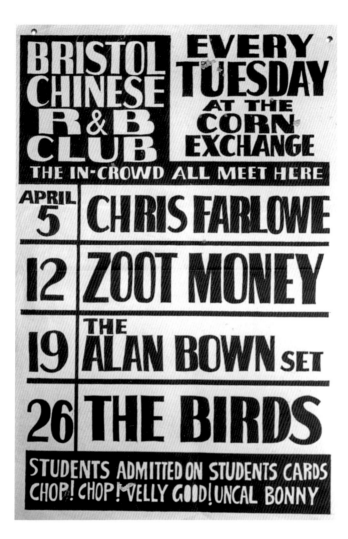

look of contempt she flounced out of the room in disgust. We all burst out laughing as it was so cruel but so funny. We knew Stan had a talent for the 'belch voice' but this was his finest moment.

We were soon back in the studio for photos of the new line up and on the 8th April, our single 'Baby Don't Push Me' was released on the Pye label. We had a review in the Evening News the following day, which said we had, '....a hoarse pounding r-and-b sound.'

Pete Burgess, our guitarist, lived in Ickenham and sometimes his parents held house parties. We used to pick him up from his house and, on days that followed one of these parties, Pete would emerge from his front door bearing plates of chicken legs and sausage rolls left over from the night before.

They would be gratefully received by the ravenous 'troops' in the van. On a sunny day, with a halo around Pete's head, it would seem like a re-enactment from the scriptures as the messiah stepped down from his lofty portal to walketh amongst the disciples and distribute vittles to feedeth the needy.

On some gigs, if we were travelling East, Jeff and Stan rendezvoused with the van at The Ace Café on the North Circular Road. The Ace Cafe was (and still is) a Mecca for bikers and a grub-stop for lorry drivers. Unlike the Gordon Ramsay type cuisines of today, the Ace had metal tables bolted to the floor and a juke box situated inside a reinforced cage to prevent bikers from giving it a good kicking when the 45's stuck or jumped. Picture then, two musicians in overcoats with overnight cases sitting at a table amongst a few of the nation's tough guys trying not to make eye contact with anyone. On one such occasion Stan and Jeff were waiting for the van to turn up and Jeff recalls; 'An hour went by but there was no sign of the van. Of course in those days there were no mobile phones and not that many phone boxes. The Ace Café didn't have a public phone so we sat and waited, feeling more conspicuous as time went by. There were about ten people in the café when the phone behind the counter rang. We looked over with vague curiosity as the burly counter assistant picked up the phone. He looked around the room and said very loudly, 'Mr Barnstable (Bannister) and Mr Al Dean (Haldane). The job's off!' Of course, everyone looked at us as we stood up and left but it gave us some cred, leaving those inside with the impression that our 'heist' had been called off at the last minute.' (What had actually happened was that the van had irreparably broken down on the way and the gig had to be cancelled).

We were still travelling in the Austin J4 and this also became known as The Bown Hotel when certain members of the band decided to save the cost of Bed and Breakfast accommodation and sleep overnight in the van, usually parked outside. These 'outsiders' would ghost their way to the breakfast room in the morning and the staff of the guesthouse would scratch their heads when finding more people at the table than they had anticipated. By the time they had worked it out, every last scrap of food had gone and we were on our way.

By now, the interior of the van was covered in graffiti, thanks mostly to Jess's artistry and boredom. This had spilled over from many messages and light-hearted insults left on dressing room walls by other bands. It was a medieval form of e-mail. Most clubs all over the country had designated rooms for bands to change in but visiting musicians hesitated to call them dressing rooms. Some were like squats. A fragment of broken mirror classified as a luxury. Little or no facilities were provided and Musician's Union representatives were never to be found venturing into places like these. Not without a pit pony anyway! However the messages brightened up everyone's day. They might have been from other bands or roadies, sometimes with groupie's names and a rating!

Bobby was still our road manager and following a gig he would usually fall asleep on the way home. On one occasion, someone in the band had a black pen, similar to a felt tip and, without Bobby waking up we managed to put black dots all over his face. When we stopped at The Blue Boar services (Watford Gap) on the M1 and queued up for a late night meal, the ladies serving the food visibly recoiled as Bobby came into view with what appeared to be a nasty attack of smallpox! No one clued him in and he ate his meal attracting strange looks from other diners, who were equally unnerved. It wasn't until Bobby went into the toilet, before continuing our journey home, that he caught a sight of himself in the mirror. Even Bob had a good laugh about it.

Not long after, our relationship with Bobby took a downturn. The old J4 was starting to crack up under the strain of the relentless demands we made upon it and one day the engine seized up on the A1. The dipstick revealed that there was no oil in the engine and Bobby got the blame. A week or two later, after some other incident, we were so infuriated with him that we left him at a petrol station, miles from London. In hindsight, I know we all regretted doing that but sometimes the frustration on the road boiled over and someone had to take the brunt, usually the roadie. From then on, the writing was not only on the wall of the van but also for Bobby who, it transpired, would eventually leave the band.

Next up for Bown mobility was a Commer walk-through van. This giant box on wheels was so high you could actually stand up in it. Hence the term 'walk-through'. Usually favoured by greengrocers, we thought it was the answer to all our transport problems. We had aircraft seats fitted in the van, leaving enough room behind them for the equipment. The downside was that, fully loaded, the van wouldn't do more than fifty miles an hour, even flat out! However, in those days there were still only two and a half motorways to speak of, the M1, the M6 and 20 miles of the M4, which terminated at Maidenhead. The A5, which is an old Roman road, connected the M1 and M6 and, although it was straight, it had about two dozen roundabouts on it. We developed a technique of keeping the accelerator flat on the floor and going round them at fifty miles an hour, no problem! The weight of the passengers and all the gear, kept it solidly on the road. It was like being on rails.

For some reason the windscreen wipers of the Commer van severely interfered with the radio reception and, as a result, Radio Luxembourg sounded more like the tapes from 'The Ipcress File'. It was certainly as much pleasure as forcing a rusty nail into the palm of your hand. With our constant attempts to relieve the boredom, we would sometimes give hitchhikers a lift and have the radio going full blast with the wipers adding to the misery. With bizarre behaviour performed by band members for the hitchhiker's attention, the poor unfortunate newcomer would soon ask to be dropped off. The contest was, to see how long he could brave it out before his bottle would go. The average was about ten minutes, following lots of nervous glances and discreet efforts to reach the door handle.

It was around this time that Richard Cowley formed his own management Company, Universal Attractions. He later teamed up with Kenny Bell and formed Cowbell. It was all looking promising now with the date-sheet filling up with more prestigious gigs.

The Winter Garden Ballroom Penzance

SUMMER SEASON 1966

Tuesdays commencing 5th July: Folk Singing
Wednesdays: Dancing to top local Groups
Thursdays: Folk Night
Fridays: ALL STAR POP NIGHT
Saturdays: Ballroom Dancing

SPECIAL ATTRACTIONS INCLUDING:

Friday, 17th June: **Unit 4 plus 2**
Friday, 24th June: **The Alan Bown Set**
Saturday, 2nd July: **The Chris Barber Band**
Friday, 8th July: **The Don Carrol Big Blues Band**
Friday, 22nd July: **THE ZOMBIES**
Saturday, 30th July: **The Mike Cotton Sound with Lucas**
Friday, 5th August: **THE APPLEJACKS**
Friday, 26th August: **THE FOUR PENNIES**
Saturday, 27th August: **The Monty Sunshine Jazzband**

Many more attractions to be booked. For details, see the *Cornishman* Newspaper.

VISIT ALSO

THE COLONY GRILL
Fully licensed Restaurant above the Ballroom. French and English cuisine. Open until 11.30. Reservations Penzance 2475.

10

THE MARQUEE CLUB AND MORE

The Marquee Club in Wardour Street, London, was regarded by most bands at the time as Mecca. If you didn't play here, you were of no consequence. It was run by the ever polite and mild mannered John Gee and his confidante Jack Barrie. I must also mention Nigel Hutchins who later administrated the club. He was always the gentleman and probably an unsung hero but it was people like him that made The Marquee special.

The odd thing about The Marquee was that, in the early years, it had no alcohol licence, which meant that bands and their entourage would walk 100 yards down Wardour Street to the nearest pub, called The Ship, which still stands today (unlike the Marquee building, since destroyed by developers). There was another more exclusive drinking den called La Chasse, which was an upstairs room at 100 Wardour Street, midway between The Marquee and The Ship. This was managed by Jack Barrie and wasn't open to the public so it was ideal for higher profile artists to escape to for a discreet drink.

The Alan Bown Set played their first Marquee gig on the 28th April 1966 and supported the Mark Leeman Five. On the 7th June we played at The Marquee again, supporting Manfred Mann.

Manfred Mann was a big enough artist at the time to insist on using the large room at the rear of the club (soon to become the Marquee Studio) as a dressing room, rather than the pokey backstage changing room. We also benefited from this arrangement and shared the room with Manfred Mann and his band. After we had played our set most of us were in the room shortly before they went on. Mike D'Abo had only recently replaced Paul Jones as vocalist and, turning to Manfred while adjusting a cravat, he said, 'How's my image?' Manfred, without a trace of humour replied, 'You haven't got one yet.' To say that in front of his band was a big enough put down but in front of us as well, I thought it was harsh. You could have heard a pin drop.

Manfred's uncompromising sense of humour revealed itself again a year or two later when we appeared at the same university ball in the provinces. Before or after our performances at universities we would look in adjacent halls to see who else was playing. On one occasion, at about 1 o'clock in the morning, we could hear music from another hall and discovered Manfred Mann playing at full tilt. We joined the 'audience' of about three roadies and when the band finished performing their song there was a deafening round of applause! It came through their PA speakers and the source of it was a tape recorder. The band members were taking exaggerated theatrical bows and Manfred was shouting above the cacophony, 'Thank you, thank you, you're very kind. No, please...' Suddenly the tape machine was switched off and there was total silence. We had to laugh. It was a classic send up.

On the 21st June, we went back into Pye Studios and recorded 'Headline News'. Jess did a great lead vocal on this and my old friend, Keith Mansfield played trombone on the intro, which gave it a great boost. On the B-side was a song, written by Jeff and myself called, 'Mr Pleasure'. Jeff sang this and we were very pleased with it at the time.

At The Marquee, on the 30th June, we supported The Action who were a very popular live band and deservedly so.

The 8th of July edition of The Evening News ran an article about the forthcoming Windsor Jazz and Blues Festival, giving all the bands a name-check, including The Alan Bown Set.

The Neath Guardian in South Wales gave us a write up on the 15th July 1966, which reviewed a gig we played at the Ritz Skewen on the 9th. The article is reproduced here;

'A double treat was in store for the dancers in Skewen last week for on Saturday, the great Alan Bown Set gave an outstanding performance. Consisting of organ, drums, bass and lead guitar, trumpet, sax and lead singer, this group gave a non-stop performance of versatility. Their new record due to be released in three weeks should be a mover. On the B-side is a song composed by Jeff Bannister, organist and Alan Bown himself. This group is booked regularly by the famous Marquee Club in London and Sheffield's Mojo Club. They deserve far more success in show business because they really knock themselves out to give a first class performance. The capacity crowd at The Ritz really went for these boys in a big way. Many of the local groups who I have spoken to rate this group as one of the best on the music scene today, although they are not receiving the credit they so richly deserve. This group of young men are not only good looking but extremely talented with it! Good luck with the new record boys, you deserve it."

The review was accompanied by a photo, which was reproduced in a later Marquee newsletter (see page 77).

We were back in Pye Studio in the morning of the 28th July and had a gig at The Marquee in the evening, supporting The Herd. The Herd were very popular, including, among others, Peter Frampton/lead vocalist, Gary Taylor/bass and my namesake, Andy Bown/keyboards (no relation to me).

The next day, on the 29th July, a half page article and photo of the band, holding a poster of the Windsor festival, appeared in the Evening News. The article gave all the members of the band a name check. The photo was captioned, 'The Alan Bown Set from Slough are on the star parade of personalities appearing at the three day Jazz Festival. They will be playing on Sunday. Holding the poster are, Alan Bown, left and Geoff Bannister. At the back – Pete Burgess, Vic Sweeney, Jess Roden, John Anthony and Stan Haldane.' It was a coup for our management, considering how many other artists would have welcomed such coverage.

Also on the 29th July 1966, The Bournemouth Times ran a half page article entitled 'Talk of the Town tonight' and this was accompanied by a photomontage of the band. The article is reproduced here;
'For sheer excitement there are few groups to beat the Alan Bown Set. In the overcrowded world of dance hall groups, they could be described as the 'apple in the apple pie' – and the cream too. The quote is taken from a line in the B-side of their new record, which is out today. Just how talented this London group are can be gauged by local audience reaction. Bournemouth Pavilion audiences have long been labelled as the most discriminating in the country. Perhaps it is because they have seen so many groups that they are only prepared to rave about the best. Yet the first time The Alan Bown Set played there, a few months ago, they had the usually reserved dancers clapping, cheering and jumping on the stage to dance. Since that Sunday in February this year they have been twice more. News of their coming has attracted record audiences and they have been labelled by many as 'Bournemouth's favourite group' The dynamic presentation of their performance, good looks and excellent musicianship are responsible for this success story, which has been repeated at dances all over the country. The group originally formed about 15 months ago. Alan Bown, who was formerly with The John Barrie* Seven, handpicked the other six musicians and together they invested a lot of their money to get themselves going. A recording contract with Pye soon followed. Their first record, Can't Let Her Go, was not a success although it sold well on the Continent, but their next release entitled, Baby Don't Push Me, did slightly better. Now, with their new disc, Headline News, out today, they could easily rocket up the charts. It is a catchy number, with a strong beat and unmistakable brass and piano sound of the Set. It will be danced to in all the discotheques and, given enough spins, should beat Edwin Starr's version hollow. The Set owe much of their success to the work of Alan himself. He arranges all their numbers, decides on their stage clothes, teaches them their dances and writes a lot of their material. The line up of the group is: Alan Bown, trumpet, vocals: Jess Rowden* vocals: Vic Sweeny* drums, vocals: Stan Haldane, bass guitar, vocals: Pete Burgess, lead guitar, vocals:

TRAVEL: By road turn off M.4 at Windsor/Eton Bypass · Thames Valley Green Line and London Country Buses · Western and Southern Region Trains **SPECIAL LATE** service to Staines, Twickenham, Richmond, Clapham and Waterloo.

THE 6th NATIONAL JAZZ &
BLUES FESTIVAL
has moved from Richmond and is now in
WINDSOR
at the ROYAL WINDSOR RACECOURSE
MAIDENHEAD ROAD (A.308)

PARTIES: Organise a party to travel by coach Car, Scooter or Rail and receive a FREE Backstage Pass to meet the Stars! For Party Ticket rates and **CAMPING** information contact NJF Secretary at 90 Wardour Street, London W.1. Telephone GER 2375

FRIDAY 29th JULY

8.00-11.30	**THE SMALL FACES · SPENCER DAVIS ·**
TICKETS	THE SOUL AGENTS · MARK BARRY ·
10/-	GENO WASHINGTON and the
	RAM JAM BAND

SATURDAY 30th JULY

2.30-5.30	**CHRIS BARBER · ALEX WELSH ·**
TICKETS	COLIN KINGWELL'S JAZZ BANDITS · KID MARTYN'S
5/-	RAGTIME BAND featuring direct from NEW ORLEANS
	LOUIS NELSON (U.S.A.)

ALL DAY TICKET 12/6

7.00-11.30	**THE WHO · THE YARDBIRDS ·**
TICKETS	CHRIS FARLOW and the THUNDERBIRDS · THE MOVE ·
10/-	GARY FARR & THE T-BONES · THE SUMMER SET ·
	JULIAN COVEY and the MACHINE ·
	Jimmy James and THE VAGABONDS ·

SUNDAY 31st JULY

2.30-5.30	**DICK MORRISSEY · STAN TRACEY ·**
TICKETS	Quartet and Big Band with KENNY BAKER ·
5/-	RONNIE SCOTT · KEITH CHRISTIE · BOBBY WELLINS ETC ·
	ERNESTINE ANDERSON (U.S.A.)

ALL DAY TICKET 12/6

7.00-11.30	**GEORGIE FAME · THE ACTION ·**
TICKETS	DIANE and NICKY · THE ALAN BOWN SET ·
10/-	THE HARRY SOUTH ORCHESTRA featuring TUBBY HAYES ·
	BLUESOLOGY · THE BLUE FLAMES ·
	ERIC CLAPTON · JACK BRUCE · GINGER BAKER

WEEKEND TICKETS 20/- IN ADVANCE ONLY

TO: **NATIONAL JAZZ FESTIVAL BOOKING DEPT.**
 MARQUEE CLUB, 90 WARDOUR STREET, LONDON, W.1

Please send me the undernoted tickets for which I enclose a cheque/postal order amount-

ing to.................................. I also enclose a stamped addressed envelope.

FRIDAY 29th JULY .... at 10/- WEEKEND TICKETS .... at £1
(SAT & SUN)

SATURDAY 30th JULY .... at 5/- .... at 10/- .... at 12/6

SUNDAY 31st JULY .... at 5/- .... at 10/- .... at 12/6

NAME..

ADDRESS..

Jeff Bannister, organ, vocals and John Anthony, tenor sax. Plans for the Continent and American tours in the autumn are on the way, so tonight may be the last chance fans will have to see them for a long time.
I forecast that the very talented Alan Bown Set will make headline news in the charts soon.' *(The press report spelling).

After this very glowing article, we were unable to attend the gig as our management secured us an appearance on Ready Steady Go! So, on the 29th July 1966, we were reunited with Cathy McGowan, as The Alan Bown Set made a guest appearance on Ready Steady Go. This was a huge accolade at the time. It was the 'in' show to do and every teenager was glued to the TV at 6.30 on Fridays. The catchphrase for the show was 'The Weekend Starts Here!' Also on the show with us were Solomon Burke, The Merseys, Manfred Mann and David & Jonathan. (David & Jonathan were Roger Greenaway and Roger Cook, who were two ex- members of The Kestrels, which The John Barry Seven had backed on the Billy Fury tour).

It was because of our successful gigs at The Marquee Club that we were offered the opportunity to appear at The Windsor Jazz festival. It was a four-day, open-air event and we played on the 31st July, the last day of the Festival. The finale of the show was opened by Georgie Fame and The Blue Flames, followed by The Harry South Big Band, (Hank Shaw, my old friend was in this band and it was great to see him. He was delighted to be there and hear my new band). Next up were The Action, then Diane Ferraz and Nicky Scott, then The Alan Bown Set, then Bluesology*, featuring Long John Baldry. The headline act was the now legendary Cream, which featured Eric Clapton, Jack Bruce and Ginger Baker.

*As history has already shown, the keyboard player in Bluesology, Reg Dwight, later re-invented himself as Elton John (see Sir Elton John's tribute on the back cover of this book).

In the evening of the very next day, we played at The Marquee. This time we were supporting Alexis Korner's Blues Incorporated.

The Alan Bown Set was the guest band at the Melody Maker's 1966 National Beat contest, which was held at the London Palladium on the 7th August. Rather than mix us up with the competing bands, the organisers decided to put us in the orchestra pit, which they explained would enable us to make a dramatic appearance. The base of the orchestra pit at the Palladium then had a floating platform, which could be raised entirely by an electronic device up to the level of the stage. In theory this was a good idea and would have been very effective except that, unknown to us, the device operated at a painfully slow speed. Once in place, in the depths of the pit and ready to play, we were given the cue to begin and on this occasion,

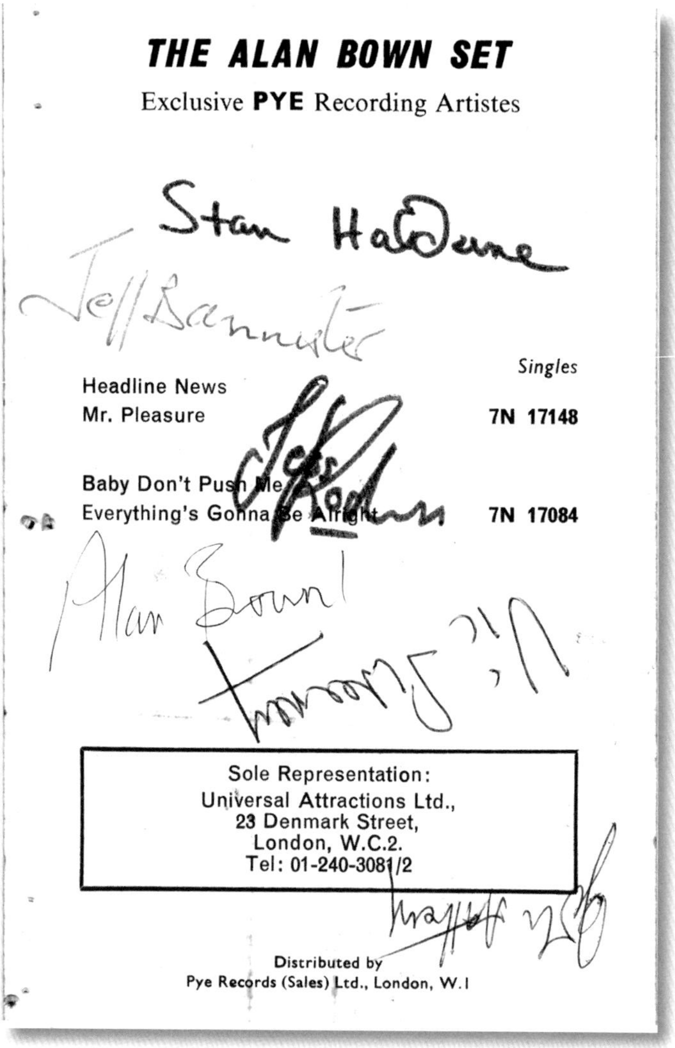

THE ALAN BOWN SET

Exclusive **PYE** Recording Artistes

Singles

Headline News
Mr. Pleasure

7N 17148

Baby Don't Push Me
Everything's Gonna Be Allright

7N 17084

Sole Representation:
Universal Attractions Ltd.,
23 Denmark Street,
London, W.C.2.
Tel: 01-240-3081/2

Distributed by
Pye Records (Sales) Ltd., London, W.1

74

anticipating what we thought would be a short intro, we opened our act with the riff from the song 'Satisfaction', Otis Reading style. This was always ideal for a brief opener but by the time the audience saw the tops of our heads, we had played the riff about 50 times!

From the time we were announced to our eventual appearance out of the pit, the audience must have wondered where the band was and where the muffled sound was coming from. After our performance of only a few songs, the platform suddenly went back down again and it was like being on a sinking ship! I do recall a front row of bemused faces in the audience, puzzled by this curious arrangement. We had a good laugh about it afterwards.

On the same day we learned that our single, 'Headline News' was number 11 in the Radio London charts. Radio London was a pirate station, broadcast from a ship moored in the Thames estuary.

Pye Records promotional handout
1966

These pirate stations didn't pay royalties but they were a great source of exposure for up and coming groups. A week later, the single went to number 7.

This was exciting news. A top ten record in the charts of a pirate radio station usually generated a lot of sales. 'Headline News' had been released on the Pye label during July and had some good reviews in the music press. Polydor records then surprised us by releasing Edwin Starr's version of the same song!

If I had known that Polydor were intending to do this, I would have doubted the wisdom of recording it in the first place. I don't deny that our recording was a cover version but the track was originally on an Edwin Starr album with, as far as we knew, no plans to release it as a single.
It appeared to be a classic record company decision to capitalise on the interest that we had generated in the song. The combined sales of both records would have guaranteed a top-ten single but with divided sales, neither achieved that goal. It was tragic, particularly as our single had a lot of radio play.

To add insult to injury, on the 21st August we played at The Stoke Hotel in Guildford and during our performance, the management complained we were too loud. Not satisfied that we had reduced the volume sufficiently, they then turned off the power! Malcolm Rose from our agency made a press statement that was published in The Times, defending us but a spokesman for the hotel said, and I quote, 'After repeatedly asking the group to tone down because neighbours had complained, we had no alternative but to switch the power off.' *Tone* down. What a classic remark!

We were back in The Marquee again on the 29th August, supporting The Steam Packet, which was lead by Brian Auger and featured Julie Driscoll and Rod Stewart. It was the final gig for The Steam Packet before their disbandment and, in the dressing room afterwards, Jeff was sitting beside Rod Stewart and asked him what he was going to do next.
Rod replied, 'I don't know. I've only got a quid.' He pulled out a crumpled pound note from his pocket to emphasise the point. Jeff said, 'Well, I'm sure something will turn up.' (And didn't it just! - Jeff).

marquee club

GERRARD 8923 | **90, WARDOUR STREET, LONDON W.1.**

SEPT 1966 Programme

THE MARQUEE PRESENTS
SONNY STITT

The first **"Jazz Spectacular"** at the Marquee is on Sunday, September 18th, and will feature one of the greatest American jazz saxophonists, **Sonny Stitt.** He will be accompanied by the **Dick Morrissey Quartet** comprising **Morrissey** (tenor sax), **Harry South** (piano), **Phil Bates** (bass), and **Bill Eyden** (drums). The programme will also feature the **Johnny Scott Quintet with David Snell on harp.**

Sonny Stitt was an early disciple of the late Charlie Parker but in recent years has evolved his own highly personal style of playing which has won for him innumerable awards. In his long career spanning over two decades Stitt has been associated with such "greats" as Dizzy Gillespie, Bud Powell, Roy Eldridge, and Oscar Peterson.

This session will take the form of a concert in miniature with a seated audience. Tickets are obtainable in advance: Members 10/– and non-Members 12/6 (from September 5th).

JOHN C. GEE,
Marquee Club Secretary

"HEADLINE NEWS"
for ALAN BOWN SET

Making "Headline News" with their record release of the same name are the **Alan Bown Set,** who move into a series of Monday evening sessions at the Marquee Club commencing September 5th. They have been appearing at the Club regularly since last April and scored an enormous success at this year's Windsor Jazz Festival. The line-up is as follows: **Alan Bown** (trumpet), **Jess Roden** (vocal), **Vic Sweeney** (drums), **Stan Haldane** (bass), **Pete Burgess** (guitar), **Jeff Banister** (organ/vocal), **John Anthony** (tenor sax).

FAIRFIELD HALL, CROYDON

Friday, October 21st, 6.45 & 9.00. The Marquee Club presents THE SPENCER DAVIS GROUP plus many other Marquee Club attractions. Full details from the Club and Fairfield Hall.

MEMBERSHIP 5/- to December 31st 1966

Membership application forms obtainable from: The Secretary, Marquee Club, 90 Wardour Street, London W.1.

Members receive a Marquee Club membership card entitling them to reduced admission, and the monthly programme which is mailed direct.

ADMISSION

The Marquee Club is open nightly from 7.30 to 11.00 p.m. Admission prices are as follows, unless otherwise stated:
Tue.: Members 7/–; non-Members 8/6. *Sun., Mon., Thurs., Fri.:* Members 5/–; non-Members 7/6. *Wed.:* Members 5/–; non-Members 6/–. *Sat.:* Members 6/–; non-Members 8/6.

Members may book advance tickets for Tuesday evening sessions one week ahead. Postal applicants must enclose membership cards and s.a.e.

REFRESHMENTS: Coffee, soft drinks, and savouries are available at reasonable prices.

PRINTED BY THE BROADWATER PRESS LTD, WELWYN GARDEN CITY, HERTFORDSHIRE

Our workload was as intense as ever as will be seen from this sample of Jeff's diary;

September 1966

1st	Stoke on Trent, Hanley – Golden Torch
2nd	Cardiff - Scene Club
3rd	Watford – Trade Hall
4th	Nottingham- Beachcomber
5th	London - Marquee
6th	London - Wood Green
7th	London - Pye Studios
8th	London – Klooks Kleek
9th	Bournemouth - Pavilion
10th	Manchester – Twisted Wheel
11th	Sheffield- Mojo
12th	Edmonton – Cooks Ferry Inn
13th	Bristol
14th	London – Magazine interviews
16th	Bath - Pavilion
17th	Uxbridge – Burtons
18th	Birmingham
19th	London – Marquee
20th	Stoke on Trent, Hanley - The Place
21st	Norwich
22nd	Eastcote
24th	Portsmouth – Birdcage
25th	London – Marquee
26th	Basingstoke
27th	Essex, Grays Civic Hall
30th	St Albans

Four days off out of 30! This was true of most months during this period. The band was constantly on the road.

We would regularly travel back from South Wales after a gig and those days there was no motorway so we had to rely on a route of A-roads. This took hours of driving and at dawn the sun would come up and shine directly into our eyes.

To add to the misery, sometimes our arrival back on the outskirts of London would correspond with the rush hour traffic. Jeff recalls, 'Because only Vic, Alan and I had a driving licence, I would sometimes not get home before 10 o'clock in the morning after driving all night and dropping everyone off.'

On the 5th September 1966, we played our first headline date at The Marquee. Supporting us was a band called Rhythm & Soul and the drummer was Dave James, an old friend of Jeff's who used to be in his band, prior to him joining The John Barry Seven. We were drawing a healthy crowd by then and the club had a respectable turn out. By Marquee standards, the evening was a great success.

Two days later, we were back in Pye studio to record 'Emergency 999' and the B-side 'Settle Down', written by Jeff and myself. The session went into extra time and Jeff had to cope with the vocals of 'Settle Down' at around 3 o'clock in the morning. Studio cleaners were actually sweeping up between takes! It was a struggle and I thought Jeff was pushed to the limit to cope with the lead vocal track after recording the backing tracks all night as well. Unfortunately we had no more studio time booked and we had no further opportunity to improve on what we had recorded. Next day, the bleary-eyed band had a photo session and interview with Fabulous 208 magazine.

Around this time two Lancashire girls, Trish and Anna, approached us and asked if they could form a fan club for us, which they did.

On the 14th September 1966 we had an interview and a photo session with Petticoat magazine. Five days later, after more gigs on the road, we were back at The Marquee, headlining and supported by The James Royal Set. Another 'Set' believe it or not.

The Melody Maker, on the 24th September, reported that The Alan Bown Set's new single, 'Emergency 999' will be released on October 24th.

On the 25th September, we recorded 'London Swings Live at The Marquee Club'. This was a live album with The Alan Bown Set featured on one side and Jimmy James and The Vagabonds on the other. The tracks on this album, for me, sum up the strength of the band in that period. It's still very exciting and the atmosphere literally jumps off the CD (vinyl, in those days). (See discography - albums).

'London Swings Live at The Marquee Club' was recorded in The Marquee Studio, which was situated in the rear of the same building so it was just a question of feeding all the multi-core leads from the stage to the studio. We did add some overdubs a day or two later to tidy up some of the vocals but there was so much 'spillage' from the amps on stage that nothing could be done about the occasional musical goof during the performance. And it was not possible to erase the voice of the idiot who ran up to the stage shouting, 'Stan, Stan, Stan'.

'London Swings Live at The Marquee Club' was also released in France in 1967. The album is now a collector's item in all territories. Expect to pay mega bucks for a copy!

We graced the stage of The Marquee once again on the 10th October, this time supported by 'The Syn'. This band, with the later addition of Rick Wakeman, became 'Yes'.

On 21st October 1966, our single, 'Emergency 999' was released on the Pye label. The song was written by Paul Korda and we applied a similar formula to it as we did for 'Headline News', using falsetto backing vocals.

The Record Mirror on 22nd October gave the new single a 4-star review. Also on the 22nd, The Melody Maker briefly reviewed the single. On the same day we played at The Ricky Tick Club in Windsor (see agreement on page 81).

There were several clubs of this name in different locations. Another was on Eel Pie Island. The promoter of the Ricky Tick clubs was Keith Mansfield's older brother, John Mansfield. All the name bands played at these clubs in the early days, in particular, The Rolling Stones.

In between gigs, we headlined at The Marquee on October the 31st, supported by 'Wynder K Frog' and back again on November the 14th, supported by 'MI Five'.

Our agency informed us that they had booked us for few days in Belgium. We always enjoyed going abroad and were looking forward to this trip knowing that the audiences in Belgium would have very little idea about our music. We could do what we liked and it would be a laugh, but, on a more serious note, all the stress of travelling around the country was getting to some of us more than others. Pete, the guitarist was drinking more than I felt was good for him, or the band. I had words with him on the subject a couple of times but it was clear the message wasn't getting through. Other members of the band were also uncomfortable with the situation and Pete's guitar playing was becoming more erratic. This was like déjà vu, for me with memories of Ernie Cox in The Seven and his drinking problem coming back to haunt me. We discussed this amongst ourselves and I decided that, sadly, Pete was no longer the man for the job. One night travelling back from the north, we stopped at the Blue Boar and it was here that I had to break the news to Pete. I told him out of earshot of the others but they knew the axe was about to fall. I found this very difficult having known Pete for years, even before I formed the band. Also, it was because of him that we had made the connections at Pye records. Outside of his playing, he had been a good friend but this decision was based purely on business. I don't think he was expecting it, though I had made it clear on several occasions that he wasn't doing himself or us any favours. Pete didn't take it that well and obviously felt that we had all betrayed him. Like the rest of us he had been looking forward to going to Belgium but in a way, it was because of that that I made the decision. I thought Pete might be tempted to regard the trip as an excuse for a booze-up. In the interests of the band, I had to avoid this. After this meeting we had a long silent journey back down the M1 with a dark cloud in the atmosphere of the van. Miles of motorway went by and then the silence was suddenly broken by John's voice, which said without any subtlety and to no one in particular, 'Do they sell cheap records in Belgium?'

11

A NEW GUITARIST

On 23rd of November 1966, Tony Catchpole joined the band, replacing Pete Burgess on guitar. Tony had previously played in a band called George Bean and the Runners and he was a friend of our drummer, Vic, who had also been a member of that band.

Teaser adverts for the album 'London Swings Live at The Marquee Club' appeared in The Disc and Music Echo and The Melody Maker on the 26th November. Our trip to Belgium on the 25th was also mentioned.

'London Swings Live at The Marquee Club', featuring The Alan Bown Set on one side and Jimmy James and the Vagabonds on the other, was released on the 25th November 1966.

We left England on the same day and travelled to Belgium. Driving such a vehicle as the Commer van on the 'wrong' side of the road was a trifle hairy to say the least. The passenger in the front seat had to be the eyes for the driver, saying when it was safe to overtake. In reality, it was never safe to overtake on those roads!

We played at a weekend festival in Liege and after the first gig, walked back through the streets to our hotel at about 2am with John blowing sax and me blowing trumpet. The rest of the band followed behind with stragglers from the audience, in carnival style! How we didn't get arrested, I don't know but when we arrived at the hotel, the night porter must have thought it was VE Day all over again.

Another English band booked for the festival was Blinky Davidson's 'Everywhichway'. Blinky was formerly the drummer with The Nice so we'd met up many times before. On the way back to Ostende we passed them on the side of the road and realised that their van had broken down. After some inspired miming in a local village shop, (no one understood the lingo) we bought a towrope and hooked up Blinky's van to ours. With their van being towed and steered by their roadie the other members Blinky's band joined us in our van. John Anthony and Blinky had been given a large bottle of Scotch by the club owner in Liege and they began to polish it off. We reached Ostende safely and the two bands came back together on the ferry to Dover.

The ferry crossing was rough that day and John and Blinky were seen holding each other up like drunken versions of Fred Astaire and Ginger Rogers! We continued to tow their van back to London but the tow-rope kept breaking and eventually we had to abandon their van on the outskirts of town.

The weekend had been a good opportunity for Tony Catchpole to get to know us and vice-versa. His guitar playing suited the band and his image fitted in well.

Pace Magazine, on October the 13th 1966, gave us a half-page review of one of our performances at The Marquee. A prominent photo of the band at the head of the article was captioned 'Atmosphere at Ignition Point for Alan Bown Performance - Hilda Baker's verdict: Fantastic.' I must hasten to add that this wasn't the Hilda Baker that used to do a vaudeville act with the catchphrase, 'She knows, you know!' This was a genuine journalist. The four column glowing review gave us all a name check and an in-depth profile.

After our return to England, on the 9th December at 2.30pm, we went into the BBC studios to record tracks for the Rhythm and Blues World Service Show. We recorded 'Do The Boomerang', 'Gonna Fix You Good' and 'Headline News'. Brian Matthew interviewed me and this was transmitted with the show. Straight after this, we drove to Leicester for a gig in the evening.

On the 12th December 1966, Bobby Pridden our roadie left the band. I felt his decision was a lot to do with Pete's departure because they were old friends. I was very disappointed that Bobby didn't stay on and when he gave me his notice I was so angry that I told him that if he left us that he would never work again. It wasn't long before I heard that he had joined The Who's road crew! He later became their chief sound technician and, I believe, he still is today. They gave him the nickname Ben Pump, which has stuck with him. At least Bobby's apprenticeship with us prepared him for more volatile encounters. Jess reported back to us that Keith Moon threw half his drum kit at Bobby on his first night!

Jess still lived at Bobby's mother's house so I was slightly concerned there might be some conflict over Bobby's departure. Fortunately it wasn't the case but it did lead to Jess guesting on vocals on The Who track, 'Magic Bus' on the 29th May two years later in 1968. Even now you can detect his distinctive voice on that track.

On the 17th December, Jeff took delivery of a Hammond Organ. Jimmy James's organist had kindly let us use his Hammond for The Marquee, London Swings album recording session and Jeff was absolutely delighted with his new acquisition. More so than our new roadies who had to lift it! However, we did get the Hammond 'split' which was a common thing in those days. The instrument was literally cut in half, horizontally and the top and bottom halves of the integral circuitry were linked with multi-core cables and connectors. In theory, it divided the weight of the organ in half. Also a 'skate-board' was fixed to bottom of the instrument so it could be pushed around without damaging the foot pedals. (That's not a skate-board with wheels, just a flat piece of wood)

We now had two new road managers, Bernie and Terry, both from Willesden, London. These two guys were like a breath of fresh air. They were good friends with each other, always a laugh and did the job with no problems. Bernie had roadied with bands previously but it was all new to Terry. With his curly blond hair and cheeky smile, Terry reminded me of Harpo Marx and it wouldn't have surprised me if he had turned up with a coaching horn tucked in his belt.

One day, on the way to a gig, we stopped to go into a grocer's shop. Bernie used to wear a trilby hat and on this occasion walked into the shop with about ten long, thin, lighted candles all around the brim of his hat! He casually surveyed the shelves to select something while astonished shoppers stood by. The shopkeeper was equally stunned and then Bernie purchased something without batting an eyelid and walked out. We were creased up. It was a one off, typical of Bernie.

Another incident, which was hilarious, happened during our stay in a guesthouse. Bernie and Terry were sharing a room and Terry had a nasty rash, which the doctor suspected might be scabies. He had given Terry a large bottle of white lotion, which had to be applied to every part of the body. So the following morning, in the room of the guesthouse, Bernie was applying the lotion to a totally naked Terry when in walked the chambermaid to service the room! Imagine her response at seeing a naked man being painted white by another man in a hat! Both of them smiling and saying, 'Good morning'. Jeff walked past the open door at the same time and viewed the scene with equal astonishment.

If we arrived in a town early, these guys had a routine, which, one day got out of hand. We would drop Bernie off, then drive around the block and, on our return, see Bernie thumbing a lift. We would pull up beside him and he would demand to be taken somewhere ridiculous and then start an argument. Terry would respond and a shouting match would develop. This particular day, Terry leapt on Bernie and they rolled around on the pavement in a mock fight, shouting obscenities, which attracted so much attention from onlookers, that someone called the police! We had some explaining to do before they let us go. Fortunately, Bernie didn't have the candles around his hat but he did get a caution.

As a footnote to this malarkey, we found that whenever we stopped to ask someone for directions, they inevitably ended with the words, 'You can't miss it'. This was the kiss of death. It was like a voodoo curse and we usually got seriously lost. We also seemed to be destined to ask the local pillock the way and while the driver was trying to interpret what was being said, one of the band would be knocking on the window and shouting from the back seat, 'Help, I'm a prisoner in here!'

On the 19th December 1966, we were back in Pye studio for demos. A series of one-nighters followed then on the 30th we appeared at The Ricky Tick Club in Windsor.

The Melody Maker reviewed our 'London Swings Live at The Marquee' album on the 24th December. The review was good and concluded, 'It's a good looking gas of an album.'

Record Mirror reported on 31st December, that we were considering another live album, recorded in Northern and Southern Clubs, for release next April.

The Melody Maker also covered this story on the 31st December but it was unfounded speculation.

We played New Years Eve 1966 at the Twisted Wheel Club in Manchester. People came from miles around to this famous all-nighter and, coincidentally, the 31st of December in 1966 was a Saturday, boosting the crowd to capacity. There was a lot of pill popping going on in those days but I have to say that we got through the nights on pure adrenaline. Visiting bands would usually play two sets from 1am onwards. It's hard to explain what the atmosphere was like in the clubs then, but to say it was electric was an understatement.

Vic Sweeney   *John Anthony Helliwell*   *Tony Catchpole*   *Jeff Bannister*

THE ALAN BOWN SET

Jess Roden *Alan Bown* *Stan Haldane*

12

THE KING MOJO AND MORE

We may have played all night at The Twisted Wheel but on the very next night, the 1st of January 1967 we played The King Mojo Club, run by Peter Stringfellow. Peter was an instantly likeable guy and unlike a lot of promoters he was totally into music. It was Peter who had suggested that we recorded 'Baby Don't Push Me'. He had built the club up from scratch mainly on the back of his personality as a host and as a DJ. I seem to remember that the Mojo was two buildings merged into one. The front part was like an old house, which you went through to access the ballroom area at the back. The atmosphere in the club was always buzzing and we had some great gigs there.

You can read more about Peter Stringfellow and The King Mojo in his excellent book, 'King of Clubs' published by Little, Brown and Co.

After one gig at The Mojo, we drove to a local Sheffield park with as many people crammed into the Commer van as possible. Several carloads of fans followed us and Peter's brother, Geoff, also came along with an ample supply of drink We had a party in the grounds of the park but it was broken up at about 2am when some park official appeared and complained about the noise. It was all innocent fun and there was no trouble but we had to wind it up and drive back to London. The 'party in the van' became part of Sheffield folk-lore.

When we stayed over in Sheffield we usually stayed at The Montgomery Hotel, run by Ivor White, an old friend of Peter Stringfellow. Two or three terraced houses had been merged into a rambling hotel with creaky floors and labyrinths of passages. It reminded me of the haunted houses you get in funfairs (without skeletons jumping out at you).
The conversion had resulted in some amusing foibles, one of which affected most guests that stayed there. Being an old Victorian terrace, the rooms in these houses were huge with high ceilings. It had been already decided that the larger rooms were candidates for partitioning thus making two rooms out of one. The large windows would have presented a problem to a less enterprising owner but the conversion had gone ahead regardless and the partitions were now in place. Checking in to the hotel after a gig and being led down many passages, through identical fire doors and up flights of

stairs meant that most musicians were so disorientated in the morning that it was virtually impossible to find your way to the dining room in time for breakfast.

We got to know the lay-out after several visits but you sometimes wondered if there was a plot to save on provisions, which were part of the 'bed & breakfast deal.'

Jeff recalls; 'One night, after getting ready for bed, in one of the partitioned rooms, I thought it might get a bit cold during the night so I closed the window. It was the old style of sash window and had to be pulled down so imagine my surprise to find it open when I awoke! Before I left the room to go down to breakfast, I closed it again thinking that I must have previously dreamt closing it. After breakfast in the dining room, which I had found by using an old Red Indian tracking technique, I returned to my room to discover the window open again! I was feeling slightly nervous now. I knew this was an old building so I began to wonder if this could be the work of a poltergeist? I shut the window again and while I stood at the sink cleaning my teeth. I became aware of some movement near the window. To my astonishment I watched immobile as the window opened itself! However, it was no poltergeist; it was another guest in the next room, on the other side of the partition wall. The conversion had literally divided one large window down the middle to serve two rooms. After observing the outside of the building from the street more closely, it was clear that some of the windows on the upper floors had a plasterboard division right down the middle!'

We regularly ate at the same Chinese restaurant in Sheffield and once, after the main course, we asked the waiter what ice creams he had. He replied, 'Strawby, chockla and valalla.' Someone in the band replied, 'Is that banana?' The waiter, slightly exasperated, said, 'No, no, not banana, valalla.' We knew he was attempting to say 'Vanilla' but kept up the pretence, asking each other in front of him if it was banana. On our next visit, we caught him out again with the valalla/banana routine and he was suitably wound up. However, on a subsequent visit when we got around to the dessert we asked him what ice creams he had and with a big smile, he replied, 'Strawby, chockla and white.'

I always had a hard time eating restaurant food on the road, particularly Indian or Chinese. It got to the point where, when a waiter asked me for my order, the band would all reply in unison, 'Egg Foo Yung!' One night we had booked into a guesthouse and Jeff and I were sharing a room. When we eventually got into the room after the gig, we discovered that there was a double bed instead of two singles! The floor had a lino covering with long mats along each side of the bed. To add to my joy, I had just eaten a dodgy Chinese meal from a local take-away and felt quite ill. I said to Jeff that I felt sick and he pointed out that there was a sink on the other side of the room.

There was no en-suite of course. It was quite late and we got into the bed, glad of the chance of some sleep and switched off the light. After about five minutes, I sat up in the darkness and felt a torrent of bile rising in my throat. In an urgent attempt to reach the sink, I got one leg out of the bed but couldn't stop the inevitable. I threw up all over the floor but I was too exhausted to do anything about it. When Jeff viewed the mess in the morning he had a stroke of inspiration. All of the vomit had landed on the mat alongside of the bed and Jeff merely rolled it up and put it under the bed! It would have been a nice surprise for the cleaning lady after we had left and could have added a new term to the glossary of carpet retailers; 'Deep bile'.

On the 2nd January, we recorded Saturday Club at The Playhouse Theatre in London. This was still a popular BBC radio show, hosted by Brian Matthew.

On the 6th January, we played in Cardiff. Tony had his guitar stolen from the van! The 7th January 1967 was Jeff's 24th birthday but his celebration of it was put on hold. The band was booked to play a 'double' (two gigs at different venues on the same night) in Birmingham. This was not unusual for us or other bands at the time but, as you can imagine, these doubles were purgatory for the roadies who had set up and break the gear down twice in one night. Mrs Regan, known by the visiting bands as Ma Regan, was the promoter for several old theatres in the Birmingham area. These were The Handsworth Plaza, The Oldhill Plaza, The Ritz Kingsheath and a club called The Brum Cavern.

It was on the way to one of these gigs that we discussed the possibility of updating the band's name. We felt that the 'Set' was beginning to sound passé but it was too late to change the name entirely. A radical suggestion was made that we just use the name 'Bown'. It was short and punchy. I sort of liked the idea. It was it the vein of 'Cream' and 'Family' so I decided to run with it.

That night, we were booked to appear first at the Handsworth Plaza and just before our performance, we spoke to Mrs Regan's husband who always introduced the bands and explained that we were not 'The Alan Bown Set' now but just 'Bown'. Mr Regan was a tall, thin black-country man, already in his 50's and looked like a bespectacled undertaker. He blinked uncomprehendingly as we repeated our new name and walked off into the wings of the stage with a not too confident air. This last minute change was doomed from then on. We were set up behind the closed curtains, awaiting the announcement, poised and ready to play. We could hear the muffled conversation of the audience and then the footsteps of Mr Regan as he approached the microphone, centre stage, on the other side of the curtains. We anticipated him saying something like, 'And now from London, your top band for tonight, Bown!' Instead, there was the predictable 'social secretary style' tapping of the mic, followed by a short pause and then, in a thick Brummie accent, just one loud word, 'Boooon!'

The curtains opened to reveal the band creased up laughing, almost unable to play. Needless to say the idea of using 'Bown' was immediately dropped although it sowed the seeds for a later adaptation of the name. To add to our evening's misery, on the second gig at The Oldhill Plaza, Jeff's organ amp blew up!

The 12th of January saw the band measured up for suits at 'Take 6' the fashionable men's boutique in Carnaby Street. To maintain a calculated individuality, each suit was tailored in a different colour. Predictably, having seven members in the band, meant that some of the colours were less popular than the others. No one wanted to be in a green suit or brown so there was a visible jostling by each musician to secure the colour of his choice with the tailor. On this occasion, Jeff ended up with a gold suit, which was too close to brown for his liking. He made up for it on the next batch by getting a white suit!* I have to say, that when we walked on stage at any gig in these suits the effect was quite something. It was part of being a visual band as well as delivering a high standard of musical performance. Jess Roden hated the suits. His high-energy performance usually resulted in the suit being drenched with perspiration and after the gig he would bundle it into a bag without any thought of how it would look on the next gig.

*The white suit was subject to an incident, which cannot go unmentioned. On one occasion we played at a venue, which had footlights along the whole width of the stage. These lights were recessed into the apron of the stage and this arrangement had created a slope, which was virtually indiscernible when the lights were on, shining directly towards the performers. At one point, during our act, Jeff emerged from behind the Hammond organ, with his mic to sing 'Heartbreak Hotel', Elvis style. Half way through the song, as he moved towards the front of the stage he misjudged the edge of the slope and completely slipped over and rolled into the recess! When he got up it was clear to everyone that, stuck to one side of the white suit, were years of dust, fluff, matchsticks, cotton buds, old tickets and a few dog-ends. The band and the audience were in hysterics as the song came to an abrupt end and the spirit of Elvis left the building!

On the 16th Jan 1967, we were back in Pye studio at 7pm to record our next single. We recorded the B-side first, which was written by Jeff and myself, called 'I Really Care'. Jess sang it really well and the brass licks sounded exciting, very raw and 'live'.

On January 23rd, we recorded the A-side, 'Gonna Fix You Good.'
We put the finishing touches to this single on 31st of January. Roger Greenaway, whom we had met on the Billy Fury Tour as a member of The Kestrels, added some backing vocals and Clem Cattini, was drafted in, on an additional drumkit to play along with Vic. We weren't happy with the final mix and I thought it had become a kitchen sink production. Compared with other Alan Bown Set singles this one failed to capture the essence of the band's style. To me, our demo sounded much more authentic.

The Alan Bown Set
Record company handout 1967

February the 26th, we were back at The Mojo in Sheffield and two days later at The Marquee in London supported by The Syn.

On Friday, the 17th of March we guested on The Joe Loss Show. It was a live transmission, afternoon radio show. We played two numbers entitled 'Come on up' and 'Gonna Fix You Good.' After the show we drove to Leicester for a one-nighter.

On the 23rd and 24th March, we played two gigs in Rotterdam, Holland. The next three days we spent in France. We played at The Locomotive Club in Paris and then appeared at The Eden Ranch, Lens, which was 100 miles from Paris. On the last day of March, 'Gonna Fix You Good' was released.

We played at Billy Walker's 'Uppercut Club' in Forest Gate, East London on the 30th March 1967. Also on the bill that night, were The Syn and The Barron Nights. I was reunited with Dave Ballinger, the drummer with The Barron Knights, whom I first met at The Slough Boys Club. We'd both come a long way since then!

Our management told us that Jacques Loussier, the celebrated French jazz pianist had been commissioned to provide music for a forthcoming film to be premiered at the Cannes Film Festival. Apparently, he wanted to capture an authentic London 'beat' sound and was coming to England to find a suitable band. We were told that he was keen to see The Alan Bown Set. For the next few gigs we were on our toes, looking out into the audience hoping to catch a glimpse of Jacques Loussier but it became a pointless exercise.

During this spell, we played at a university function, which featured several bands, placed in different halls around the campus. When we went on, it was quite late and there were only about three roadies and a couple of stragglers in the hall. At the end of our act, seeing little response, we lost our usual composure and started clowning around. John began playing The Conga on sax and we got behind him, shuffling around the stage. Jess was on the drums and a couple of us dropped our trousers to spice up the proceedings and our roadies were out front, falling about. More rude gestures followed and the band eventually collapsed into a heap of legs and arms. We came off stage still laughing and jostling each other and a few minutes later a total stranger put his round the dressing room door. He asked politely if he could come in for a word or two. The French accent was an immediate give away. It was Jacques Loussier! He had seen the whole of our act and before we had time to explain all the lunacy, he said how much he had enjoyed it!

At the beginning of April 1967, we were excited to discover that our single was No 27 in the Radio London charts. Next day we recorded Saturday Club at The BBC Playhouse Theatre with Brian Matthew then we played Cooks Ferry Inn, Edmonton in the evening. This venue was an old pub by the river Lea and all the name bands played there at the time.

The Melody Maker, on the 8th April, ran an advert for our appearance that night at The Night Owl in Leicester, one of our regular gigs that drew a big crowd. Also on the 8th, Disc and Music Echo reported on the music that we had recorded for the film 'The Killing Game' to be shown at The Cannes Film festival.

On the 9th April we learned that 'Gonna Fix You Good' was No. 20 in Radio London charts. It was also getting plays on BBC radio programmes and prospects were looking good.

We had an interview with 'Jackie', which was then one of the most popular magazines. Melody Maker reported on the 15th April that we were flying to Cannes for the premier of the film, 'The Killing Game.' The report also mentioned, 'On April 16th they make their debut at London's Saville Theatre, on the bill with Bo Diddley and Ben E King.'

By now we had too much equipment to transport in one vehicle so we bought a car for the band and a Ford Transit van for the roadies. We also had a change of roadie at this time. Bernie left and was replaced by Steve Hackett from Sheffield. In those early days, only Jeff, Vic and I had driving licences but now, at last, we could gain some pleasure out of driving. The automatic transmission of the car meant no more 'stirring puddings' in worn out gearboxes.

Melody Maker on the 4th March 1967 reported; 'Alan Bown Set's new 12-seat Ford Galaxy belonged to King Hussein and has electronically operated windows, record player, tape deck, TV, cocktail cabinet and change colour windscreen!' Our publicist, Keith Goodwin, had excelled himself with hype.

In the April 15th issue of Trend, an article and photograph of the band was accompanied with the headline, 'The Wonderful Car in The Alan Bown Set Up'. It also reported that we'd bought a 12-seater, American Ford that used to belong to King Hussein and the car had tinted windows, a TV and cocktail cabinet.

In truth, we had bought a Ford Galaxy 9-seater saloon with bench seats, electric windows and a monster V6 engine. (The registration number of the car was 7 YMY). Yes, it was American. No, it didn't have tinted windows, record player, tape deck, TV or cocktail cabinet. What it did have was a habit of blowing gaskets and a tendency to break down in the most remote places. It was the envy of many other bands on the road but it came at a heavy price. All spare parts were quadruple the cost of English components and we could only take the car to a specialist garage in London, so breaking down in somewhere like Upper Wallop in Cheshire was a nightmare.

Out of curiosity, to see how fast the car would go we once actually got the speedometer up to 120 miles an hour on the M1, which was a scary to say the least. Seven white faces broke into nervous laughter when the speed dropped back to 70 mph. We soon found that, in icy conditions, the car was not the most secure vehicle on the road and, on the way to one gig, we snaked up the M1 with the back end trying to overtake the front! It was like some fairground ride but without the fun.

The speaker for the car radio was on top of the dashboard and Jess Roden would spend most of the journeys home huddled over it to hear the latest records on Radio Luxembourg. The signal of this station was notorious for fading in and out and Jess's torso would become more contorted as the journey went on with his attempts to hear every musical morsel. At the signature tune of Disney's 'When You Wish Upon a Star', Jess would slide off the dashboard into the seat and, within seconds, fall asleep.

Once, on the way to South Wales, the brake calipers on the right front wheel seized up and, as we pulled over, we could see smoke coming from behind the wheel. We all quickly got out and someone wisely suggested getting far away from the car, in case the petrol ignited and blew up the tank. John Anthony was having none of it. He went to the back of the car and, ignoring our shouts of warning, opened the back door. One of the band called out, 'John, you're crazy, what are you doing?' He turned round and waving a rolled up newspaper at us, replied, 'I'm getting my bloody Melody Maker'. Evidently it was much more valuable than the life of a saxophonist! We stood there in dismay, in the middle of nowhere, observing flames consuming the front tyre. In those days, there were no mobile phones so we were helpless. Then an enormous articulated truck pulled up behind the car and the driver jumped down. Without saying a word he released the cap on a fire extinguisher and put out the flames in about 5 seconds. We were very grateful but that wasn't the end of our troubles. One of us did manage to get a lift to a local garage and send out a tow truck. Now, not many people believe this part of the story but the tow truck actually broke down on the way to the car! Another tow truck had to come out to tow the first one back and then come back to tow us to a garage. I can't remember if we ever got to that gig but I think we had to hire a van so any chances of a profit on that day were truly scuppered.

We used to have our car repaired and serviced in Hammersmith at Galena Garage. This was run by American car specialists and one of them was called Harry. After successive visits for replacement parts, mostly half shafts, we nicknamed him 'Half-Shaft-Harry'.

On the 16th April 1967 we appeared at The Saville Theatre, London, in a concert with Ben E King & The Drifters and Bo Diddley. A band called The Bunch opened the show and we followed. The finale of our act featured a rock 'n' roll medley, which unexpectedly enraged the purist fans in the audience. They were so incensed that they started running towards the stage, shouting, waving their fists and throwing missiles. Jess had the good sense to duck down behind the amps but Jeff was hit in the mouth with a coin and it broke off the end of a tooth. At this point, compere Rick Dane came on to the stage to try and calm things down. Even though he had on a token teddy-boy jacket, he too was booed and threatened.

Ben E King was on next and he must have wondered why the crowd were so hostile but they settled down when he came on, showing some respect for a legend with considerably more cred than us upstarts! We sensibly decided to leave the theatre, via the back door, before the concert finished.

Two different press reviews of the show reported that we were lucky to escape with our lives! It was a frightening experience and Jeff still has one tooth shorter than the others.

On reflection, the souvenir programme of the show didn't help, featuring a rare photo of the band all guffawing!

Photo from the Saville Theatre Programme
April 1967

We were back in the recording studio on the 29th April for demos, then played a gig in the evening at The Ricky Tick Club, Maidenhead.

May the 2nd saw us back at The Marquee, supported by 'Darlings'.

13

JEU DE MASSACRE

On 4th May 1967 we flew to the France with Richard Cowley, whom we had now appointed as our manager.

An extract from John Anthony Helliwell's diary reads;

May 1967

4th	London to Paris. Meal in Paris
5th	TV recording, Paris 10.00am. Paris-Nice 3.30pm. TV in Cannes at 8.00pm. Meal after with Jacques Loussier.
6th	TV in Monte Carlo 6.00pm. Play Whisky-a-go-go in Cannes at 12.30am.
7th	Bed at 6.00am. Saw film (Jeu De Massacre) at night.

After our arrival at Nice airport, a porter came up with a trolley and we all put our cases on it. Richard our manager had not seen this manoeuvre but when he spotted us strolling behind the trolley he rushed over and asked us how much this extravagance was going to cost. When we told him it would be nine centimes he hastily began to take the cases off the trolley. The porter and other travellers looked on in astonishment as Richard piled our cases up as though we were being taken to the French cleaners. It was embarrassing and hilarious at the same time.

When we made our exit from the terminal, the concourse was bathed in brilliant sunshine. It was so dazzling that Stan had not seen the large shallow artificial pond outside and walked straight into it. Suddenly realising his mistake and with water filling his shoes, he kept on walking as though it wasn't there while the rest of us watched, wondering if there was a deep trough in the middle. Fortunately for Stan there wasn't and he walked the whole width of the pond and stepped out at the other side unperturbed. Other travellers emerging from the terminal halted and looked on in astonishment.

Jacques Loussier's company had arranged accommodation for us just outside Cannes, which was hard to come by during the festival.

VOGUE

SERIE MEDIUM

EPL 8 537

GRAND JEU
des PORTE-CLEFS
vogue
1
8 537
VIGNETTE
45' EP
VALABLE JUSQU'AU
31 AOUT 1968

BANDE SONORE ORIGINALE DU FILM :

PRODUCTION
vogue
international

Imprimé en France

JEU DE MASSACRE

Réalisation Alain JESSUA — Production René THEVENET — Films FRANCINOR

REPRESENTE LA FRANCE AU FESTIVAL DE CANNES 1967

avec

Jean-Pierre CASSEL
Claudine AUGER
Michel DUCHAUSSOY
Eléonore HIRT
Anna GAYLOR
Guy SAINT JEAN
Nancy HOLLOWAY

Musique composée et dirigée par **JACQUES LOUSSIER**
avec THE ALAN BOWN SET dans « KILLING GAME »
Jacques Loussier — Alain Jessua
Courtesy of PYE Records LTD.
Editions Vogue International

Dessins : Guy PEELLAERT

DILLARD et Cie. Imp. Paris

GRAND JEU
DES PORTE-CLEFS
VOGUE

Découpez les vignettes se trouvant au verso de vos disques VOGUE, et vous gagnerez de magnifiques porte-clefs en métal argenté à l'effigie de vos vedettes préférées, numérotés de 1 à 8 et un Joker. Tirage limité à 1 000 exemplaires.
Les porte-clefs en votre possession vous permettent de participer aux jeux VOGUE qui passent sur les antennes de Radio et dans la Presse.
Les gagnants recevront de nombreux prix et participeront à la « Grande Finale » du « Grand Jeu VOGUE ».
Vogueman

1 ANTOINE
2 PETULA CLARK
3 FRANÇOISE HARDY
4 JACQUES DUTRONC
5 AIMABLE
6 PIERRE PERRET
7 SIDNEY BECHET
8 CLAUDE LUTER
Le Joker J.-J. DEBOUT

Envoyez vos vignettes :
Disques VOGUE
« GRAND JEU DES
PORTE-CLEFS »
93-VILLETANEUSE
20 vignettes de 45 Tours
pour 1 Porte-clefs
10 vignettes de 33 Tours
pour 1 Porte-clefs

Ce disque est un enregistrement **VOGUE** Haute Fidélité, le matériel galvanoplastique et le pressage ont été réalisés par la **Manufacture de Productions Phonographiques VOGUE**

C'EST UNE RÉALISATION Villetaneuse (Seine)

We could even walk to the beach and mingle with the jet-set, swollen by many visitors in the film industry. We soon discovered that restaurant prices were exorbitant and you had to take out a mortgage on a cup of coffee.

On the 6th May 1967, we made a live appearance at a Monte Carlo TV station at 6pm. It was quite a small studio and I remember the band being cramped into a corner and only one camera available. French TV seemed to be in it's infancy in those days and I recall a certain amount of what can only be described as mayhem going on, with us in one corner and something else like a circus act happening in the opposite corner. Us 'veterans' thought it was very amateur.

I suppose, in reality and being the South of France, it was just a more laid back approach. Heaven knows what viewers made of it (all ten of them!). After the TV show, we went back to Cannes to play a gig at The Whisky a-Go-Go, which began after midnight. The club was packed with film people; starlets, producers and hustlers, all jostling to be seen. So much so, we were virtually ignored! As John recalls, we were there all night.

The evening of the next day we went to the screening of the movie, which Jacques Loussier had commissioned us for. It was called 'Jeu De Massacre' or in English, 'The Killing Game'. The movie starred Claudine Auger and the dialogue was all in French, so we sat there bored and clueless until pieces of our music came and went on various parts of the soundtrack. I remember it being a typical French film with car chases on empty roads, stressed out heroines and a lot of shooting. Jacques greeted us afterwards and asked us if we had enjoyed it. We all nodded and smiled in agreement. I think we saw him once again in London some time later but no more film offers followed after that.

We flew back to London on the 8th May and two days later recorded a session for a BBC radio show called Swingalong.

On May 13th, The New Musical Express printed a letter from C.A.Jackson, Kearsley, Lancs who wrote, 'Isn't it about time we gave the Alan Bown Set a break? On stage they are marvellous…'

On the same day, The Disc and Music Echo, reported, 'Alan Bown stood on his head for four minutes 25 seconds on stage at London's Marquee Club last Tuesday, breaking a record. But not his head.' This was a reference to my yoga routines which had gradually become part of our act. Our stage show now contained a lot of action and improvised dance movement.

Trend Magazine on 20th May, in their 'Private Ear' column,

featured a photo of the band with the caption, 'A flash car for Mike Nesmith, Zoot Money takes to the Air and the Alan Bown Set to hit the American scene'. (An American promoter had approached us, after he had seen our performance at a London gig. He was convinced we would go down well in The States and he had all the necessary contacts there to make arrangements. It all seemed promising at first but rumours went around that the guy wasn't kosher and bands he had dealt with before had been knocked (unpaid). The risk appeared too great for our management and consequently no deal was agreed. In retrospect, I think we should have taken a chance. The 'playing safe' policy denied us the opportunity to appear in front of American audiences who had already embraced bands like 'Blood Sweat and Tears' and 'Chicago'. I was not alone in thinking that we had the talent and the image to do some serious damage over there but it wasn't to be).

Back in the real world, we were doing a gig in Oxford on the 25th May and Bobby Pridden our ex-roadie (and now with The Who road crew), had told Jess that The Who were in town and Roger Daltrey had invited the band to join him for a drink in a quiet local pub that afternoon. We had crossed paths with The Who many times and we responded to the call, finding Roger in a discreet corner of the pub. He was the first person that we saw wearing a kaftan. He was also wearing white sailor's trousers and white sneakers (there were no 'trainers' in those days). With a pair of shades to complete the image, he looked a million dollars. I mention all this because it had quite an influence on our image, which was pure Carnaby at the time as you can see from some of the photographs in this book.

The amusing sequel to this meeting was that, on our trip to the Isle of Wight two days later, Vic, Tony and Jess all turned up in kaftans and Jeff, Stan, John and I couldn't resist the temptation to say, 'Blimey, the band's been Rogered!' or words to that effect. After the leg pulling, I was the next to succumb to the idea and went out and bought a kaftan. Stan, who lived in Edmonton, not known for its tolerance of androgyny, thought better of it and John and Jeff just raised an eyebrow. We were all into the Carnaby Street and Kings Road shops on our rare days off and I have to say that the clothes around at the time were more exciting than anything you see today. You could wear a diver's outfit and still be cool, providing you didn't want to run for a bus!

The gig on the Isle of Wight was in Ryde but there was no mini-break there, as we played in Chertsey the following night.

The Blue Boar at Watford Gap on the M1 motorway was a popular watering hole for all the gigging bands at the time and over the years it had many tales to tell but one comes to mind that illustrates how the clothes the band wore sometimes provoked insults or even aggression.

One night, we filed in to the restaurant for our meal or 'oil-change' as we sometimes called it and already seated were two Hell's Angels. They took immediate exception to our appearance and started making remarks. They singled out Tony Catchpole who, to them, looked the most feminine and one of them called over, 'Oi! Are you a tart or a woman?' Not wanting to point out to this cretin that a 'tart' was, by gender, a woman, we tried to ignore him but unsatisfied with our reaction he got up from his seat and came over to us with the obvious intent of tormenting us further. Just at that moment, our roadies, Algy and Steve walked in and the pair of them relished any opportunity for a good scrap. They told the Hell's Angel to return to his seat but he refused to back down. The other Hell's Angel came over making menacing remarks and a scuffle broke out. The women who served the food were shouting to stop it as fists were flying and bodies rolled around the floor. After a brief scrap, the Hell's Angels were unceremoniously bundled towards the door, mouthing off incoherent death threats. At that moment, in walked The Jimi Hendrix Experience with their roadies, followed by The Small Faces of similar flamboyant appearance. The Hell's Angels were stunned and severely outnumbered by, what must have appeared to them, as a troupe of circus performers! As they scuttled away, the looks on their faces were priceless.

One of the most indelible memories of The Blue Boar was one of karma. We had played a gig in the Midlands and were returning to London. This night Jimmy James and the Vagabonds were already in the Blue Boar, having a late night meal. We all knew each other (they also recorded at The Marquee and featured on one side of the 'London Swings' album) so there was a friendly rapport between us before they left to resume their journey. We watched them through the window of the restaurant as they piled into their van. There were about six or seven of them and with their gear as well, we could imagine how cramped they must have been. We quietly congratulated ourselves that our mode of transport, the Ford Galaxy, was far superior. We left about ten minutes later and sped down the M1. It wasn't long before we saw The Vag's in the distance and we shot passed their van doing about 90 miles an hour, giving them a smug 'royal wave' (looking straight ahead but waving one hand for effect). To our dismay we soon noticed that the needle of the water temperature gauge on the Galaxy's dashboard was in the red, indicating imminent trouble. With the Vag's van still a dot in the rear view mirror we had to make a quick decision. Pull over onto the hard shoulder and face humiliation or keep going with the hope that a turn-off would present itself. Pride made the decision for us and we kept going. Fortunately, in about a mile down the road, our prayers were answered. A motorway turn-off loomed up ahead! We reached it in a few minutes but by now the car's engine was coughing and sputtering so we had to jump out and push the Galaxy up the last 20 yards of the slip-road. We switched off the lights then, crouching down behind the car and, under the cover of darkness, we watched Jimmy James and the Vagabonds drive past without a glance in our direction. It was a close call but our dignity remained intact. We had to wait for the engine to cool down until we could persuade the car to crawl to the next services where we filled up the radiator with water. Another late night but the secret was never revealed, until now.

To give another example of our workload, the dates (from Jeff's diary) for the next couple of weeks, looked like this,

July 1967

1st	Norfolk - The Tavern, East Dereham
2nd	Oxon - Bridge Hotel, Wheatley
3rd	Bristol - Corn Exchange
4th	London - Marquee
5th	Bournemouth
7th	Uxbridge - Burtons
8th	Plymouth - The Purple Fez Club
10th	Worcester
11th	Cleethorpes - Winter Gardens
12th	Solihull
13th	Salisbury - City Hall
14th	Romford
15th	Matlock Bath - Pavilion
16th	Stoke on Trent - The Place, Hanley
17th	Warrington
18th	Sunderland - Kirklevington Country Club,
20th	Newcastle - Club A-go-go
21st	Redcar - Jazz Club
22nd	Sheffield - Mojo
24th	London - Studio
25th	London - Klooks Kleek
26th	Stevenage

A rather tall girl who regularly attended our gigs at The Bridge Hotel, Wheatley took a shine to two members of the band (who shall remain nameless). They discovered to their delight that she was an expert at fellatio and for them gigs at this venue took on extra appeal. On one of our subsequent visits to The Bridge she wasn't there and, after mentioning her to the promoter, he revealed the reason. He showed us an expose from The News of the World about a transvestite who lived in the Oxford area. The face in the accompanying photo looked all too familiar. Yes it was the tall girl with the sexpertise. She was a man!

We played The Lafayette Club in Wolverhampton many times and it was not far from Jess's hometown, Kidderminster. There was a local guy who used to hang around outside and ask us if he could sing a number with the band. To be honest, he looked a bit of a mess with long unkempt hair, ragged jeans, an old jean jacket and plimsolls with holes in. The bouncers in the club didn't want him coming in because there was a 'no jeans' dress code. However, the guy was very persistent and the bouncers said they would agree to let him in for one number, if we agreed to back him. We weren't keen but Jess knew the guy was a local singer and was embarrassed to say no, so to keep the peace, I agreed to let him sing one number. We launched into a 12 bar blues which seem to go on forever. There was a lot of vocal gymnastics going on and I didn't think it suited The Alan Bown Set at all so I was glad when it was over. True, the guy had an amazing voice but it seemed to be well over the top. The audience didn't seem to be impressed either and there was a sense of relief when the guest singer left the stage to muted applause. After we finished our set, I said to Jess, 'What was the name of that guy who sat in?' Jess replied, 'Robert Plant'. It showed Jess's strength of character that he was able to let someone of that calibre sit in with the band even though Led Zeppelin was yet to come!

Mac Poole, former drummer with renowned 60's band, Warhorse, has this recollection;
'The Alan Bown Set stood alone for sheer talent. They had honed their craft to such an extent that bands would fear to be on the same bill as them! Their lead singer, Jess Roden, was somewhere between Otis Redding and Janis Joplin and on one occasion, when Jess was in The Shakedown Sound, I remember seeing Robert Plant in the audience being visibly shaken by Jess's performance. The fusion of Jess Roden with all the great players in The Alan Bown Set created a devastating unit, capable of stealing both the audience and the night from even the most reputable name bands of the time'.

Around this time I was approached by Maurice Jones who ran an agency in the Midlands called Astra. Our meeting developed into a long productive relationship, which put many gigs our way.

Trend Magazine on the 15th July, featured us in their column 'You've Said It'. It was a series of replies to readers questions. John, Jess, John and myself gave the answers. A photo of the band was also included.

On the 27th July 1967, Jeff went into hospital. Not with exhaustion but finally to have his tonsils out! We carried on without him and he returned on the 10th August to play the Streatham Locarno, a huge Mecca ballroom. Whilst the roadies were carrying in the Hammond organ, it jammed in a doorway and one of the white notes snapped off, right in the middle of the upper keyboard! It couldn't have been worse and throughout the gig, Jeff had to try to avoid the gaping hole. What a welcome back!

BALLOON MEADOW ROYAL WINDSOR RACECOURSE
Maidenhead Road (A 308)

Friday 11th August 8—11.30 pm
Tickets 12/6
SMALL FACES THE MOVE
The Nite People · The Syn
THE MARMALADE · Tomorrow

Saturday 12th August 2.30—5.30 pm
Tickets 7/6
JEANNIE LAMBE · DANNY MOSS
Mike Carr Trio with **Harold McNair**
Graham Collier Septet
& FROM THE U.S.A. **YUSEF LATEEF**

JAZZ & POP

ZOOT SIMS & AL COHN

PAUL JONES
Richard Kent Style

Saturday 12th August 7—11.30 pm
Tickets 15/-

THE PINK FLOYD

ZOOT MONEY · AMEN CORNER · TIME BOX
The Crazy World of ARTHUR BROWN · 10 Years After
Aynsley Dunbar Retaliation · ADAMS Recital

For Special
PARTY RATES
and all enquiries
contact the
NJF secretary
at the
MARQUEE
GER 6601

Sunday 13th August 2.30—5.30 pm
Tickets 7/6
THE DONOVAN SHOW

OTTILIE PATTERSON
John Slaughter Trio
Al Stewart · Picadilly Line

Why not make a weekend of it?
Stay at our beautiful riverside
 CAMP SITE
Bring your own tent etc
We provide water, toilets and
shop. For details contact NJF secretary

BALLADS & BLUES

TRAVEL: By road turn
off M.4 at Windsor/Eton
Bypass. Thames Valley
Green Line and London
Country Buses. Western
& Southern Region Trains
SPECIAL LATE service
to Staines, Twickenham,
Richmond, Clapham and
Waterloo.

THE CREAM
Sunday 13th August 7—11.30 pm
Tickets 15/-

JEFF BECK · P. P. ARNOLD · ALAN BOWN
JOHN MAYALL · Chicken Shack · Blossom Toes

Debut of
PETER GREEN'S
Fleetwood Mac

The Pentangle with
BERT JANSCH

DENNY LAINE
strings

To **NJF BOX OFFICE**
MARQUEE 90 Wardour Street W1
Please send me the undernoted tickets for
which I enclose a cheque/postal order for
I also enclose a stamped addressed envelope

SPECIAL TICKETS* in advance only
·SEASON @ £2
·WEEKEND (Sat & Sun) @ 30/-

FRIDAY 11th AUGUST @ 12/6
SATURDAY 12th AUGUST @ 7/6 Aft @ 15/- Evg @ 20/- All day
SUNDAY 13th AUGUST @ 7/6 Aft @ 15/- Evg @ 20/- All day
Name
Address

Office:

14

THE ALAN BOWN!

It was during 1967 that I decided to streamline the name of the band. We dropped the 'Set' added an exclamation mark and became The Alan Bown!

On the 13th August, we appeared at The Windsor Jazz Festival for the second time. This year we were on the same programme as Cream, Jeff Beck, P.P. Arnold, John Mayall, Chicken Shack, Blossom Toes, Peter Green's Fleetwood Mac, The Pentangle with Bert Jansch and Denny Lane. Tickets for the whole day were 15/- (fifteen shillings). Today that's 75p! (see poster on page 107).

Some people believe that cars have a personality of their own. Over the course of time, the efficiency of the Galaxy's rear electric window mechanism became erratic and to help it to open, we developed a technique of pummelling the glass with our fists in a downward direction thus assisting the motor to lower the window. This was accompanied with much turning on and off of the key to kick-start the motor. Eventually, even this method resulted in a stubborn response and only an inch or so gap at the top of the window would present itself. There was just enough space to insert several fingers to pull down the window with an extra tug.

This worked ok until one disastrous day when we arrived outside a venue, which already had a long queue of people waiting to go in. Jess Roden pushed both fingers in the gap and attempted to force the window down but in the heat of the moment, the person in the front seat operating the key turned it the wrong way and the window went up again, trapping Jess's fingers. In the time that followed, Jess was in agony and all of the key turning and pummeling was to no avail. The window was tightly jammed! The queue of people stood watching in silent bewilderment at The Alan Bown Set, shouting, swearing and dancing around the back of the car in a frantic attempt to release Jess's fingers, until finally the window gave up its trophies. We couldn't believe our eyes. Jess's fingers were blue and the ends were swollen like balloons. A lizard would have been proud of them and could have scaled the tallest tree in three seconds. The 'fingers-in-the-window-technique' was abandoned after that and a new motor installed.

The 20th August 1967 was Peter Stringfellow's wedding day. We had known Peter and Coral for some time now and after the ceremony, we played at their reception in The Mojo Club. They had become good friends of ours and it was a nice gesture from Peter, to book us for that day. (See Peter Stringfellow's tribute to The Alan Bown Set in the opening pages of this book).

On August the 22nd we were back headlining at The Marquee, supported by Timebox. After our live recording that we had made at the club, we used to pack the place out. We had a great rapport with all the management and I would always ask John Gee, the manager, who his favourite singer was and he would reply, 'Frank Sinatra.' I would say with mock surprise, 'Who?' and John would reply, 'Jess Roden, of course.'

On the 30th August, we had a 3pm photo session in Berkeley Square (see photograph below). Jeff remembers this particularly because, even then, it was difficult to park around the Square and he had to walk two blocks to the session. There were some repairs being carried out on the roadside and Jeff's outfit caused a torrent of comments from the workmen. This happened to us all now and again but it was annoying and sometimes aggressive. To hear workmen shouting, 'Allo darlin', give us a kiss!' wasn't the most flattering remark you wanted to hear. In fact, I heard a story that Steve Marriott was accosted in a similar way and went over and gave the workman a bit fat kiss on the lips!

On the 9th September, The Melody Maker published a letter from two fans in Bournemouth, who were disenchanted with The Crazy World of Arthur Brown. '...give recognition to groups like the Alan Bown Set who have talent to communicate, captivate and entertain their audiences without screaming obscenities and setting fire to their hair.'

On the 27th September 1967 we had a recording session for BBC Radio 1. It was for a programme called Happening Sunday and we performed, 'Penny For Your Thoughts', 'Technicolour Dream' and 'My Girl The Month Of May'.

The Melody Maker, on 30th September, published a letter from me about yoga and warning about it becoming trendy but meaningless.

In the same edition of the MM, another letter from a reader had this to say, 'All I seem to see in your paper today is Psychedelic, Flower Power and Hippies – what a load of tripe! Having seen Eric Burdon, Arthur Brown, Soft Machine and Pink Floyd I'm shocked that anyone should like such pathetic acts. As far as audience participation goes, it is dead compared with the real ravers and real hippies – the fans of Geno Washington, Alan Bown, Jimmy James and the Vagabonds, Herbie Goins and of course that fantastic Stax Show. Yet they get no publicity. Instead we get pictures of painted morons, who are just using the poor brainwashed English teenagers. J.S. Parish in Chelmsford, Essex.'

Our fan Club was in full swing now, run by Maggie and Ann based in Queens Avenue, Hanworth, Middlesex. They regularly printed our itinerary in their newsletter and the October dates are reproduced here.

October 1967

1st	Wembley – Starlight Ballroom
2nd	Edmonton – Cooks Ferry Inn
3rd	Kidderminster
4th	Brighton – Sussex University
6th	Chelsea – Kings College
7th	London – Queen Mary's College
8th	Coventry – Leofric Hotel
9th	Bournemouth – Ritz
10th	London – Marquee
12th	York
13th	Birmingham - High Hall, Edgbaston
14th	London - Chelsea College
15th	Nottingham

18th	Weymouth – Steering Wheel Club
19th	South Wales – The Ritz, Skewen
20th	South Wales – Pengam
21st	Leicester – University
22nd	Manchester*
24th	London – Playhouse – (Recording Saturday Club)
25th	Newcastle – Majestic Ballroom
26th	Stoke on Trent – Golden Torch, Tunstall
28th	Port Talbot
31st	London – Klooks Kleek

*We were due to play at the Mojo Club in Sheffield on the 22nd but later heard that it had been closed down by Sheffield Council. This was a blow to us but more so to our old friend, Peter Stringfellow. Peter would soon open another venue in Sheffield, called the Penthouse. The club premises were on the 7th floor of a high-rise building and there was no lift! Imagine what the roadies thought of that with the Hammond organ to carry up.

On the 10th October, we made another appearance at The Marquee, and were supported again by 'Timebox'.

The 24th October 1967 found us back in The BBC Playhouse, London to record Saturday Club.

Three days later, our new single was released on our new label MGM - Music Factory. 'Toyland' was the A-side, and 'Technicolour Dream' was the B-side. Mike Hurst produced both sides of the single and added excellent string parts, which made each track very special. They were both potential A-sides to me.

There had been quite a protracted discussion over these two songs. 'Toyland' had been written by Jess Roden and Tony Catchpole while 'Technicolour Dream' was written by Jeff and myself.

Our management played both tracks to various people for their comments and a window cleaner proclaimed that 'Toyland' was easy to whistle to and therefore more instantly commercial! Thanks to the window cleaner, 'Technicolour Dream' was relegated to the B-side and became lost to public consciousness and potential radio plays.

It's easy in retrospect to say that we should have reserved 'Technicolour Dream for the next single but the management was convinced that 'Toyland' would be a hit so we went with the flow. History has since shown that 'Toyland', even after good reviews and extensive radio plays failed to make the charts. Would 'Technicolour Dream' have had more success? We will never know. However, it was (and still is) a great track. It was right for the time and in my opinion, had a more ingenious lyric.

'Toyland' was released in the last week of October. Half page adverts, featuring the band's new psychedelic photo, appeared in 'Top Pops' on 24th October also 'Melody Maker' and 'New Musical Express' on 28th October.

Also on the 28th, New Musical Express favourably reviewed both sides of the single;
'Can't imagine why The Alan Bown Set has become The Alan Bown! – maybe it's because this is quite different from anything they've done before. Enchanting words set to an up-to-the-minute backing, incorporating flute, cellos and organ. Mid-tempo beat. Well worth your attention. Flip; I've heard this song before (Technicolour Dream) and I specially like Alan's styling. Imaginative scoring with falsetto counter harmonies supporting the soloist.'

In The Melody Maker, on the 28th October, Chris Welch reviewed 'Toyland'; 'Too much! A great record from a great group or G.R.G.G. for short. This must mark the long awaited chart breakthrough of trumpeter and leader Alan and his exceptional young singer, Jess Roden. The lyrics are, loathe as I am to use the word, 'kookie'. No, that damns it from the start. Let us say 'quaint'. Children's voice open and close the side while Jess sings in a new, clear non-screaming voice, tales of mind blowing in toyland, where things aren't quite so square and teddy bears have the scene sown up. It's clever, cute and a hit or my name's not Ronald K Sprothole.'

Record Mirror, again on the 28th, gave the single a four star rating with this mini-review;
'This group are on a fast rising commercial kick here and this class job must stand big chances. Fantasy. Almost fantastic.'

The Disc and Music Echo, on the 28th, gave the single a 'Quick Spin'; 'Beautiful production on Alan Bown's Toyland but I'm a bit tired of songs saying how turned on childhood is. We all know that. Now why don't we leave it alone?'

The November newsletter of The Alan Bown Fan Club included this itinerary;

November 1967

2nd	Newcastle – Club a Go-Go
3rd	Redcar – Jazz Club
4th	Matlock Bath – Pavilion
5th	Hanley – The Place
9th	Flintshire – Connah's Quay Civic Hall
10th	Wolverhampton – Civic Hall
11th	Manchester – Twisted Wheel (all nighter)
12th	Birmingham – Kyle Hall
13th	Wolverhampton
14th	High Wycombe
15th	Hull – Skyline Ballroom
16th	Oxford
17th	Oxford – St Michael's Hall
18th	London – School of Economics
19th	The Londoner Hotel
20th	Sheffield – City Hall
23rd	Yoevil – Liberal Club
24th	Bristol – College of St Matthias
25th	Margate – Dreamland
26th	Harlow – Birdcage Club
27th	Ipswich – St Matthews Baths Hall

One of our gigs at Oxford University had an amusing sequel. We had arrived early to discover that we had been scheduled to play well after midnight. Although none of us were heavy drinkers, we ended up in the bar out of sheer boredom. University bars always seemed to be staffed by two people when thirty were waiting to be served. It was the same story everywhere but tonight a solution suddenly presented itself. One of the barmen took a fancy to Vic our drummer and said in a very camp voice something like, 'Yes love, what you like?' Vic bought a couple of drinks then, when given his change, the barman added, 'My name's Larry but you can call me Lola! Anything you want just let me know love!' Then the free drinks started to flow. It was obvious that Larry/Lola was trying to get off with Vic and may even have 'laced' a drink in the process. However, the result was that Vic was really ill. Jeff relates the remainder of the story;

'I had gone to the gig in my car with Stan, John and Vic. When it was time to leave, Vic was in a state of advanced inebriation (pissed). My car, a Ford Anglia was only a two-door model, so on the way back we let Vic sit in the front passenger seat, in case I had to stop quickly for him to get out. The road out of Oxford was a long winding hill and, on this night, never ending. Half way up Vic said, 'Stop the car, I have to be sick.' The road had double yellow lines all the way up and I replied, 'I have to get to the top of the hill. If you feel sick open the window.' Vic, by now a whiter shade of green, opened the window, put his head out and emptied the contents of his stomach in an almighty gush. Unfortunately a combination of the wind and lack of Vic's accuracy meant that a large proportion of the puke came back into the car splattering the occupants of the back seat. I could see John and Stan in my rear view mirror trying in vain to dodge the incoming technicolour yawn. When I was able to finally stop the car, the hapless occupants of the back seat emerged completely pebble-dashed! It took me a week to get the smell of sick out of my car.'

John recalls; 'I'd just bought a new suede jacket and it took the full force of Vic's vomit. Afterwards, I never really managed to get the stain out of it. I remember that Jeff was so angry with Vic that, when he stopped the car, he literally booted him out onto the grass verge. When we eventually got to Vic's house, he had passed out and we couldn't find his keys so we had to wake his mother up. Instead of being furious, she said, 'Oh Vic, you are a silly boy.' That's not what we had called him!'

Top Pops on the 7th November, published a colour photo of the band, taken at The Marquee in London. The accompanying article gave us a plug for the single and each member of the band a name check. In the same issue, their 'Single Releases' column gave us a prominent and positive review.

Our shirts were made just off The Old Kent Road by Mrs Trott, who used to make them for the famous Kings Road boutique, 'Granny Takes a Trip'. We used to buy the material and take it to her to be measured up. It cost two pounds for a plain shirt to be made and two pounds ten shillings for patterned material (because she had to line up the pattern).

It was considerably more reasonable than going to the King's Road or Carnaby Street, where you had to pay through the nose. Our made to measure suits were fashioned by a tailor in Seven Sisters Road. It was then the vogue to have flared trousers that were very tight around the hips and top of the legs. This resulted in the occasional seam bursting on stage. Jeff recalls; 'I had one go during my Elvis Presley routine and didn't realise until I saw a bunch of girls in the front row laughing. I looked down and saw that the inside-seam of one trouser leg has split from the knee to the crotch!'

The spate of gigs was briefly interrupted on the 7th November, by a recording session for demos in The Marquee Studios.

**The Alan Bown!
live on stage
in
bespoke
shirts and suits**

15

ELECTRIC BLUE TRUMPET

The Melody Maker on the 11th November 1967, reported that 'The Alan Bown! will be heard on Radio One throughout the whole of December. They start a week on The Pete Brady Show on November the 25th. They follow with two weeks on Top Gear, the David Symonds Show and a return to the Pete Brady Show.' In the same issue, Chris Welch briefly interviewed me and mentioned our subtle name change, from 'Set' to exclamation mark.

Top Pops on the 25th November reported a curious story about an overcoat that Jess bought, which seemed to bring us bad luck with vehicles. Every time he wore it, the car broke down.

There followed more recording at The Olympic Studio in Barnes on the 28th and 30th November 1967. In between these dates, on the 29th, we recorded for the BBC radio show, Top Gear, performing 'Toyland', 'Pandoras Golden Heebie Geebies' and 'Love Is A Beautiful Thing.' (Top Gear was a trendy music show at the time and nothing to do with cars - Alan)

The December newsletter of The Alan Bown Fan Club included these dates;

<u>December 1967</u>

1st	Bristol – Hyatt Baker Hall
2nd	Loughborough University
3rd	Grantham – Cat Ballou Club
4th	London – BBC David Symonds Show
5th	Portsmouth – Savoy Ballroom
6th	London – Olympic Studio
7th	Sheffield City Hall
8th	Bridgend – Zachary Rack Disco
9th	Sheffield University
10th	Cleethorpes – Purple Onion Club
12th	Exeter University
13th	Reading – Bulmershe College
15th	Leicester – El Rondo Club
16th	London - Burtons Uxbridge

17th	Guildford – Wooden Bridge
19th	Bournemouth – Ritz Ballroom
20th	Lyme Regis – Marine Ballroom
21st	Nottingham - Langley Mill
22nd	Portsmouth – Manor Court School
23rd	Norfolk – Dereham Tavern
24th	Harlow – Birdcage Club
26th	Middlesborough - Kirklevington Country Club
29th	York – Assembly Rooms
30th	Manchester – Twisted Wheel

You may think that after a month of such a schedule we would have some time off but that was not the case. We had very few days off – period.

In Melody Maker on the 2nd December, The Cat Ballou Club in Grantham announced our appearance at the club on the following day. In the same issue the forthcoming Radio One sessions were also mentioned.

December 4th we recorded BBC Radio One's David Symond's Show from 5.30 to 8.30. That was for two tracks, overdubs and mixing! The next day we had a one-nighter in The Savoy Ballroom Portsmouth then back into Olympic Studios from 2pm the day after.

The Melody Maker on the 16th December, published a photo of the band, (minus myself and Stan for some reason) examining a breathalyser which was about to be introduced by Transport Minister, Barbara Cartland. The article said, 'The Alan Bown! guests of honour at The Waldorf Hotel last week to launch a new non-alcoholic drink.....Tenorist John Anthony surprised everyone by breathing on the crystals and turning green himself.'

MGM advertised the new single, 'Toyland' in Top Pops magazine on 23rd December. The ad carried a photo of the band.

It was around this time that I went to Ronnie Scott's Club in Soho, to see The Don Ellis Orchestra. What I heard changed my whole concept of musical thinking. Ellis's use of electronic devices opened up a whole new world of trumpet playing. I could see a future for the instrument in amplified rock music. After Don Ellis's performance, Pete King introduced me to him. Don was a really nice guy and told me all about the electronic bug he used and the octave divider, which was marketed as an octivider.

After that night, I decided to pay a visit to an old friend of mine, Phil Parker, who ran a shop for brass musical instruments and he suggested I go to Bill Lewingtons at Cambridge Circus. John Hemmings, a trombone player and assistant at Bill Lewingtons, arranged to have a bug fitted to a mouthpiece, which I could use with any trumpet. I also bought an octivider, a wah wah pedal and an echo chamber from them. (Funny enough, Vic Sweeney, our drummer at the time, used to work for Chas Foote in Denman Street with John Hemmings). Soon after that, Yamaha contacted me through John Hemmings and offered to supply me with a trumpet of my choice. I asked them to customise my blue lacquered trumpet and angle the bell at 27 degrees, styled on Dizzy Gillespie's famous horn. I wanted something that looked unusual on stage. My old friend Hank Shaw thought it was hilarious but gave me his blessing. The result was a triumph visually but, because of the angle of the bell, I had to lean forward to blow into the microphone. This didn't help my inherent back problem!

In the December 1967 issue of 'Beat Instrumental' magazine, we had a full-page article and photograph of the band. We all got a mention in the review, including Richard Cowley, who was still our manager at this point.

The band had an unwelcome early Christmas present on the 23rd December. We were appearing at the Wellington Club in East Dereham, Norfolk and a pre-gig scuffle occurred between our roadies, Algy and Steve and a bunch of disgruntled bikers.

There was an obvious culture clash going on in outposts like this. Local lads were still into the Gene Vincent look and bands like us were pure 'flower power' as it was labelled by the press. With brightly coloured frilly shirts and tailored flared trousers with stack-heeled boots, you could say our image was more DC than AC. It was the 60's fashion, but not in the outback! Consequently, although our appearance appealed to the girls in the audience, it was red rags to a bull for many of the guys. Add that ingredient plus alcohol consumption to verbal abuse exchanged with the roadies and it was not surprising that we were taunted throughout our set with jibes and threatening gestures. Half way through a song, some guy tried to pull a microphone-stand off the stage and he got clobbered and pushed back by Steve, our roadie. This incensed the other guys and it was clear that tempers were about to boil over. Looking back, I can't recall any officials of the club doing much to calm things down or coming to our assistance.
It was clearly a 'them and us' situation. At the end of our performance we hastily scurried down the stairs into our dressing room, which was under the stage. Only one door served this room and we had no escape. It was rat-trap! The support band was already in the dressing room unaware of the fracas until we frantically piled in with our roadies in close pursuit, slamming the door behind them. Then we heard the ominous trampling of feet on the wooden stairs and much shouting. Algy stood behind the door to prevent anyone entering but the pounding on it from the other side suddenly produced a terrifying result. The door burst inwards and flattened Algy in one movement. He lay under the door, prostrate and unconscious,

as the angry mob burst in. Realising that Algy was under the door they started jumping up and down on in and we watched in horror unable to go to his aid. We were shouting out for help from the management and for someone to call the police but we had no idea that anyone could hear us. The only illumination in the room was one bare light bulb, hanging from the centre of the ceiling. Steve had the sense to grab some object and smash the bulb, leaving the room in darkness. Now all we could see was silhouettes and the bikers tried to make out where we were in the room. In the gloom I heard Tony call out them, saying that we were only musicians and didn't want trouble. It was slightly too late for negotiating! Several of them lunged forward, punching and kicking. I saw two guys go for Jeff and he grabbed an arm and spun one of them round into the wall. The guy seemed to hit the wall and collapse in a heap. His cohort attacked Jeff with a knuckle-duster or screwdriver and gashed his head with it. It was just about to develop into an all out brawl when the police arrived and broke it all up. Algy was revived and we checked each other out. There were no serious injuries thank goodness but we had to wake up the local doctor to look at the cuts and scrapes and give Algy an examination for concussion. The hair on one side of Jeff's head was caked in blood and the doctor suggested he might need three stitches. Jeff declined, wanting only to get home. There wasn't any sign of our attackers now but the police gave us an escort out of the area. I think they were glad to see the back of us. The feeling was mutual.

A few weeks after this incident, we were booked to do a gig in Cromer in Norfolk, but for the safety of the band, I cancelled the engagement. The promoter threatened to sue me but the threat wasn't fulfilled. However, as a postscript, I heard that when it was announced in the Cromer ballroom that we would not be appearing, some biker shouted out, 'We done 'em!' I was told that the guy who shouted was standing on a balcony and someone promptly threw him over it! Proving that not everyone was pleased with our fate. In fairness, I was sad that we had to decline to return to Dereham as there were some genuine fans in that area and we always had a good gig there. With the exception of that night in December 1967!

On the 30th December, we played the all-nighter again at The Twisted Wheel in Manchester. For a change we saw the New Year in at home on a day off.

Jeu De Massacre, the movie that Jacques Loussier commissioned us to play on the soundtrack, was shown in January at The Cinephone Cinema in Oxford Street, London. In the wisdom of the distributors they decided to rename it 'Comic Strip Hero'. Maggie, our fan club secretary, went along to see it and, in the January newsletter, she commented that the film had won 'Best Screenplay Award' in France at the Cannes Film Festival. Maggie also reported that my dog 'Dizzy' named after Dizzy Gillespie, had had seven pups and I was looking for good homes for them.

The Eastern Evening News on the 1st January 1968, reported, 'After ugly incident at Dereham Club. Not Again Says Alan Bown - Group May Boycott Norfolk Bookings.' The comprehensive article and interview about the attack from the hostile bikers included a photo of the band captioned, 'The Alan Bown – trapped in dressing room' and a photo of myself captioned, 'Alan Bown, kiss of life.' I told the interviewer that I had to give Algy, the roadie, the kiss of life!

On the 3rd January, we recorded our next single called 'Story Book'. Jeff and I wrote this one and the B-side was 'Little Lesley', written by Jess and Tony. The production was by Mike Hurst once again and he put an effect on the intro, which was quite hypnotic. Jess sang the song really well and we were all very pleased with it. In retrospect, recording and completing two sides of a single in one day was asking a lot from all concerned. It makes the results even more remarkable.

The Melody Maker on 6th January, covered the Dereham news item with a few lines.

Also on the 6th January, Top Pops published a letter from the band refuting the idea that 'Toyland' was released to be a 'Christmas cash-in'.

The Sheffield Star, 'Top Stars Special', January Edition 1968, published a photo of the band, captioned, 'The Alan Bown Group to visit Worksop.' The article gave us all a name check and reported that …'The Alan Bown group are firm favourites with Sheffield audiences and they will be back again on January 12th, playing at Worksop Town Supporters Club, 'Big Night In' at Worksop Palais Ballroom.'

The Melody Maker, on the 13th January, gave a more full report on the incident in Dereham.

Top Pops on the 20th January published a 'Top Pops Special Report' headed, 'Violence in Pop'. It was another report on our experience in Dereham and incidents concerning other musicians that had faced similar problems.

In a lighter vein, Jackie Magazine, also on the 20th, published a colour photo of the band in their 'Pop Gossip' column. The article is reproduced here;
'Most people have paintings on their walls, some have paintings on their faces but The Alan Bown have come up with something different. What is it?

They have the most colourful equipment this side of the Aurora Borealis! The guy responsible for this is Robert Adams, a 16 year-old commercial artist friend of the group's singer, Jess Roden. 'He did Tony's guitar first,' enthused Jess, 'and we were so knocked out with it that we got him to paint the drums and organ as well. Fans are going for our 'National Gallery' in a big way. The paint is luminous, so it looks really great under ultra violet lights!' The Alan Bown already have one of the most entertaining acts on the scene today and now with those bright, strong designs on their gear, they are certainly among the most colourful.'

This innovative artwork from Robert Adams was really something to behold and, with my electric blue trumpet, the visual aspects of the band were now enhanced to the full.

During a trip to Holland on the 6th January, we travelled from Southend airport on a charter flight. Also on the plane was Status Quo, bound for the same destination. The plane was an old propeller aircraft and the two bands exchanged nervous jokes about it, like 'Who's sitting next the rear gunner?' etc. The lone stewardess ran through her safety instructions with the customary lifejacket routine and added, 'We will take off as soon as we've checked the hold.' Algy, our road manager replied very gallantly, 'I'd like to check your hold love!' This brought a roar of laughter and the stewardess realised that formality was a lost cause on this flight. However, she took it in her stride and knew that nothing offensive was intended.

Quo were booked into the same hotel as us and soon after we had checked in we heard a commotion coming from one of their rooms. We went along to investigate and found one of their band furiously banging on the floor with a shoe while the other guys stood around watching intently. On closer inspection it could be seen that the focus of their attention was a large spider, which was splayed out motionless on the carpet. Satisfied that the spider was dead, we all then went off to make our respective recordings for a TV programme in Rotterdam but when we returned, a disturbing discovery was made. The spider had disappeared! The disturbing part was, where to?

The Melody Maker on the 17th February reported;
'Alan Bown's new single will be 'Story Book', released by MGM on March 1st. They guest on The Jimmy Young Show from February 19-23.'

MGM our recording company placed a teaser advert for 'Story Book' in The New Musical Express on 24th February.

On the 25th February, we played at The Place in Hanley. By now we had built a very enthusiastic following here and we all got on really well with the guys that ran the club, Kevin, Bill and Barry. We could do no wrong at this club with the exception of one night when John recited a line from a Frank Zappa album track. The line was 'Be a jerk and go to work.' After our performance, a guy came up to us and complained saying, that he had to go to work and didn't regard himself as 'a jerk'. John had to apologise which made the rest of us laugh, knowing his habit for putting his foot in it. However, John had the last laugh when we were leaving a variety club somewhere in Yorkshire. We had played a gig there and the club was now closed but, just on the way out, as we walked through the foyer, John put a coin in a large fruit machine and pulled the handle. To everyone's surprise, when the drums came to rest, the machine started to spew out handfuls of coins. John had won the jackpot! We all laughed and congratulated him but the manager of the club stepped in vigorously protesting. 'You can't take that money,' he blustered, 'that's for our members!' John had suddenly gone deaf and was scooping the coins into his pocket (he was also a Yorkshireman). We all leapt to John's defence pointing out that the manager had made no attempt to prevent John putting a coin in the machine, not expecting him to win. 'My members have been feeding that bloody machine for weeks,' he said. 'They'll go bloody mad when I tell them.' 'Well don't tell them,' we chorused through spates of laughter while pushing each other through the exit door.

On the 28th February 1968, we recorded the Alan Freeman show in Manchester. Alan, or 'Fluff', as he became affectionately known, was a really nice man. Always positive and complimentary, he loved his job as one of the top DJ's and presenters of the era.

The Alan Freeman Show was on the 1st March, the same day that our second single, 'Story Book', was released on MGM.

Disc and Music Echo on 2nd March reported that 'Alan's a Dad!' with news of my daughter Nicole's birth on the 22nd of February and also our appearance on the Alan Freeman Show, performing 'Story Book'.

Record Mirror, on the 2nd March, gave the single, 'Story Book' a 'chart possibility'.

MGM Records placed an advert with The New Musical Express on 2nd March for 'Story Book', featuring a photo of the band.

Also on the 2nd March, Melody Maker published a bellicose Blind Date record review of 'Story Book' by Don Partridge. He said that the intro made him feel sick!

My Association with Universal Attractions came to a close around this time. I felt that they had done everything they could for the band but we needed to raise our game so early in March I signed the band to The Harold Davidson Agency and a management deal with Mel Collins of Active Management, based in Dean Street, London.

There were no parking meters in those days so there was no hassle going to meetings! Mel had a big sign on the office wall that said, 'Today is the first day of the rest of your life.' It didn't mention tomorrow...

Jackie Magazine on the 9th March gave us a half page article and a colour photo of the band.

We mostly stayed in guest-houses in those days because there were no 'Travelodges' or 'Travel Inns'. There was rarely any economic middle ground between guest houses and 5-star hotels so we had little choice when staying away. On one occasion we checked into a place that was run by two middle-aged women. They looked a bit startled by our appearance when we arrived and it was clear that the phrase 'we don't get many strangers round here' applied in this case. Their main concern seemed to be the fact that we all had long hair and as they were ushering Stan and John into their room, one of the women said nervously, 'We don't want you boys washing your hair in the sink. We had two girls with long hair staying here once who washed their hair and blocked the sink up.' (Needless to say, the rooms were not en-suit and washing your hair in the communal bathroom after a lorry driver had emptied the contents of his bowels was not a desirable option!). Stan took great exception to this remark and hatched an idea for retribution. He found an old vase in the room and from then on, every time he or John needed to urinate they did so in the vase.

By the time we were due to leave the next morning, the vase was quite full and Stan stood on a chair and placed it on top of an old wardrobe. He positioned it centrally, right above the wardrobe door so it was quite visible to anyone entering the room. Stan's theory was that one of the 'old girls' as he respectfully referred to them, would come into the room, see the vase on top of the wardrobe and reach up to retrieve it, thinking it had just been placed there for a prank but not suspecting that there was anything in it. It only had to tip over at a small angle for the contents to pour out, over the head of the person holding it. The most undesirable 'hair wash' of all!

We recorded the David Symonds show again on the 18th March and two days later, Top Gear for the BBC. A week later, another photo session was held in London.

16

OUTWARD BOWN - THE ALBUM

On the 28th March, we rehearsed songs in preparation for the new album, 'Outward Bown'.

The Melody Maker, on 20th April, published a short interview with Jeff Bannister.

During April 1968, namely the 3rd, 8th, 17th and 23rd, we recorded and completed our first album entitled, 'Outward Bown', produced once again by Mike Hurst and recorded in Olympic Studio, Barnes. There were, of course, gigs between all of these dates but in a way it knocked any new songs into shape and by the time we recorded them, they were note perfect. There was a great studio vibe recording the tracks and even our roadies sang on the chorus of 'Mutiny'. (See discography - albums).

I must also point out that we wanted to release 'All Along the Watchtower' as a single but the record company in their wisdom considered it not to be commercial. We had first heard a rough demo of the song by Bob Dylan just playing guitar and singing. From that demo we created an arrangement of the song, which became a highpoint in our act but it was Jimi Hendrix who was to prove how commercial the song was.

We were actually supported by Jimi Hendrix on one of our gigs on the circuit, in Guildford Civic Hall. Chas Chandler, his new manager had driven him down from London and it was his first gig in the provinces. Hendrix didn't even have a guitar with him and Chas asked our guitarist, Tony Catchpole, if he had a spare that he could borrow. Tony complied but Hendrix had to re-string the guitar because he was left-handed. His band, which would soon become the famous Jimi Hendrix Experience, already comprised of Noel Redding/bass and Mitch Mitchell/drums. The evening began with their performance and Tony looked on nervously as Hendrix, in full flow, scraped the guitar against the mic stand and detuned it for extra effects. We were quite fascinated by this but the crowd were not impressed and started booing! Whether or not he had intended to play for more than 30 minutes is not clear but it was a short uncomfortable set for the superstar that was yet to come.

After our performance, which always went down well at this venue, Noel Redding came up to us and said how much he had enjoyed our version of 'All Along the Watchtower'. Soon after that gig Hendrix recorded his own version, which history has shown was a big hit. He actually went on record, personally crediting The Alan Bown Set for 'inspiration on the arrangement'! A nice tribute but I would have rather seen our version of the song in the charts.

MGM issued a brochure of the band to coincide with the release of our new album. Each of us was given a condensed personal biography with an accompanying photo.

Beat Instrumental interviewed me in their April 1968 issue and published a photo of the band with the article.

A letter printed in the Disc and Music Echo on the 25th May, mourning the break-up of The Zombies, was written by Stan our bass player. Colin Blunstone, the singer of the Zombies' biggest hit, 'She's Not There' eventually emerged as a solo artist and the keyboard player, Rod Argent went on to form Argent, who later had a massive hit with 'Hold Your Head Up'.

In May, Beat Instrumental proclaimed me as Player of the Month! John Ford wrote the article with a half page photograph of me blowing my Super Olds trumpet.

Around this time, Algy Ross, our roadie decided to leave and was replaced by Paul Stringfellow, Peter's younger brother. Paul was only a teenager then, but he did have a driving licence, which was essential because Steve Hackett, our remaining roadie, hadn't passed his test.

At the end of this month, we recorded 'We Can Help You'.

It was Mike Hurst's suggestion that we should record this song, originally recorded by the English band 'Nirvana', but at first we were not convinced it was right for us. Although the melody was catchy (derived from Handel's Hallelujah Chorus), we would have preferred to have released a track from our forthcoming album. Also, we were not happy with the lyrics of the verses and Mike promptly persuaded the songwriters, Patrick Campbell-Lyons and Alex Spyropoulos to let us change them. They agreed, apparently with some reluctance, to let us change the verses and we hurriedly cobbled together an alternative lyric. It was all done in too much haste and I regretted not spending more time on it. I know Jess secretly hated singing the final version, although as always, he did a great vocal. Mike Hurst produced it and added a superb string arrangement. John blew some cool clarinet on it and it certainly had all the hallmarks of a hit.

At best, we looked upon it as a chance to finally break into the charts. At worst, it was a blatant commercial enterprise, which did little to enhance our reputation with dedicated fans. Funny enough, it was more recently suggested that it could still make a great jingle for a TV advert. The B-side of the single, 'Magic Handkerchief', was on the album and was

written by Jeff and myself. Jeff had got the idea for the song from a teacher who used to come to the rescue of young schoolchildren in distress and stop them crying by telling them she had a magic handkerchief. Apparently, it always worked. For me, this track had more magic than 'We Can Help You.' The irony is that Mike Hurst was right about the song's commerciality and it was to take us into the national charts for the first time, but more about that later.

A series of gigs took us up to 10th June 1968, when we recorded the Dave Symonds Show again for BBC radio.

On June 15th we played at the London College of Printing, for their Summer Dance. Other bands on the bill were The Who, Aynsley Dunbar's Retaliation and The Nice.

Top Pops magazine on 29th June reported the release of our new single 'We Can Help You' with the headline, 'Alan Bown launch MGM label'. In 'Post Bag' of the same Top Pops issue, fans wrote in asking for 'more

photographs and articles on the fantastic Alan Bown! It's about time, not to say long overdue, that such talented and dedicated musicians gained recognition and chart success.'

Then on the 2nd of July we were back at The Playhouse Theatre, London to record tracks for Saturday Club. Later, on the same day, we recorded for the Jimmy Young Show! Positively no slacking!

On the 5th of July, 'We Can Help You' was released on MGM's new Music Factory label and our management organised an afternoon press reception for the band at The Pair of Shoes Club, in London. After that we drove up to Nottingham to play at the University.

On 6th July, adverts appeared for 'We Can Help You' in The New Musical Express, The Melody Maker, The Disc and Music Echo and Top Pops, all big circulation weekly music papers at the time. The adverts all carried a photo of the band.

The Melody Maker on the 6th July gave us 'Pick of the Week.' The review is reproduced here;
'Alan Bown - We Can Help You.' - 'Hooray! Here it is, the first big hit by Alan Bown, or my name isn't. A great song by Alex Spyropoulos and Patrick Campbell Lyons, which they featured on Nirvana's original 'Story of Simon Simopath' science fiction pantomime album. A tremendous orchestral backing arranged by Harry Robinson and the great vocal performance one expects from Alan's vastly underrated singer, Jess Roden. This must be The Alan Bown's best single yet and one to finally establish them in the chart.'

In the same issue of the MM, it was reported that 'The group guests in Saturday Club this weekend (July 6) and is at The Royal Albert Hall on Sunday (7).'

Also on the 6th July, The Record Mirror had this to say;
'We Can Help You/Magic Handkerchief.' – 'Debut on a new label and this could give the boys, at long last, that biggie. It's a splendid, repetitive, lively, string backed sort of song, which is darned catchy – and a complete change of style for one of the groups I most admire. A lovely mixture of the old and the new, musically speaking. Hope it makes it. Chart possibility.'

Further positive write-ups on the single appeared on the 6th July in Disc and Music Echo and The New Musical Express. It was looking good.

On Sunday the 7th July 1968, we appeared at The Albert Hall.
It was a charity event for 'Keystone', the National Association of Boy's Clubs. On the same bill as The Alan Bown were, Grapefruit, Bobby Goldsboro,

Joe Cocker, The Easybeats, The Bonzo Dog Doo Dah Band and American band The Byrds, featuring Roger McGuinn. They'd had big hits in the UK with the Bob Dylan song, 'Mr Tambourine Man, also 'Turn Turn Turn and 'Eight Miles High'. The Albert Hall was packed for the occasion. It was good exposure for us and we went down well. The show was closed by The Move who had the biggest PA stacks anyone had seen and it blasted everyone into submission.

Top Pops on the 13th July published another advert for the single, combined with a band photo.

Also on 13th July, in New Musical Express, we shared a Music Factory advert with Chris Rayburn. In the same issue of NME a miniscule report said, 'The Alan Bown is a group that has been without a hit for too long and worked hard on an entertaining and exciting act - Amen Corner, Nice, Crazy World of Arthur Brown, Joe Cocker and Alan Bown, in All-Day Rave at Burton Constable Hall, near Hull on August 3rd.'

I was interviewed by Ian Middleton of the Record Mirror on 20th July. The half-page article was headed; 'It Must Be The Only Trumpet Lead Group Around'. The caption under a photo of the band read, 'The Alan Bown – Things happening at last'. The single had a positive mention. Also on the 20th July, The Daily Express reported in a supercilious article that, '...The Alan Bown keep distant from the barber's chair...' – 'Tonight, a rave up on Dee Time (BBC 1, 6.15pm)'.

On the 20th July, as reported, we appeared on the Simon Dee BBC 1 TV Show, which was called 'Dee Time'. This was a popular Saturday evening show with large viewing figures and we performed our single, 'We Can Help You'.

Top Pops on 27th July, published a half page colour photo of the band captioned, 'Alan Bown! – We Can Help You.'

On the 2nd August 1968, we recorded the Eamon Andrews 'Today' programme, to be screened on ATV later in the month. News of our forthcoming show with Jack Good was reported in Record Mirror, New Musical Express and also in Melody Maker on 3rd August.

The August 1968 edition of Beat Magazine featured a full-page article and photo of the band. The piece was entitled, 'The Very Commercial Alan Bown!'

17

TOP OF THE POPS

In the late 1950's, Jack Good launched the legendary ABC TV Rock 'n' Roll show, 'Oh Boy'. It was in direct competition to the popular music show on BBC TV at the time, 'The 6-5 Special', which Jack Good had originally produced.

All the major British artists had appeared on 'Oh Boy' in its time; Adam Faith, Cliff Richard, Billy Fury, Marty Wilde, Joe Brown, The Dallas Boys, Ronnie Carroll, Lord Rockingham's X1, Cherry Wainer on organ and The Vernons Girls. The John Barry Seven had also made guest appearances on the early shows (before my time).

A spectacular recreation of those early days was to be screened by Yorkshire Television in the autumn of 1968. The title of the show was 'Innocence, Anarchy and Soul' and would be produced by Jack Good.

We began rehearsals at Elstree Studios on the 30th, 31st July then the 1st August followed by the 4th, 6th, 9th, 10th and 11th August, 1968. Also booked for the show were Lulu, Lonnie Donegan, Chris Farlowe, The Flirtations, Dominic Grant, The Breakaways, The Chants and Ian Whitcombe who was a sort of Rock 'n' Roll poet. Lance LeGault, an old buddy of Jack Good's came over from America to do some Elvis Presley songs, having apparently sung on many demos of songs for Elvis.

Jack Good wanted to include an element of reality in this production and enlisted the help of local bikers and rockers. This was all very well but once again we had that prickly feeling that our presence wasn't held with much reverence. These 'outsiders' were the same breed as the Dereham gang that had attempted to beat us to pulp. They were given banners with words like 'Rockers', 'Hippies Go Home' and 'Come Home Jerry Lee'. In all honesty, this part of the show wasn't our scene and it had a sort of pantomime atmosphere about it. What didn't help was that Jack decided in his wisdom that we should also dress up like teddy boys, with drape jackets and string ties. The Rockers took exception to this and some remarks from them brought back memories of The Saville Theatre debacle. However, disregarding all that, we had a lot of fun doing the show.

After a dispute between the technicians and the management at ITV, the Jack Good Show, originally scheduled for the 12th October, was eventually screened on Saturday, the 26th October.

Top Pops 10th -17th August 1968 edition, included us in a four column article entitled 'Behind the chart front...' It was about bands currently on the scene. Our recent band photo headed the article and was captioned, 'Alan Bown! – Drawing crowds.'

On the 12th August, The Eastern Evening News reported on 'New Look Mayall debut in Norfolk.' A photo of The Alan Bown! appeared alongside, mentioning that we were 'among the groups booked for The Gala, Norwich, next month.'

The Melody Maker on the 17th August reported, 'Wage Dispute Hits £50,000 TV Pop Show.' Headshots of Julie Driscoll, Lulu and myself were included. This article was about the technicians' dispute affecting The Jack Good Show

The Eamon Andrews 'Today' programme was shown on ATV on the 22nd August. The following day we had a photo session.

Two days later, we learned that 'We Can Help You' had gone into the New Musical Express charts at number 29. A top thirty record was big news in those days and we were well pleased. We then heard the news that BBC TV wanted us to do Top of the Pops! It was the news every band wanted to hear. Not least The Alan Bown!

It was then brought to my attention that all members of the band had to be in the Musician's Union. This was a must to appear on TOTP because resident musicians were involved and if it was found out that non-union musicians were being employed there could be a dispute, which could jeopardise our appearance.

In Disc, also on 24th August, an item headed 'Peel for Nice, Price Show' said that John Peel would compere The Nice/ Alan Price/ Alan Bown/ Spooky Tooth/ Eclection/ Tim Buckley concert at Croydon's Fairfield Halls on September 29th in aid of the British Olympics Appeal Fund. The show will be filmed by BBC2 for their production, 'Colour Me Pop.' The South London Press, Sunday Telegraph, Evening News, Record Mirror and Disc also covered this report and mentioned the band but, as it turned out, we had to resume recording the Jack Good Show on that date, which had been delayed by a technicians dispute.

Also on the 24th August, another item appeared in the NME

and mentioned that our first album, 'The Alan Bown!' would be released on October 1st.

Top Pops 24th-31st August 1968 edition, reported, 'Alan Bown booked for Jack Good.' The single was also mentioned and forthcoming dates; 'Georges Ballroom, Hinkley (24) Chesford Grange, Kenilworth (26) Guild Hall, Portsmouth (28) The Pavilion, Bournemouth (30) Middlesbrough Festival (31)

The New Musical Express headlined an article on the 24th August, 'Nice-Bown-Price Charity Show for Two Part BBC Screening.' On another page of the same edition of the NME was an article devoted to us under the heading, 'New To the Charts' and sub-headed, 'Alan Bown – soft and hard music.' In the same issue, the NME Top 30 (week ending August 21, 1968) showed 'We Can Help You' at number 29.

We appeared on 'Top of The Pops' on Thursday, 29th August 1968.

This was the biggest TV music show at the time. Shown on BBC TV, it was compulsory viewing for all teenagers and guaranteed increased record sales. We were on with only one other act, The Flirtations who, by coincidence, were also on the Jack Good Show. The rest of the 'acts' televised that day were on video so we had the benefit of a five-camera shoot. For convenience, even in those days, artists would perform to a backing track that was pre-recorded at the TOTP studio. We recorded ours, with the resident orchestra, playing the string parts, so we didn't actually mime to the record, just a version of it. However, the vocals were live and Jess breezed through the song with backing vocals from the band. Before our performance, the TOTP photographer came in to our dressing room to take some shots of us for the following week's show. He said, 'You lads will be back next week, no trouble.' Two days later the single had moved up to number 26 in the NME charts.

'We Can Help You' was being played on all the major radio stations. It looked as though Mike Hurst had been right all along.

The Middlesborough Evening Gazette on 29th August included an article headed, 'Top Pop Comes To Big T for £2,500.' The report gave details of the forthcoming pop festival in Teesside. We were mentioned amongst a host of other names. Promoter John McCoy booked us. We played many times at his Kirklevington Country Club, near Middlesborough. I say 'near Middlesborough', in fact it was in the middle of nowhere! The venue was a building over a garage on the side of a remote road. However, it was a very popular club and attracted people from miles around. John had his own band 'Tramline' so he understood musicians more than the average promoter.

We got on well and had a mutual respect for each other.

In the Bournemouth Evening Echo on the 29th August, our single was given a plug, 'We Can Help You is by the Alan Bown, who are at The Pavilion tomorrow night.'

In The Leamington Spa Courier on 30th August, an article headed, 'Music Music' gave details of Chesford Grange where we recently appeared.

The same day, The Kettering Leader, mentioned our single, 'We Can Help You', saying it originated from the band Nirvana.

The 31st August issue of Jackie Magazine printed a long letter from Maggie of our Fan Club, headed, 'She Has All the Low-down on The Alan Bown.'

Also on 31st August, the Melody Maker published a letter of apology from a member of the public, about an incident at a gig; 'At a recent dance in Newcastle, where Family and Alan Bown were appearing, some idiot threw a glass at The Alan Bown, on stage. I hope that Alan Bown do not judge Newcastle teenagers by one idiot'.

This is an example of the vulnerability of playing in public for any musicians. On another gig, elsewhere, a half drunk member of the audience climbed onto the stage and, without even realising it, managed to bang his head into the end of my trumpet. I was blowing at the time with my eyes shut so I didn't see him coming. The impact of the collision split my lip but the guy staggered off, completely oblivious!

An article in Disc on 31st August 1968 reported that 'Long John Baldry turns compere again when he hosts a pop festival in Middlesborough this Saturday. Traffic, The Bonzo Dog Doo Dah Band, Ben E King, Family, Alan Bown and Joe Cocker are among the guest artists'. Another report in the same issue of the newspaper mentioned our forthcoming (but later withdrawn) appearance the Fairfield Hall, on September 29th. An article more about Tim Buckley appeared in the same issue in Disc and gave us another mention. The Northern Echo, on the 31st August also reported on the festival.

The Nuneaton Evening Tribune on the 31st August, also reviewed our single, 'We Can Help You,' The article, headed, 'It Looks a Winner', concluded, 'Undoubtedly it could prove to be their first big success.'

NME TOP 30

(Week ending Wednesday, August 28, 1868)

LAST WEEK	THIS WEEK			WEEKS IN CHART	HIGHEST POSITION
1	1	HELP YOURSELF	Tom Jones (Decca)	8	1
5	2	I'VE GOTTA GET A MESSAGE TO YOU	Bee Gees (Polydor)	4	2
4	3	THIS GUY'S IN LOVE WITH YOU	Herb Alpert (A. & M.)	8	3
6	4	DO IT AGAIN	Beach Boys (Capitol)	5	4
2	5	MONY MONY	Tommy James & the Shondells (Major Minor)	10	1
13	6	I SAY A LITTLE PRAYER	Aretha Franklin (Atlantic)	3	6
3	7	FIRE	Arthur Brown (Track)	9	2
12	8	HIGH IN THE SKY	Amen Corner (Deram)	4	8
7	9	SUNSHINE GIRL	Herman's Hermits (Columbia)	6	7
10	10	DANCE TO THE MUSIC	Sly & the Family Stone (Direction)	6	10
18	11	HOLD ME TIGHT	Johnny Nash (Regal Zonophone)	2	11
8	12	I CLOSE MY EYES AND COUNT TO TEN	Dusty Springfield (Philips)	9	6
17	13	ON THE ROAD AGAIN	Canned Heat (Liberty)	3	13
9	14	I PRETEND	Des O'Connor (Columbia)	15	3
14	15	KEEP ON	Bruce Channel (Bell)	7	11
11	16	MRS. ROBINSON	Simon and Garfunkel (CBS	8	4
16	17	DAYS	Kinks (Pye)	7	14
25	18	DREAM A LITTLE DREAM OF ME	Mama Cass (RCA)	2	18
24	19	YOUR TIME HASN'T COME YET BABY	Elvis Presley (RCA)	4	19
	20	JESAMINE	Casuals (Decca)	1	20
21	21	DREAM A LITTLE DREAM OF ME	Anita Harris (CBS)	3	21
15	22	LAST NIGHT IN SOHO	Dave Dee, Dozy, Beaky, Mick and Tich (Fontana)	8	8
23	23	HARD TO HANDLE	Otis Redding (Atlantic)	4	23
26	24	LADY WILLPOWER	Gary Puckett & the Union Gap (CBS)	3	24
	25	ELEANOR RIGBY	Ray Charles (Stateside)	1	25
29	26	WE CAN HELP YOU	Alan Bown (Music Factory)	2	26
	27	VOICES IN THE SKY	Moody Blues (Deram)	1	27
22	28	SON OF HICKORY HOLLER'S TRAMP	O. C. Smith (CBS)	13	2
19	29	UNIVERSAL	Small Faces (Immediate)	7	16
	30	LAUREL AND HARDY	Equals (President)	2	26

Alan Bown £500,000 world deal?

THE Alan Bown has received a lucrative five-year offer for world-wide representation from a major American agency. The terms guarantee the group a minimum income of £87,000 per year. If the deal is clinched, the Alan Bown would undertake extensive tours of America, Japan, the Philippines and the Far East every year for the duration of the contract — and would probably be involved in a Hollywood film deal.

The group's manager Mel Collins is at present discussing the terms with its agent Harold Davison—who, in the event of the offer being accepted, would retain the Alan Bown's British representation.

Four days have been set aside during the first half of next month for the group to record its next single under Mike Hurst's supervision. It will be in the studios for three days from next Wednesday (4) and again on September 10. Next Tuesday, the Alan Bown records a guest spot in Radio I's " Pop North " for transmission two days later (5).

One-nighters set for the group include Bournemouth Pavilion (tonight, Friday), Malvern Winter Gardens (next Monday), Gillingham Aurora (September 7), Harlow Youth Centre (12), Isle of Wight Seagull (14), Yeovil Liberal Club (19), Devizes Corn Exchange (20), Norwich Gala (21) and Streatham Philippa Fawcetta College (27).

The New Musical Express on the 31st August, published their NME Top 30 (week ending August 28, 1968). 'We Can Help You' had moved up to number 26! It was our second week in the charts (see page 134).

In the same issue of NME a prominent article was headlined; 'Alan Bown £500,000 world deal?'

Record Mirror, also on the 31st August (busy week!) published a half page article by Peter Jones, entitled, 'Nobody Knows Our Faces!' A band photo was at the top of the page and captioned, 'The Alan Bown! At last achieving success they deserve.' The article gave an in depth profile of each member of the band, concluding with, 'Jeff is compiling a book of short stories, drawings and satire.' (This has now been published by Banland Publishing Ltd – 38 years later! The book is entitled, 'The Blue Book – Tonto Greenberg').

On the 3rd September 1968, we travelled to Manchester to record Pop North for BBC Radio 1. After the show, when we left the theatre, which was in the middle of a slum clearance project, hordes of girls surrounded us and attempted to rip souvenirs off our clothes. For the first few seconds it seemed like fun, then it got far too physical and, before we managed to scramble into our car, I think Jess or Tony lost a clump of hair!

I was interviewed by the Dundee Courier, on 4th September. I recalled our early days in the J.M. Ballroom in Dundee and mentioned the new single.

Also on the 4th September, The Yorkshire Evening Press reported that we were appearing in York. Next Friday - the 13th – not unlucky for The Alan Bown!' They're at The Assembly Rooms for the first time since they notched Top 30 with 'We Can Help You.'

On the 5th September, the band had an interview and photo session with New Musical Express. Afterwards we had a meeting with our manager, Mel Collins at his office in Dean Street. We were in a good mood after the interview, which were always a laugh, but Mel had some bad news for us. It couldn't have been worse.

The pressing plant that processed the records for our label, MGM – Music Factory, had gone on strike! Mel had taken legal action but meanwhile our single would not be processed and consequently, there would be no deliveries to the record shops. It was an absolute disaster.

Here we were, in the Top 30, with a very recent Top of the Pops appearance, radio plays every day, good reviews in the music press but no product available in the shops! By the time the dispute had been resolved, our single had disappeared from public consciousness. It was an all time low for the band's morale.

The New Musical Express on the 7th September, in their 'Countdown' section, listed the week's events including Pop North. Apart from us, the show also featured The Move, The Equals and Status Quo. Also, in the same issue of the NME, an item headed, 'Radio 1 Highlights' reported on the forthcoming guests on the Jimmy Young Show. 'The Alan Bown! and The Move top the bill.'

Also on the 7th, Fabulous Magazine gave us a plug for 'We Can Help You'. Their article was headed, 'Westward Bown!' (Cringe!)

In Disc on 7th September, Vicki Wickam wrote a scathing article saying 'Top of the Pops should ditch D.J.'s. She berated the programme's old fashioned sets and disinterested audiences. She said, 'Alan Bown won slightly 'cos they at least looked a bit happy.'

Also on 7th September, The New Musical Express reported on our performance at a festival. The article headed, 'At Middlesborough', is reproduced here;
'The festival was promoted by John McCoy, a Northern agent who owns The Kirklevinton Country Club. The Alan Bown played for over an hour, including tracks from their new LP, plus things like 'Toyland', 'The Violin Shop', 'Morning Dew' and 'We Can Help You.' 'The band puts on a complete show with leaping around, vocal harmonies, good instrumentalisation and colourful outfits. They launched into a rock medley which featured jiving amid 'Tutti Frutti and 'Whole Lotta Shakin' Going On'. No wonder they're so popular.'

On 12th September, The Yorkshire Evening Press included us in an article, which mentioned us appearing at The Assembly Rooms in York, on

Friday the 13th for Peter Stringfellow's Mojo Soul Show.

On the 13th September, The New Musical Express', Who's Where' section included us on their gig list saying, 'Alan Bown; Ryde - Seagull (14th) and Yoevil - Liberal Club (19th)'.

On the same day, the NME ran a big feature article on the forthcoming Jack Good Show. The article opened with, 'Lulu, Julie Driscoll and The Brian Auger Trinity, Jerry Lee Lewis and The Alan Bown are the stars of a Yorkshire TV special, which Jack Good is producing for autumn networking.'

Also on the 13th September, The Luton Evening Post reported on the forthcoming concert at Fairfield Hall, Croydon and gave the band a name check.

Valentine magazine gave us a full-page feature with a photograph on the 14th September. The photo was boldly captioned, 'Bown! To Happen!' The article was written by Pat Brennan who had seen the band and commented that, after the gig; 'I came out raving then and I'm still raving now!' (Not raving mad, I hope - Alan).

The Record Mirror, on the 14th September, an article headed Olympic Pop Fest, also mentioned the Fairfield Hall and The Alan Bown booked for the concert.

In Fab Magazine, on the 14th September, Sandra Wright, from Norfolk wrote a letter requesting info on the band.

Fabulous Magazine on the 21st September, reported, 'Pop Stars to raise Olympic Funds.' The article referred to the forthcoming concert at the Fairfield Hall, which was to be recorded by the BBC. It was accompanied by a photo of the band captioned; 'The Alan Bown! One of the groups taking part in the concert.' I have to give full credit here to our publicity department, which was often on the ball with this kind of article. This one for example, could have featured a photo of any other band, some of which were big names at the time. As it can be seen, we certainly didn't suffer a low profile in the press.

In the 27th September issue of 'What's On' magazine, a brief article mentioned 'Olympop', a special show at Croydon's Fairfield Hall on the 29th September, to aid the British Olympic Appeal Fund. The show was to be compered by John Peel. On the bill were, Julie Driscoll, The Brian Auger Trinity, Alan Price, The Nice, The Alan Bown and Spooky Tooth.'

The Melody Maker on 28th September, published an article about me, entitled 'Pop Trumpet Leader'. The article was a personal profile and the accompanying photo was captioned 'Alan Bown: lacquered trumpet.'

The disputes that halted the Jack Good Show were also resolved and we resumed recording at Elstree Studios on the 26th, 27th, 28th and 29th of September.

Rave magazine gave The Alan Bown a feature in their October 1968 issue. The piece was entitled 'Autumn Almanac', subtitled, 'So you think you're in tune with the pop scene? Well, here's your chance to find out with Rave's guide to some of the best sounds around.' T Rex and Family were also featured.

Alan Bown
1968

18

SWEDEN UP IN SMOKE

On October 1st 1968, The Alan Bown! flew to Sweden for a short
Scandinavian tour.

We arrived in Malmo and had the first evening off. We were taken
out for a sumptuous meal by our hosts who had booked us after seeing
performances of the band in England. We didn't play in Malmo but went on
to Stockholm on the 3rd October.

We discovered that, compared to London, Malmo city centre
was very clean and tidy. In fact, all the people seemed to be equally clean
and tidy! During the afternoon, Jeff and I were strolling through the main
shopping centre, sightseeing, when we noticed a crowd of people in a large
store transfixed by some activity that we were unable to see. Being curious,
we went in to find out what was attracting so much attention. All the people
were in a semi circle around what appeared to be a seated area in the middle.
They stood in silence as though something very strange was happening. By
now, we had established that it was a shoe shop and we could see a man with
long hair, trying on ladies boots. Jeff and I looked at each other and said the
same word. 'Stan'!
A red - faced female assistant was standing next to Stan with a selection of
boots that he had chosen. In Sweden, in the 1960's, the idea of men wearing
ladies boots was about as common as topless female accordionists and
about as scandalous. I hasten to add that the fashion at the time in England
embraced stack-heeled boots and some women's boots were butch enough
for us followers of pop fashion, so it was nothing new to us. However, by the
expressions on people's faces, I wouldn't be surprised if Stan's performance
was considered to be so outrageous that it became part of Swedish folklore!

The first gig in Stockholm on the 4th October 1968 went well and
on the 5th we appeared on a TV show and played another gig in Stockholm
in the evening. That also went well but after the gig some guys who had been
in the audience invited Jess Roden back to their place. Jess spent the night in
the company of guys smoking some heavy stuff and when he turned up at the
hotel the next morning he could hardly speak!

On the evening of that same day, the 6th October, we had our next gig in Jonkoping. The venue was quite a large ballroom and by the time we were due to perform, a large crowd had built up. Jess looked very pale when we went on, almost as though he was anticipating the worst. Then, following the intro of our first song, Jess opened his mouth to sing but after a few croaky notes his throat closed up and that was it. His voice had gone! The crowd watched with incredulity as Jess strained every muscle in his larynx to emit a sound but with no result. He turned and looked at us like a rabbit caught in the headlights. It was an awful moment for us all. Soon the mood of the audience turned sour as they could see our vain attempts to save the situation.

Jeff, by now, had taken a back seat with lead vocals and only did a couple of songs in the set. After those and a few instrumentals, Jess was still unable to sing a note so we had to apologise to the audience and leave the stage. As soon as we came off, the promoter came up to me and threatened me maliciously with all kinds of action, claiming that the crowd wanted their money back and his reputation was also an issue. It was humiliating and once we got into the dressing room, I went ballistic. None of the band did drugs and I had no sympathy for Jess. I knew he smoked the occasional spliff but this had gone too far. I was so furious that I told him right there, in front of the rest of the band that he was sacked! With only a whisper of a voice, Jess pleaded his case with heartfelt apologies, repeating to all of us that he didn't want to leave the band. It was obvious he hadn't done this on purpose but the gig had gone up in smoke and so had our prospects of being re-booked.

The next day, during our return trip to England, I had a talk with Jess and he again asked me, in a whisper, to let him stay on with the band. He convinced me that this would never happen again so I agreed. With an album in the pipeline, it would have been a negative move for all concerned if he had left. Nevertheless, in retrospect, I think the damage had been done and the episode sowed the seeds for Jess's eventual departure. The camaraderie that had glued us together all this time was never the same again.

The New Musical Express, on October 5th, published a half page report on The Jack Good Show. Headlined; 'Jack Good Rolls us back to Rock.' The article included a great photo of Jeff, Jess, John and myself. In the middle of the shot, in German Army helmet and flying jacket was Chris Farlowe. Most people thought it was our drummer Vic. (Even Vic!).

On the 18th October 1968 we played at The Lyceum in London. It was an all-nighter, commencing at midnight. Top of the bill was The Who with The Crazy World of Arthur Brown, Elmer Gantry's Velvet Opera and Skip Bifferty also on the bill. We appeared around 1am.

The Jack Good Show on ATV October 1968
Left to right:
Jeff Bannister, Jess Roden, Chris Farlowe, Alan Bown and John Anthony Helliwell

brunel university students' union

Groups booked through Hadley Artists Limited

midnite rave

**12.30 to 7 a.m., fri. night, oct. 18th/19th
at the lyceum, strand, w.c.2**

WHO

CRAZY WORLD OF ARTHUR BROWN

ALAN BOWN ★ ELMER GANTRY

★ SKIP BIFFERTY, etc.

Licensed Bars till 3 a.m.
21/- at door (SU-ULU-NUS or Club Cards)
advance tickets from lyceum
dress anyhow — now you can enter "mecca" in your hippiest gear!

The Jack Good Show was finally screened by ATV on the 26th October and was watched nationwide by all avid music devotees.

Paul Stringfellow, who was our roadie at the time, unfortunately lost his licence after a speeding offence and had to leave us during November. Paul recalls; 'I was driving the van through a village on the A10 and the speed limit was 30mph. I must have been doing around 45 miles an hour when I was pulled over by a police car. The previous night I had been in Olympic Studio in Barnes with The Alan Bown! and the Rolling Stones had been recording before us and left bottles of alcohol in the studio. There was a nearly full bottle of whisky and I decided to take it home for my Dad. Unfortunately, I couldn't find the top of the bottle so I decided to strap it to the side of the driving seat, to prevent it falling over. When the police officer saw this he asked me if I had been drinking and made me walk along a white line. I was stone cold sober as it happens so he did me for speeding instead and I was eventually banned for 6 months.' (It was probably the long straw coming out of the bottle that made him suspicious – Jeff)

We were sorry to see Paul go but Steve Hackett stayed on and was joined by Keith, a former roadie for 'The Nice'. The Nice had nicknamed Keith 'The Snail' because of his expertise in the art of slow motion. We never saw him hurry anywhere so the name stuck but he always got the job done so I had no complaints. In fact, I must say that all the roadies we had were great.

John Peel on his 'Underground' page in Disc and Music Echo on 2nd November, presented, 'My ABC of Beauty' which gave his opinion, alphabetically, of most bands around at the time. He said of us, 'Alan Bown, not just a dance band as many seem to think. They've done some very nice things for radio'.

Top Pops on the 2nd November reviewed the new album, 'The Alan Bown : Outward Bown (Music Factory)'.
Jeff Tarry gave the album this review;
'Here is the first solo album from the most under-rated and sadly neglected bands in Britain, if not the world. On stage they are superb visually, with power and humour combining effortlessly. This is a collection of their own songs, which have excited audiences at live gigs all over Europe. 'Toyland' was nearly a Top Thirty record, while 'Sally Green', 'Technicolour Dream', 'Story Book' and 'Penny for Your Thoughts' are all very good numbers. Their version of 'All Along the Watchtower', the Bob Dylan song, is infinitely better than the Hendrix offering. 'My Girl in the Month of May' has an almost hypnotic appeal. Yes, this album has lived up to all my high expectations. Please give it a listen and don't miss your next chance to see them on stage.'

Also, on the 2nd November, New Musical Express reported on upcoming guests for The Radio One Club.
'Appearing throughout the November 11-15 week are the Alan Bown...'

Around this time, our loyal mechanics at Galena Garage obtained a much newer Ford Galaxy for us This was another 9-seater, which apparently had only one previous owner. This was a great improvement on the old clapped out original Ford Galaxy. However, several golden memories of the old car live on like this one:-

We were travelling back from South Wales (to London) after a gig and it started to rain. Then, to our dismay, we discovered that the windscreen wiper motor had seized up! Our ingenuity came to the rescue and we pulled over to tie two long pieces of string to each wiper arm and thread them through the top of the window of each side/rear door. The two lucky passengers in the back seat had to pull the strings alternately, thus making the wipers traverse the windscreen. Bearing in mind that, in pre-motorway days, this journey took about four hours and the momentum had to be maintained, there were some serious complaints from the back! Complying with 'Murphy's Law', the rain inevitably continued throughout the journey. One of the 'wiper-motor detail', John Anthony, complained next day of having 'tennis elbow'!

One of our roadies at the time, Algy Ross, regarded himself as a custom-car buff and we told him that the new Galaxy had a supercharger. It was a ruse to get him to look under the bonnet (hood, for American readers) and as he searched in vain for the prized piece of kit, he forced his head further and further into the recess. At that point someone pressed the car horn, which on that car was very loud. He jumped up so quickly that he banged his head on the bonnet with an audible clang! Needless to say, he wasn't at all impressed with our little joke and for a split second there was violence in the air but then he started laughing. He knew it wasn't malicious, just another prank, born out of boredom.

On the 10th November 1968, we appeared once again with The Who. This time at Colston Hall, Bristol. They were doing an autumn tour sponsored by Kit Lambert and Chris Stamp in conjunction with Kennedy Street Enterprises. The show was compered by Tony Hall. The Crazy World of Arthur Brown was top of the bill, supported by The Who, The Mindbenders and The Alan Bown!

On the 11th November, The Western Daily Press, a review of 'Last night's pop show at The Colston Hall, Bristol.' All the bands were mentioned (as above).

The Eastern Evening News on the 11th November, in 'Here and Now' published an article about the current pop scene and gave us a mention.

In the Western Daily Press on 14th November, Brian K Jones in his 'The Long Thin Column' reviewed the concert at Colston Hall; 'Alan Bown was Alan Bown their usual high standard. Enough said.'

An article written by Keith Altham about The Who, appeared in the New Musical Express, 16th November, Jess Roden was given a mention for having sung backing vocals on The Who's track, 'Magic Bus'.

In The Portsmouth News on 21st November, a short article in 'Pop Chatter' reported, 'Manor Court Club have The Alan Bown! for their Christmas dance, which last year attracted 1,000 youngsters.'

In Melody Maker on the 23rd November, a feature entitled 'Club Scene' mentioned The Opposite Lock Club in Birmingham, celebrating its second anniversary with a host of artists, including Alan Bown on December 6th at the Lock's Factory.

The Western Daily Press on the 24th November interviewed the whole band and gave us all a name check. Unfortunately Jess was named Jess Voden!

The 26th of November, we were back at the BBC recording The Dave Symonds Show from 7pm to 10.30pm.

The Birmingham Evening Mail on 29th November, also reported on the Opposite Lock Club in Gas Street, Birmingham and its extension, The Factory, where we eventually played.

The New Musical Express on the 30th November gave us four stars for our new album 'The Alan Bown – Outward Bown'. The review was good and all the tracks were mentioned.

Also on the 30th, in The Gloucester News column, 'Disc Talk by Tony' gave results to 'last week's quiz; 3. Edwin Starr and Alan Bown are the two artists who recorded a version of 'Headline News'.'

The Radio Times on 3rd December 1968 had a column on The Radio 1 Club, which reported; 'Tuesday: Keith Skues's guest D.J. is Jonathan King. The Alan Bown will be there, too.'

In The Portsmouth News, on the 5th December, in their column 'Pop Chatter', headed 'Best of Beat on the Pier', reported that the 'Fairport Convention, Idle Race , The Alan Bown and local group Tangerine Slyde, are all set for 'star-loaded' beat dance at South Parade Pier tonight. Tyrannosaurus Rex, strongly tipped as a future booking.'

Jackie magazine on the 7th December featured a photo of me and a column explaining, 'The Loves and Hates of Alan Bown.'

In The Dorset Evening Echo on the 10th December it was reported that 'The Traffic', the group booked for South Dorset Technical College annual dance on December the 19th will not be fulfilling their engagement because the break up of the three man team last week. It is now hoped to book the Alan Bown group in time for the dance in nine days time.' (Yes, we did play in Weymouth on the 19th December instead of The Traffic).

On the 14th December, The Melody Maker gave us brief review of the album 'Outward Bown'. It said, 'A fine band who have had difficulty crystallising their approach but always record quality pop. Tracks include 'Toyland'. Jess Roden's vocals are excellent as always.'

The Scunthorpe Star on the 17th December, in their column, 'On the Steelbeat', reported that we were appearing at The York Technical College on New Year's Eve. Also on the 17th December, The Loughborough Monitor reported on Loughborough College's forthcoming attractions. '...the entertainments committee have already booked top line artists in the pop world for two rag dances; Top radio and TV disc-jockey, Stuart Henry has agreed to appear on one of them. Also booked are Chris Farlowe, Alan Bown and the Moody Blues.'

In the 'Pop Chatter' column of the Portsmouth News on the 19th December, we had this mention; 'The Alan Bown Set for The Manor Court Club, Drayton, dance tomorrow night. The group played for a Christmas dance at the club last year, attracting 1,000 fans.'

In the New Musical Express on the 21st December, their 'Latest on Radio' column reported that Alan Bown were lined up for The David Symonds Show.

In The Disc and Music Echo on the 28th December, Jonathan King in his column said, '...The Alan Bown deserve a hit...'
On another page of this issue, in the 'Tune In' column, it was reported that we were guesting on the David Symonds Show. Also on the 28th December, a report in the Middlesborough Evening Gazette, said, 'The Alan Bown, the soul band, make a return to Redcar Jazz club tomorrow after illness had forced them to cancel an earlier booking.' Unfortunately, we couldn't get there after all because the North East was completely snowed up!

The December 1968 issue of Beat Instrumental gave the new album, 'The Alan Bown - Outward Bown' an outstanding review (see below). Also in the same issue of Beat Instrumental it was reported that Mel Collins, our manager was lining us up for an international promotional tour.

OUTWARD BOWN

THE ALAN BOWN!
MUSIC FACTORY
CUBLM I

The Alan Bown! have always been very honest in their approach to music. They say they are a commercial group, which is true, but it's commercial music saturated with class. All but three of the numbers on this album are their own, with *Sally Green* outstanding enough to be a single, and *Toyland* and *Technicolor Dream* full of individuality and technique. The powerful brass line of Alan Bown and John Anthony play clever harmony phrases throughout, and the voice of Jess Roden blasts and soars through every number. It's albums like this which are the life blood of English pop music.

Side One: Toyland; Magic Handkerchief; Mutiny; All Along The Watchtower; Sally Green; Penny For Your Thoughts.
Side Two: Story Book; Technicolor Dream; Love Is A Beautiful Thing; Violin Shop; You're Not In My Class; My Girl; The Month Of May.

19

THE PRESS TURN UP THE HEAT

On the 4th January 1969, Disc reported, 'Alan Bown's baby daughter, Nicole aged 10 months is the proud winner of 'Beautiful Baby of the Year' title from Johnson's baby products.'
In the same edition of the Disc, it said, 'Four frozen groups – Pretty Things, Eire Apparent, Alan Bown and Tyrannosaurus Rex – waited five hours for a plane to take them to Utrecht, Holland on Saturday. It didn't turn up!' (More snow chaos).

Also on the 4th January, The Melody Maker ran the same story but put us first, 'Alan Bown, Tyrannosaurus Rex, The Pretty Things and Heir Apparent (spot the different spelling - Alan) waited 5 hours at Gatwick airport on Saturday for a plane to take them to Utrecht Pop festival. The plane never showed up. Bad weather also prevented Alan Bown reaching a date at Redcar the following day. The group is guesting on The Jimmy Young Show this week.'

On the 6th January in the morning, we recorded The Jimmy Young Show in London and later that afternoon we had a photo session. Then it was back on the road for a further succession of gigs throughout February and March.

In The Western Evening News on the 7th January an article about Bob Dylan mentioned that we had recorded one of his songs, 'All Along the Watchtower'.

On the 11th January, The Folkestone Herald gave us a positive review. The article was headed, 'Big year for The Alan Bown' and featured a large, page-width head & shoulders photo of the band. All the band members were given a name check. The article began, 'One two three ...seven faces all belonging to The Alan Bown, who played to an audience of 700 at Folkestone's Leas Cliff Hall on Saturday.'

In Fabulous Magazine on the 12th January, in the 'Where They're At' column, it reported that Alan Bown were at The Top Rank Suite Leicester (15) - Oakleaf Hotel, Middlesborough (16) - Civic Hall, Wolverhampton (17) - Southampton University (18) - The Coatham Hotel, Redcar (19).

In The Portsmouth Evening News, on the 16th January, the Pop Chatter column mentioned, 'Dance at Portsmouth Mecca on Tuesday January 21st in aid of Isle of Wight International Children's Society will feature Pretty Things, Alan Bown, plus two local groups Concrete Parachute and Halcyon Order.'
In the same edition, results of a reader's popularity poll for visiting groups gave us 3rd position with 136 votes.

On the 17th January, The Evening News printed a photo of Nicole on my wife's lap pretending to play my trumpet with me putting my fingers in my ears. The photo was captioned 'Blowing Her Trumpet.'

The Daily Mirror on the 18th January reported that 'Pop Star Alan Bown's ten month old daughter Nicole, wins a national baby contest – and parents get a years free supply of talc and nappies!'

On the 24th January, the Yorkshire Evening Press column, The Night People, headlined an article with, 'Alan Bown group has York date.' The article began, 'The Alan Bown...the group they really appreciate in York...due at The Assembly Rooms this Saturday the 1st February.'

Fabulous Magazine on the 25th January, printed a photo of Nicole with a heading, 'Alan Bown's Daughter is Top Beauty.' The accompanying article began, 'Presenting the most beautiful baby in Britain.' In the same edition, the band was mentioned in their 'Where They're At' column. 'Alan Bown, Sloopy's, Middlesborough (30).'

In the February 1969 issue of Honey, Steve Marvel's column, 'Marvel Music' included this; Sallie says: 'Alan Bown is beezer' and she's been to Emperor Rosko's flat, so I had to include their first album, 'Outward Bown'. Their sound is sometimes reminiscent of the Beatles but is usually original and always worth hearing. The first track on side one, Toyland is double beezer.'

The Yorkshire Post on the 1st February ran an article about the local pop-scene. The article was headed, 'Getting on the pop map' and featured a photo, captioned, 'The Alan Bown, who appear in York tonight.' The article included these words; 'Guaranteed to fill any club with an appreciative young audience are The Alan Bown, one of Europe's highest paid groups, should be worth the trip to The Assembly Rooms, York, tonight.' Also on this date, Fabulous Magazine featured us in their column, 'Where They're At' – 'Alan Bown: City Hall, Newcastle (6)'

'What's On' magazine on the 7th February, reported on a 'Midnight to 6am shindig at Goldsmith's College, New Cross on 14th February with

I WISH YOU WELL.

REGARDS

Peter Rutland

M.D.   Barnard Publishing
       Desire Smart
       Power Print World . Com

PLSE. Confirm Receipt

Alan

ENCL. 1) ONE OF THE FIVE
ADVANCED COPIES.

AS A THANK YOU I HAVE ARRANGED
FOR A HANDWRITTEN THANK YOU +
SIGNATURE FROM ALAN.

THIS IS NOT A COPY OR REPRODUCTION
BUT A COLLECTABLE 1 OF 5. (ENCLOSED)

The Moody Blues, Elmer Gantry, Alan Bown, Deviants and the Good Earth.'

We had an amusing routine when sharing dressing rooms with other bands. When one of our band members went out of the room we would make malicious remarks like, 'Can't stand that tosser.' 'We're getting rid of him soon but he doesn't know yet.' 'He stinks of BO.' 'He's a right misery.' The remarks would be uncomfortably received by the members of other bands. Some would unwittingly be drawn into the plot and agree with us!

The Melody Maker, on 8th February, mentioned us in an article about The Place in Hanley, Stoke on Trent; 'There are times when there are more famous faces in the audience than on stage at The Place Hanley. Among those who have unexpectedly dropped in over recent weeks are Freddie and the Dreamers, England and Stoke City Goalkeeper, Gordon Banks, Georgie Fame, Alan Bown and The Peddlers.'

The Staffordshire Advertiser on the 13th February reported; 'On March 21, the Rag Ball at the Beaconside College, Stafford will feature, The Alan Bown, Episode Six, the Carribbean Steel Band, The Old Fashioned Love Band and May Fisher.'

The Melody Maker on 15th February, gave us a mention about playing at Goldsmith's College, in their 'News Extra' column

In Fabulous Magazine on 18th February, we had a mention in the 'Where They're At' column. 'Alan Bown; Skyline Ballroom, Hull (20) Concord Club Southampton (18) Town Hall Aylesbury (22).'

The Yorkshire Evening Post on 19th February, reported on the demise of The New Marquee Club Leeds. This was supposed to be a spin off from the London Marquee Club but it failed to gain support from the young people in Leeds and had to close. The headline said it all, 'Sad End To An Experiment'. The report included; 'When Alan Bown appeared at The New Marquee only 500 turned up, but the next night at York there was a marvellous reception from a capacity audience.' (*only* 500? - Alan)

On 26th February 1969 we recorded at the BBC for The Jimmy Young Show, from 10-1pm.

The Loughborough Monitor, on the 7th March, published a half page article with a photo of the band. The article had the headline; 'Rag kicks off with the group who put the show in show business' – 'University rag week kicks off with a dance tomorrow night, when Chris Farlowe and The Alan Bown will be providing the music with Stuart Henry choosing the rag queen. The Alan Bown have been big in this country and on the Continent for some time and they have played regularly to packed houses.'

The Middlesborough Evening Gazette on the 8th March gave us a mention;
'The Alan Bown soul group returns to Redcar Jazz Club tomorrow. An earlier appearance was postponed to allow one member of the group to undergo a throat operation.' (This was the official reason we gave out for Jess losing his voice in Sweden).

Also on the 8th March, The Melody Maker reported, 'The Alan Bown record a guest spot in Mike Yarwood's ATV Show on March 14th for transmission next month.'

The Record Mirror on 14th March, reported, 'Alan Bown have signed a three year recording contract with Decca, said to be worth more than £40,000.'

On the same day, The Weston Mercury ran this headline; 'The Alan Bown in The Pavilion' – 'Entertainment at The Winter Gardens Pavilion tomorrow night features, Saturday Dance Date with The Alan Bown and supported by the Ken Birch Band and The Mike Slocombe Combo.' The Winter Gardens at Weston Super Mare had been a regular gig for me since The John Barry Seven days.

The same report appeared in The Melody Maker on 18th March.

The Melody Maker on the 29th March reported; 'An all-night dance will be held at The Lyceum Ballroom, Strand on May 2 featuring the Move, Spooky Tooth, Alan Bown, Herbie Goins and Portrait.'

Also on the 29th March, The New Musical Express published a head-shot of myself with a report on the new Decca record deal.

The Western Telegraph on the 3rd April, mentioned the new Decca record deal.

The New Musical Express on 12th April announced; 'The Jimmy Young Show, April 21-25, Tremeloes, Harmony Grass, Alan Bown, Art Movement, Jackie Trent, Sight and Sound, Cat's Eyes, Happy Magazine, Onyx, Katch 22 and Kenny Ball's Jazzmen.'

The Melody Maker on the 12th April, The Isley Brothers new single, 'Behind a Painted Smile' was reviewed by someone who thought it was us! On the same day, the 12th, we went to the Isle of Wight for a one-off gig.

Disc on the 19th April, mentioned Radio One programmes in their column, 'Tune In' 'Over at Jim's Inn, they only serve coffee and corn (!) Tremeloes, Harmony Grass, Alan Bown! And Jackie Trent (Radio One Mon-Fri 10.00-noon.)'

On the 25th April 1969, we were back at the BBC for another recording.

What's On, in their 25th April issue, mentioned another forthcoming Lyceum gig; 'All-Nighter jazz* from Alan Bown, Spooky Tooth etc (midnight to 6am) at the Lyceum Ballroom.' *(jazz? – wake up! - Alan).

In Rave Magazine's May edition, 'Dodo's Datebook' noted;
'All-night rave - May 2nd – Lyceum Ballroom, Strand - Move, Spooky Tooth, Alan Bown, Herbie Goins.'

We were still gigging across the country and the May date-sheet was as follows;

May 1969

2nd	London – Lyceum
5th	Edmonton – Cooks Ferry Inn
6th	London – Marquee
8th	London – Recording demos
9th	Newport, Lincolshire – Bishop Grosseteste Girls College
10th	Northumberland Ashington – Lamp Glass Cellar
13th	Swansea Town Hall – Swansea University
15th	Bournemouth
16th	London - Northampton Hall
17th	York – Assembly Rooms
22nd	Scarborough
23rd	Oxford – North Oxford Technical College
26th	Redcar - Coatham Hotel
27th	London – Decca Studio – recording
31st	Oxford – Lincoln College

May the 6th we headlined at The Marquee, London, supported by 'The Maddening Crowd'.

The Bournemouth Times on 9th May, reported on the May Ball at The Royal Ballrooms for The Bournemouth Municipal College. 'Next Thursday, The Equals, Alan Bown and Blossom Toes are at the College Ball.'

Top Pops on 14th May reported;
'All-star pop festival for Albert Hall. London's all-star pop festival is to be held at The Royal Albert Hall between Sunday 29th June and Saturday 5th July. Roy Guest of Nems Enterprises is to produce this festival, affectionately known as 'The Pop Proms' and each evening will feature a different musical theme and all-star pop names from the pop music world. Artists so far booked for the concerts include; Sunday 29th June, Led Zeppelin, The Liverpool Scene, Mick Abrahams, Blodwyn Pig. Monday 30th June, Fleetwood Mac, The Pentangle, Duster Bennet. Tuesday 1st July, Amen Corner, The Marmalade, Bob Kerr's Whoopie Band, The Web. Wednesday 2nd July, The Incredible String band, Fairport Convention. Friday 4th, (2 shows) Chuck Berry, Chicken Shack, The Alan Bown.'

The Melody Maker and The New Musical Express on the 17th May also covered the story on The Albert Hall, both mentioning Alan Bown.

The Wolverhampton Express on the 22nd May 1969 also reported on The Albert Hall Concert with a name check for the band.

THE DECCA RECORD COMPANY LIMITED

DECCA HOUSE · 9 ALBERT EMBANKMENT · LONDON · S·E·1
TELEPHONE: 01-735 8111 (34 LINES)   TELEGRAMS: DECCORD, LONDON, S.E.1   CABLES: DECCORD, LONDON   TELEX 28568, LONDON

RECORDED DELIVERY

GJM/KR   6th March, 1969

Mr. Mel Collins,
Active Management Limited,
Townsend House,
22/23 Dean Street,
London, W.1.

Dear Mr. Collins,

THE ALAN BOWN

I enclose herewith a recording Agreement for the services of the above named Group, in accordance with details contained in your letter of 21st February, 1969, and advice received from Mr. R. B. Rowe.

We look forward to an exchange of contracts with the parties concerned in the terms thereof in the immediate future.

I note that the matter of the existing tapes is receiving attention, Mr. Rowe having replied in this connexion, on the 23rd February, 1969.

Yours very truly,
THE DECCA RECORD COMPANY LIMITED

G. J. McGarrick
Artists Contracts Office
The Legal Department

Enc: 1318 dated 4th March, 1969 and copy.

DIRECTORS
SIR EDWARD LEWIS (CHAIRMAN)   A. C. W. HADDY   M. A. ROSENGARTEN (SWISS)   H. F. SCHWARZ (U.S.A.)   W. W. TOWNSLEY

20

DERAM - A NEW ALBUM

In Spring 1969, we signed to a new record label, Deram.

Deram was a new venture by Decca records, in a bid to update their image with the young generation. The Alan Bown! was one of the first bands to be signed so there was an exciting buzz going round the studio at West Hampstead. The studio was two minutes walk from The Railway Hotel, home of Klooks Kleek, the club run by Dick Jordan where we often appeared.

Our first recording sessions for Deram were on the 27th and 28th May 1969. The next session was a week later on the 3rd June. We completed both sides of our next single during these sessions. The A-side was entitled, 'Still as Stone', which was written by Jess and Tony. The B-side, 'Wrong Idea' was written by Jeff and myself. We came to an agreement that both sides would be credited to the four writers, hence the names on the record labels.

Our agents were still The Harold Davison Organisation and our management was still Mel Collins for Active Management. The single was produced by Mike Hurst so, in effect, all that had changed in our organisation was the record label.

Record Mirror on the 31st May mentioned our new single in their 'New Releases' column.

Also on the 31st May, The Melody Maker reported that '....Deram spending a lot of money to promote new Alan Bown single....' In the same issue, we were mentioned in an article that was headed; 'Peel for Proms'. John Peel was being courted to appear as a guest DJ at The Albert Hall.

The New Musical Express on the 31st May reported on new single releases; 'Also out on June 6th, is the Alan Bown's first for Deram, 'Still As Stone.''

Around this time Jean and I moved from Stafford Avenue in Slough to a detached house called 'Garlands', in Hammersley Lane, Tylers Green, Penn. Jean felt that there were strange vibes in this house and never felt relaxed here. One night when I returned from a gig, she told me that the kitchen light had switched itself on! After some research, we found that the house had been built on the site of an old pub so perhaps 'last orders' were still being called in some parallel dimension.

Record Retailer on the 4th June 1969 reported Mike Hurst's involvement with Decca; 'He is responsible for three of the new June releases, by Cat Stevens, Neil MacArthur and Alan Bown.' Decca executive producer, Dick Rowe and label manager, Wayne Bickerton were both mentioned. In the same issue, rather cheekily, Mike reviewed our new single 'Still As Stone' (which he neglected to say, he had produced!). He concluded his review with; 'there's a lot of talent here.'

We had a photo session on the same day, the 4th, so we were more or less ready for the official launch on the new label, which was during the same week of June.

Heralded as 'The Deram Explosion' our single was reviewed on the 7th June 1969 in Record Mirror, Disc and Music Echo, Top Pops, The Melody Maker and The Kensington Post. All the reviews were encouraging and positive that we were once again on the threshold of having a hit. We also had significant half page adverts placed in the press.

The Melody Maker, also on the 7th June, reported that; 'Among future guest artists at Durham University are Freddy King, Sam Gopal's Dream and Mike Hart (June 14) and the Hollies, Alan Bown and Edgar Broughton Band (20)

Top Pops, on the 14th June, reported on our single release, 'Still as Stone.'

Disc on the 13th June mentioned the NEMS Pop Proms at The Albert Hall; 'July 4th (5.30 and 8.30 pm): Chuck Berry, Chicken Shack, Alan Bown.'

The Melody Maker on the 14th June reported; 'Alan Bown LP - Alan Bown, who's new Deram single is 'Still as Stone' has completed a new LP for the label. The group guests in The Tony Brandon Show on June 16th and records a Stuart Henry Show on June 29th. On July 4th they play The Royal Albert Hall with Chuck Berry and Chicken Shack.'

Also on the 14th, The Gloucester Journal mentioned; 'There are many other interesting records on the market which are worth noting. They are, 'Still as Stone' – The Alan Bown (Deram) 'Baby Make it Soon - Marmalade (CBS) and 'A Salty Dog' by the Procol Harum.'

Record Retailer on the 17th June 1969 reported that Len Levy, the president of Metromedia records in America, flew into London this month to finalise a deal with Mel Collins of Active Management.' This deal signed Mike Hurst for 'special projects' and should have benefited The Alan Bown! but very little materialised.

Also on the 17th June, The Yorkshire Evening Post reported, under the heading 'Singles to watch out for: 'The Alan Bown, 'Still as Stone'. Strange attractive record, not unlike the great Zombies hit of a few years ago, 'She's Not There'. This review was also published in The Doncaster Evening Post on 21st June. Top Pops on the 20th June also covered the above story.

In The Kensington Post on 20th June Ray Hammond reviewed the single in his 'Pop Scene' column. Headed, 'Latest from Bown', it began, 'One of the finest and underrated groups in the country must be Alan Bown...'

The Hants and Berks Gazette on the 20th June also reviewed the single;
'The Alan Bown have never had a chart success but such is their popularity that they are able to play to packed halls wherever they appear. So far, little of their on-stage magic has rubbed off on their recordings but let's hope they get the success they deserve with 'Still As Stone' and 'Wrong Idea' (Deram DM 259)'.

Also on the 20th June, The East London Advertiser reviewed the single, Still As Stone; 'Often in the Top Thirty but never in the top ten is the story of the Alan Bown group. I think this will be a continuation of that story. Good enough to climb into the lower reaches of the charts.'

The Herald Express, Torquay, on the 20th June published a photo of the band and a report boldly headlined, 'Cover up topless dancers, orders Town Clerk' We had been booked to play at Torquay Town Hall on the 28th June and the promoter, in his wisdom, had arranged for topless dancers called 'The Birds of Paradise' to appear. We did fulfil the engagement but only one Bird of Paradise showed up, with strict instructions not to dance topless. All the posters promoting the show in Torquay had the word 'topless' crossed out!

The Melody Maker, on 21st June, published an article on the Pop Proms at The Albert Hall, beginning 29th June. We were mentioned amongst the roll call.

The Melody Maker on 20th June published a 'Complete Programme' of the Pop Proms at The Royal Albert Hall, including; 'Friday July 4th (8.30pm) Chuck Berry, Chicken Shack, Misunderstood, The Alan Bown!'

What's On magazine, on 27th June, also covered the Pop Proms concert in full.

The Weston Mercury on 27th June published an article on The Winter Gardens which concluded; '...next Saturday there is a return of The Alan Bown, a group successful and popular in a previous appearance as the stars of Dance Date.'

I was interviewed in The Watford Evening Echo, on the 28th June, by Patrick Stoddart in his 'Showplace' column. The half page article was headlined 'No shark will grab my loot, says Alan'. It chronicled my career and included a portrait photo of me.

A half page article appeared in Top Pops on 28th June. Karen de Groot interviewed Jeff and the piece included a photo of the band.

On the 29th June 1969 at 2.30pm, we were back at the BBC to record tracks for Radio One Club hosted by Stuart Henry. We recorded 'Movie Star Baby' and 'Gypsy Girl' and returned to the BBC on the following day at 7.30pm for mixing and overdubs.

We had also been recording tracks in the Decca studios to complete our next album, simply entitled, 'The Alan Bown!' (See discography-albums).

Soon after all the vocals had been added and we were into the mixing, Jess came to me with a bombshell. He told me that he had decided to leave the band! I tried to persuade him to stay but to no avail. We all felt he was part of the band's identity and he had always been a great front-man. The Alan Bown! had developed over the years into the perfect vehicle for Jess's style of performance and I was really sorry to see him go. In fact none us wanted him to leave. I took the news with a mixture of sadness and frustration. I thought the album had pulled us more together than ever before but in the back of my mind I now felt that the showdown in Sweden may have influenced his decision. Also, the lack of success of the single 'Still as Stone', which Jess co - wrote, probably made him feel that the band was slipping from popularity. He seemed genuinely disillusioned but agreed to stay on until we found a replacement. However, why he didn't tell me this before the vocals were completed, I don't know but it meant that we had our second album scheduled for release at the end of August with no lead singer to promote it! I had to tell Mel Collins our manager and he arranged with Deram to put the release date of the album on hold.

The plan now was to try to find a replacement in time to re-record the vocals. It was a tough assignment but someone had stuck in my mind that we had seen on the circuit, not too long ago, playing in a band called The Mandrakes. He was a flamboyant young singer and the next weekend I went up to Scarborough to locate him.

It was like something out of the movie, 'Get Carter'! I went to several music venues and put the word out that I was looking for Alan Palmer. The following day, I heard that he was playing at a club gig in Scarborough and went along to see him to offer him the position with the band. Alan took little persuading to join The Alan Bown! He'd already seen the band performing and this was undoubtedly a big break for him. The week after our meeting, Alan Palmer (real name Allen Robert Palmer), came down to stay at my mother's house in Slough. John Anthony was already living there so it wasn't too strange for Alan to fit in. He was an easy going guy and came from a very good family. After some consideration, Alan Palmer decided to use his middle name to avoid confusion with my name. So the stage was set for our new singer, Robert Palmer.

We rehearsed with Robert at our usual hall in Hanwell Community Centre.

The sequel to this period in time was that, on one of Robert's train journeys to Slough, he met a girl called Sue, whom he eventually married!

The Bournemouth Evening Echo on the 3rd July, reported on bands soon appearing at the Bournemouth Pavilion; 'Friday, September the 5th brings The Searchers to the Pavilion and the series closes on the 12th with Alan Bown.'

On the 4th July 1969 we played at The Albert Hall once more. The headlining artist was the legendary Chuck Berry. At the time, we were still finishing our act with a rock'n'roll medley and some of us took turns to sing parts of a song. Jeff used to come out from behind the Hammond organ and sing the Elvis Presley classic, 'Heartbreak Hotel', followed by Jess singing 'Tutti Frutti' or something similar. This routine used to go down really well in the clubs but, as we had experienced before, some purists took exception to it. Tony recalled that just as Jeff had ended his song and turned around to regain his place at the keyboard, a 'lump of metal' fell on the stage where Jeff had been standing. Luckily, Jeff was oblivious to this. However the band was not unaware of a large number of hostile faces in the audience, not to mention the yelling and angry gestures. It was a shame because we were paying tribute to the era, which was always intended to entertain people and not provoke them.

The Weston Mercury on the 4th July reported, 'The Alan Bown Return to the Pavilion.' The report is reproduced here;
'After their last appearance at Weston-Super-Mare, in March, the demand

was great for a return visit of The Alan Bown, one of the most popular groups on the 'pop' scene. They will be back tomorrow night to fill the star spot for Dance Date at the Winter Gardens Pavilion. Also appearing will be The Ken Birch band and The Mike Slocombe Combo.'

The Morning Star on the 7th July, reported on The Pop Proms at The Albert Hall. The three column article gave us a mention.

The Record Mirror on the 8th July, in their 'Face' column mentioned; 'Mel Collins who represents Alan Bown, Mike Hurst, Neil McArthur etc to launch nationwide tape cartridge distribution set-up in the summer.'

Disc on 8th July, published a letter from an American reader in New York, which began; 'Reading the charts in Disc, I can only feel sorry for the waste of British talent and pop buyers neglect. Your charts are getting as bad as ours with all these soul-type and Motown dribble.' (dribble? Don't you mean drivel? - Alan). 'Why don't you support more rock groups? You made Moody Blues, Led Zeppelin and Jethro Tull big sellers, now how about Ten Years After, Deep Purple, Cartoone and The Alan Bown?'

The Gloucester Globe on 10th July, reported on The Albert Hall Pop Proms;
'Like apparitions from another era, the rockers appeared at The Chuck Berry Pop Prom concerts at The Royal Albert Hall. Aged around the 30 mark, probably married and family men, they brought out carefully preserved drape suits, string ties and thick crepe soles for a nostalgic reunion with their hero. Unfortunately, the rockers have not matured mentally over the years. Anybody else on the bill preceding Chuck Berry was dismissed as 'so-and-so rubbish'. Those who particularly felt their scorn were The Alan Bown band and Chicken Shack, who's lead guitarist, Stan Webb, managed to momentarily silence his Teddy-suited critics with one withering retort. 'Yeah well' he told one of the unconverted in the second row, 'I happen to think I can play guitar better'n you can ride a BSA.'

Valentine Magazine on 12th July 1969 published a photo of the band and devoted a half page to answering questions about various bands and singers. Hazel Ward from Sutton asked;
'Can you please tell me where the members of the group The Alan Bown were born? Also when was their single disc, Still as Stone released?'
Answer; 'Alan Bown (trumpet) was born in Slough. John Anthony (tenor sax and recorder) was born in Todmorden. Bass player Stan Haldane started life in Edmonton. Jeff Bannister was born in London. Drummer Vic Sweeney's birthplace is Chelsea and lead guitarist Tony Catchpole was born in Klagenfurt, Austria. Still as Stone was released on the 6th June.'

The New Musical Express on the 12th July reported 'New Radio 1 Names.' We were among the host of bands mentioned; 'Desmond Dekker and The Aces are joined by The Alan Bown in 'Symonds on Sunday' this weekend (13).'

The Disc on 12th July in their 'Tune In' column reported, 'Three cheers for the return of David to ' Symonds on Sunday' thereby ending all malicious rumours. Introducing Desmond Dekker and The Alan Bown (Radio 1, 10.00-noon).'
In the same issue of Disc, an article by Gavin Petrie about the Albert Hall Proms was headed, 'Rockers crash the Pop Proms'. This began;
'Friday's Prom was ruined somewhat by members of the audience who believe that pop music ceased to exist at the end of the first rock 'n' roll era that encompassed Chuck Berry, Eddie Cochran and Bill Haley. Consequently, these Teds, Rockers, or what have you, refused to give an ear to the other groups on the bill topped by Chuck Berry by yelling his name and generally causing a disturbance. Groups, who undoubtedly dug Chuck Berry, but had moved on musically. First to come under fire were The Alan Bown, who struggled bravely through a short set. They seem to be moving towards an individual sound that could be a breakthrough for them. Their last number, 'The Prisoner' a sort of story in words and sound, gave the feeling of a Moody Blues of the future.'

The Melody Maker on 12th July a report headlined, 'Bown Visit US' said; 'The Alan Bown is set for their first visit to America. They will make a ten-week coast-to-coast tour starting in the first week of October. Their current Deram single, 'Still as Stone' is released in the States this week. They have a new album, 'The Prisoner,' released in both Britain and America at the end of this month.'

This USA visit never happened and was a tragic missed opportunity. I think a tour was being planned but it never materialised because of economics. Having seven musicians in the band and a two man roadcrew meant that our management, Active Management, would have been overstretched financially. It was high risk and Mel Collins, our manager, was not prepared to take it.

The Scarborough Mercury on the 13th July ran the headline, 'Scarborough pop vocalist to join top British group.' A photo of Allen (Robert) Palmer was also included.

The Scarborough Evening News on the 14th July 1969 ran the headline; 'Scarborough Singer Joins Leading British Pop Group'.
The article reproduced below, was accompanied by a headshot photo captioned, 'Allen Palmer'.
'20-year-old Allen Palmer, has landed a job with an internationally famous

British pop group, The Alan Bown. Getting the job as lead singer constitutes the biggest achievement ever for a pop musician from Scarborough. Mr Palmer has been the lead singer with the local group The Mandrakes for the last six years and always said, 'I'm not interested in going professional.' The job with The Alan Bown, formerly the Alan Bown Set, became open when lead singer Jess Roden decided to pull out and start his own group. Competition for the job was fierce. To take the job Mr Palmer will give up his apprenticeship as a process engraver with The Evening News. For The Mandrakes the news comes as a bit of a blow but despite the fact that they are losing their vocalist, the group aims to carry on and plans for a girl vocalist to take Mr Palmer's place are being considered. The Mandrakes had perhaps their most successful moments last month when they made a 16-day tour of Denmark and were widely acclaimed. One of the highlights of the near future for Mr Palmer and The Alan Bown will be a 10-week tour of the US, starting in September. Some of the past hits of The Alan Bown were 'Toyland' and 'Headline News'. In their early days they were described as a soul group but later as a folk-blues group. Mr Palmer is a former pupil of the Scarborough High School for Boys. He expects to take his place with the group in the near future. From then on he is to be known as Robert Palmer because there is already an Alan in the group.'

NB. It's interesting to note that Robert gave up an 'apprenticeship as a process engraver' to join The Alan Bown. This was a major step for him and it could be argued that, without this move, Robert Palmer may never have become a professional singer.

The Lincolnshire Echo on 14th July reported on the Pop Proms at The Royal Albert Hall. The article was a reprint of the Gloucester Globe's on the 10th (already included).

On the 15th July 1969, Jess Roden sang for the last time with The Alan Bown! The gig was at The Showboat Club in Middlesborough.

Jess went on to form his own band with some old friends of his from Kidderminster. It was a country rock style band, called 'Bronco'. (Jess invited Jeff Bannister to play piano on a couple of tracks of the Bronco album, which he did).

For The Alan Bown! it was the end of an era and the beginning of a new one.

The South Devon Journal on 16th July ran the headline, 'Pop Mania at The Town Hall.' The article began; 'Total mania is to be the aim of the organisers of Torquay Town Hall's summer dance spectaculars which sport top groups until the end of August. On Saturday's the names include Alan Bown, The Bedrocks, Troggs, The Herd, The Casuals,

The Who, Marsha Hunt and the Moody Blues.'

The Melody Maker on the 19th July devoted almost a full page to their 'Caught in the Act' feature, headlined; 'Pop Proms-from teenyboppers to the Teds'. The article covered the whole event at The Alber Hall, including this report on the night we appeared;
'There was idiocy afoot at The Chicken Shack-Chuck Berry night of the Pop Proms on Friday, writes Chris Welch. As occurred the following night when Chuck was billed with The Who, The Teddy Boys were out in force, following their traditional pursuits of throwing pennies and shouting abuse at all acts other than Mr Berry. Alan Bown, Chicken Shack and The Misunderstood all received 'the treatment' and if they had played like gods there would still have been howls and the quaint practice of holding the nose while miming the act of pulling a lavatory chain, one of the Ted's favourite japes. Chuck Berry played an embarrassing corny and tasteless comedy number called 'Ting-a-Ling', which sounded more suitable for eight year olds and went into his usual medley of hits. He is a fine singer, guitarist and writer. It's a pity he has to play down to a dim witted audience, instead of forming a good group and getting back into music.'

Also on the 19th July, The New Musical Express reported;
'Alan Bown group set for its debut US tour, commencing first week of October and lasting 10 weeks.'

The Scarborough Mercury on the 24th July reported;
'The Mandrakes played their last gig with vocalist Allen Palmer at the Penthouse Club Scarborough, last night. Allen leaves Scarborough tonight for London and his top pop job with The Alan Bown. For his first week in London he will stay with Alan Bown and learn the numbers performed by the group. The Alan Bown have made many TV appearances and could be only a matter of time before local teenagers turn on the television to see former Mandrake Allen at the microphone. 'We have a radio date on 6th August,' said Allen 'and we hope to make a single before we go over to the States.' Allen has had a lot of reaction to his leaving the Mandrakes from his fans. In Cottingham near Hull last week a group of girls made a mock kidnap attempt. 'I have had lots of letters wishing me good luck,' he said. The Mandrakes are to carry on locally with a girl vocalist called 'Angie' from Hull.'

The Melody Maker, on the 26th July, reprinted their 12th July report on our American 'visit' but headlined it; 'Bown's US Debut.'

In the same issue of The Melody Maker; with the headline 'Roden May Quit', it was reported; 'Singer Jess Roden, who has been with The Alan Bown for four years may quit the group soon, said Alan Bown. Jess wants to do something different on his own. We are still very good friends and it's up to Jess to decide. Jess's replacement in the group is expected to be Alan Palmer, a 20 year old singer from Scarborough who has worked with The Mandrakes group. Roden's plans are not yet decided.'

The Eastern Evening News on the 28th July 1969, reported; 'Howard Platt is lining up some big names for the Gala in the Autumn. Thunderclap Newman brings his band along on September 13th followed by Alan Bown on the 20th and Family on the 27th. Names like Marmalade, Move and Pyramids are planned for later dates.'

The Alan Bown! in rehearsal with Robert Palmer 1969
Left to right:
Alan Bown, Vic Sweeney, Tony Catchpole, Robert Palmer,
John Anthony Helliwell, Stan Haldane and Jeff Bannister

21

EXIT JESS RODEN - ENTER ROBERT PALMER

THE ALAN BOWN !

MANAGEMENT:
ACTIVE MANAGEMENT LTD.,
FLAT 3, TOWNSEND HOUSE,
22,DEAN STREET,
LONDON, W.1.
01- 437 7220

AGENCY:
HAROLD DAVISON ORGANISATION
REGENT HOUSE,
235/241 REGENT STREET,
LONDON, W.1.
01- 734 7961

Robert Palmer's first gig with the band was at The Dunstable Civic Hall on the 2nd August 1969. The gig went well and the loyal fans took to Robert rather cautiously at first, although the girls were soon impressed. Robert had obvious charisma but his voice fell short of the power that Jess Roden had, so there was a plus and minus to the new lead singer regime. However, there was no doubt in my mind that Robert was the man for the job and he got on very well with us all.

I recall an amusing incident when Robert joined the Musician's Union. Arthur Eagle was still at the helm of The North London Branch and had an over-familiar way of abbreviating member's names. So if you were

Charles, you would be referred to as Chas and so on. Imagine Robert's face when he received his card back from the MU with the name on the envelope 'Bob Palmer'! We all had a good laugh about that and Robert was suitably insulted at the suggestion that he was a mere 'Bob'.

In the August edition of Beat Instrumental 1969 we had another full page article, entitled, 'Stronger and Stronger, The Alan Bown!' Unfortunately, it was a pre-Robert article and the photograph featured Jess. However, there was a positive vibe expressed about the new album. In the same issue, we were again reported to be embarking on an American tour in October.

The Dorset Evening Echo on the 8th August reported on DJ Ed Stewart's recent visit to Weymouth with The Radio One Club. 'Tapes of a live session by Tuesday's Children and The Alan Bown were played on the show.'

Top Pops on the 9th August reported, 'New vocalist' – 'Jess Roden, vocalist with The Alan Bown has been replaced by 21 year old Robert Palmer who was previously with The Mandrake Paddlesteamer. Palmer has so far worked two dates with Alan Bown and Alan stated, 'Robert really gives the group a new image'. The Alan Bown fly to the States in the first week of October for the start of their 10 week tour.'

Also on 9th August, The Melody Maker reported;
'New Bown Singer' – 'Robert Palmer, previously with a Middlesborough group, Mandrake Paddlesteamer, is the new lead singer with The Alan Bown. He takes over from Jess Roden who has been forced to take a rest on doctor's orders. The Alan Bown! make their first American tour in October.'

This illustrates how some oddities show up in the press now and again. Robert was in a band called the Mandrakes but the 'Paddlesteamer' part was a mystery to him. Also Jess wasn't forced to quit on doctor's orders. As far as I know he had no health problems at the time and he left for reasons already stated.

On the 10th August 1969, during our first run of gigs with Robert, we played in The Redcar Jazz Club at The Coatham Hotel. The band had already played here on numerous occasions and we had a big following so I was a little apprehensive about how they would receive Jess's replacement. We opened our set with an instrumental and Robert stood on the side of the stage waiting for its conclusion. There were no wings so he was aware that the audience could see him and he was self-consciously smoking a cigarette. When the opening number finished he flicked the cigarette to the ground and virtually flounced towards the mic. The expressions on the faces of the front row of the crowd were in suspended animation, each person on the threshold of making a judgement. To Robert's credit, he won them over and stamped his authority on the whole event.

The Wolverhampton Star on the 14th August, reported; 'Top names booked for Club Lafayette, Wolverhampton include Wayne Fontana (August 22) Jason Cord (August 26) Fat Mattress (September 11) and Alan Bown (September 26).'

The Stage, on the 14th August, reported on summer events in Torquay; 'At the Town Hall are presented concerts by name groups such as Alan Bown, Bedrocks, Troggs, Who, Herd, Casuals, MoodyBlues...'

Record Retailer on the 16th August in a short item headed, 'Palmer to Bown' reported; 'Jess Roden has left The Alan Bown group and has been replaced by 21-year old Robert Palmer. The group is set for its visit to the States on October 1 for a ten week tour.'

Also on 16th August the new Musical Express, in their 'Popliners' column reported; 'Robert Palmer, formerly with Mandrake Paddlesteamer is now lead singer with the Alan Bown.'

Robert Palmer would often sing along to the radio during our car journeys to gigs. He would mimic vocal lines with perfect synchronisation, saying that listening to the phrasing of other singers helped his development as a vocalist. I wasn't so sure about this concept and felt he should develop his own style. He did a very convincing sing-a-long rendition of 'All Right Now' by Free, which was very popular at the time.

For the remainder of August and all of September, we were back on the road but the itinerary, with only two or three gigs a week, wasn't as demanding as the same period during the previous year. It gave us all a chance to get to know Robert and vice-versa. Even then, I thought he had star quality. All we needed now was that elusive hit.

The new Musical Express on the 23rd August headlined a report; 'Latest Radio 1 Star Bookings. Live Interviews from the I.O.W Festival' – 'Latest bookings for Radio 1 Shows include; Sounds Like Tony Brandon; Vanity fare, Equals, Jimmy Ruffin, Jimmy James and The Vagabonds, Jimmy Powell and the Dimensions, Sons and Lovers, Settlers and the Johnny Howard Band (all next week); Status Quo, Symbols, The Alan Bown, Timebox, Californians...'

The September 1969 issue of Beat Instrumental headlined a report; 'Alan Bown Replacement' – 'Robert Palmer, formerly with Mandrake

Paddlesteamer, has replaced Jess Roden as lead singer with The Alan Bown. Rob is already working with the group who fly to the USA the first week in October to promote their new single 'Still as Stone'. This report was a double cringe for Robert, still being haunted by the Paddlesteamer and then being called Rob!

Fabulous Magazine on the 12th September in their 'Where They're At' column, subtitled, 'Here's where the big names are' reported; 'Alan Bown, Gala Ballroom Norwich (20).'

We had a BBC session on the 24th September 1969 for The Dave Cash Radio Programme. We recorded, 'Friends in St. Louis' and 'Got a Line on You'.

We went into the Decca Studio on the 14th October, to replace Jess's vocals on the album. Robert had knocked all the songs into shape on the road and he handled the recording really well. My instinct had paid off and I had no reservations about him. We were all very pleased with the result.

On the 31st October 1969, our new single 'Gypsy Girl' was released on Deram with Robert Palmer on lead vocals. Jeff and I had written the song and it was a much brighter track than 'Still as Stone', the previous single. John added a catchy recorder intro, which set the mood. The B-side 'All I Can', was written by Tony Catchpole. We had a variety of ads in the music press, which featured an attractive model, posing in Romany costume (see page 168).

Top Pops and Music Now, on the 1st November, published a review of 'Gypsy Girl' by Karen de Groot, headed, 'A Chance for Alan Bown!' It is reproduced here;
'This is terrific. Written by Alan Bown and Jeff Bannister and incorporating what is rapidly turning out to be my favourite instrument – the school recorder. 'Still as Stone' was perhaps a little too advanced for general release but whereas this doesn't compromise the group in any way, it's far more simple and commercial. Vocally excellent and nicely broken up with aforementioned instrument. I'm certain that barring fire, floods and fickle public tastes this will take the strangely mal-fortuned Alan Bown & Co to the top. At least I sincerely hope so.'

Penny Valentine also reviewed 'Gypsy Girl' on November 1st, for The Disc and Music Echo. She liked it and she was a huge influence to readers at the time. Her review, headed, 'Alan Bown', said; 'This group has been making records for a long time and always rather missed the boat. Certainly none have come anywhere near the commercial appeal of this. Absolutely instant hit with little piping flutes and drums, tight verse, good commercial chorus, nice tune. What more do you need? Nothing.'

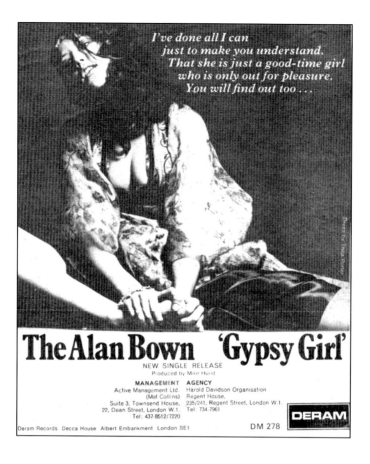

The South Wales Argus on the 20th November 1969 took exception to our advert for our new single, 'Gypsy Girl'. The photo from the advert was reproduced and captioned 'Cherry in the Picture – and out'.

The article is reproduced here;

'This is how model Cherry Brownhill looked in a poster to advertise a new record called Gypsy Girl by Alan Bown. But Bown's recording company, Decca banned the poster and described it as rubbish. This did not exactly make Cherry happy because it was her first modelling job. 'I can't see what they're complaining about.' she said. But Decca make it quite plain what they are complaining about. Their promotions manager, Chris Denning said, 'We don't need sex to sell records. We think the record is good enough to be successful on its own merits without using this sort of advertising.' The poster was designed by Alan Bown's manager, Mel Collins who once managed the late Donald Campbell. 'I can't see how anyone can describe the girl in this picture as looking sexy. In fact, we spent days searching for a girl who had not done any modelling before for the very reason that we didn't want a picture that depicted a sort of professional sex.' But the decision is made, Cherry must go.'

(This illustrates just how much things have changed - Alan).
There is a footnote to this story. We heard that the photographer was so smitten with Cherry that he married her!

The Basingstoke Gazette on the 21st November, reviewed the single; 'The Alan Bown are one of our best groups though we don't often see them in the charts. Provided their latest single Gypsy Girl gets enough airings it should do well for them. It was penned by group members Alan Bown and Jeff Bannister.'

On November 27th 1969 we had a meeting with Mel Collins at Active Management. It was a morale-boosting meeting with a positive outlook on the future. In general, the gigs had thinned out compared to last year and it was important to know that the management were still 100% behind us. The next day we had another recording session for the BBC.

Top Pops and Music Now, on November 29th, published an interview I had with Karen de Groot. The half page article was headed, 'Cream Cake Looks or Not, It's the Music that Counts'. Karen wrote an intelligent profile of the band's recent progress, giving us a plug for 'Gypsy Girl' and the new album. The article also featured the photo from the back of the new album, which included Robert Palmer.

A quarter page advert for 'Gypsy Girl' was published in the December issue of The Music Business News.

December the 19th 1969 found us back at The Marquee, this time supported by 'Audience'. It was Robert's first appearance at the club and he was well received by the London followers of the band.

Also on the 19th, The York Evening Press headlined a report; 'Sensational Welcome for Santa' – 'Santa Clause will get a sensational welcome in York, on Christmas Eve from… The Alan Bown. Just back from their US tour, The Alan Bown launch a rave-up Yule at Joint Promotion session in York Assembly Rooms.'

Robert Palmer had got into the London scene now and knew a girl who ran a boutique in the King's Road. He had obtained a pattern and paper templates for suede trousers, which were made in sections, glued, then laced together with a leather thong down each side. On long journeys, he would sit in the car and spend quite sometime making these trousers. The result was very appealing to the King's Road clientele and a small source of extra income for Robert. However, he only made about ten pairs before finding it too much of a chore.

On the 26th December 1969 we played at The Place, Hanley once again. It was packed with Boxing Day revellers. The year came to a close rather quietly and our first gig in the New Year was at Dreamland in Margate.

On the 11th of January 1970 at 2.30pm, we recorded more tracks at the BBC for The Dave Cash Radio Programme. These were 'Loosen Up' and 'Strange Little Friend'. We returned to the BBC on the 13th at 7.30pm for mixing and overdubs. The show was broadcast on the 30th January.

The 19th of January 1970 was Robert's 21st. We had the day off and didn't see him until the following day for a band rehearsal.

We recorded demos of new songs at Decca Studio on the 21st of January from 3pm – midnight.

On the 28th January, we played in Robert's hometown, Scarborough. His parents ran a hotel there and the band stayed the night. His mother and father were very pleasant people, obviously very proud of their son.

The Bromley & Kentish Times on the 6th February ran this report, with the headline;
'Band That Deserves Success' - 'Judging by their performance at The Mistrale Club, Beckenham last Friday, The Alan Bown band deserve more success than they have enjoyed in the four years that they have been together as a progressive group. The seven piece band whose new LP is due to be released next week gave a slick powerful performance. All their numbers, with the exception of Steve Miller's 'My Friend' were original many having appeared on their two previous albums. A number, which has not been recorded entitled, 'Make Up your Mind', gave members of the group the opportunity to demonstrate their individual skill. Impressive solos came from sax player John Anthony, organist Jeff Bannister and Alan Bown on trumpet. Lead guitarist Tony Catchpole took over the band's penultimate number 'Crash Landing.' Vocals throughout were provided by Robert Palmer.'

Disc, on 21st February, gave the album a three star review;
'The Alan Bown, an underrated sevensome, very pop-based with a heavy/jazzy feel. Their brass contribution to the sound is a bit uninspired and their tracks a bit short, just when they're getting into something good – the songs finish. Their songs, however, are melodic and they get a good sound on a record that has long pauses between tracks and abrupt endings.'

February the 22nd saw us back at the Lafayette Club in Wolverhampton. There was no sign of Robert Plant now. Far too busy with Led Zeppelin!

The News, Portsmouth on 5th March 1970, reviewed the album with this headline;
'Good Work from The Alan Bown' – 'The Alan Bown! Once highly thought of in Portsmouth and this could be a step towards re-affirming their talent. Straight unpretentious pop ranging from the mildly heavy to well constructed ballads like, 'Perfect Day'. Good, although it tends to be a little too workmanlike in parts.'

On the same day, The Ilford Recorder featured us in their 'Disc of the Week' column. The article is reproduced here;
'An LP this week and what an LP. It's one of the best I've heard in a long time. Alan Bown are seven in number and produce a sound that is completely their own – the singing is tremendous on all of the ten tracks. Coupled with the beautiful backing sound they have themselves an LP hit. Alan Bown should be a name we will be hearing a lot of lately – their music is both commercial and nice to listen to while being vaguely progressive. Fave track was Gypsy Girl – the last one on the LP – though if you buy this gem of a record I'm sure you will like the lot. And congrats to Decca and their subsidiaries – they are giving us some great records now.'

The Melody Maker on 7th March gave us a mini album review;
'A band who seem to have missed the boat in acceptance but always produce worthwhile albums. Robert Palmer is a good replacement for Jess Roden as lead vocalist and they obtain a hot brass sound.'
In the same issue of the MM, an article headed; 'New Look Radio 1 Star Line-Up' included this mention; 'Line-up for the first two weeks of Radio 1's new daily show 'Sounds of the 70's' to be broadcast in the 6-7pm spot, has been announced. '…and Blodwyn Pig and Alan Bown (14).'

The Bournemouth Evening Echo on the 9th March reviewed the album;
'Haven't heard The Alan Bown in better form than on their new album which simply carries the group's name. All the numbers have been thoughtfully put together and the best are: Strange Little Friend, Elope, Friends in St Louis, The Prisoner and Children of the Night.'

The North Wales Chronicle on the 12th March gave us this review;
'Album: The Alan Bown – Remember their Gypsy Girl single? Well that is included on this their first album. The Alan Bown produce a rather attractive big band noise, which is certain to pep up a party and make the neighbours complain. Although I don't see this as a sell out album, it wouldn't surprise me if the band did pretty well with it.'

Also on the 12th March, The Cumberland Evening News & Star, remarked on the album; 'Apart from their latest single, Gypsy Girl there are no outstanding tracks on the new LP by The Alan Bown! which is named after the group. However, there is a consistently attractive style throughout the record.'

The New Musical Express on 14th March 1970 in their 'One-Nighters' column mentioned, 'Booked for Hanley Place are O'Hara's Playboys (tomorrow, Saturday) Alan Bown (Sunday).'

Also on 14th March, The Southern Evening Echo reported on Jess's new band Bronco. Jess had this to say to the journalist;
'I left Bown because it was not giving me the outlet I wanted. I was not doing anything with him. I was earning good money with Bown but that's not everything. So I gave it all up to start all over again. The group is still a bit stiff but that is only understandable seeing how we have only been together a very short time. In the end though, I think we shall definitely have something new to offer.'

I felt that Jess's statement, 'I left Bown because it was not giving me the outlet I wanted' was unfair and misleading. I always welcomed Jess's song writing contribution. In fact he had writing credits for several of The Alan Bown! singles and many of his songs were included on the albums. I can't honestly recall vetoing any of his work. We all had faith in his self-penned single, 'Still as Stone' but unfortunately, the record-buying public didn't appear to share it.

In the Melody Maker, 21stMarch 1970, Chris Welch gave us this review of a recent gig;
'An exciting new band roared into action at Edmonton's Cook's Ferry Inn last week – The Alan Bown. The music fought back against the wall of apathy that can build up against a band when they have been around for a long time and by the end of the evening the audience were convinced and responded with cheers that seemed to surprise themselves. For the band have a strong line-up with a variety of instrumentation they have used for years and now considered the prerogative of 'Chicago' jazz rock type groups. Yet they are not playing jazz. John Anthony blows some powerful and free tenor and alto solos and Alan uses trumpet and flugel horn to good effect. But the overall effect is of good contemporary music that holds no allegiance to any particular category. Robert Palmer is an outstanding new singer. He has been with the band only a few months but is obviously instrumental in changing their image and approach.'
In the same issue of the MM, Brian Auger in 'Blind Date' reviewed 'My Friend' and 'Strange Little Friend' from our new album. He concluded, 'I'm glad I listened to this. Nice.'

The Record Mirror on 21st March reviewed the album, 'The Alan Bown';

'When I was a young lad down in the depth's of Plymouth in Devon, our three monthly treat was the visit of one Alan Bown Set to yon local discotheque. In those days it was 'Extraaa! Extraaa! Read All About it!' Then they made a radical change to more progressive scenes culminating in their latest album. A very pleasant and inventive group, they have the talent and the writing power to break through.'

The Eastern Evening News on the 23rd March also reviewed the album; 'The Alan Bown';
'A fair old powerhouse of a sound that just about sums up Alan Bown and his men on this album. Driving beat on most numbers many of which are given their first airing. On the quiet side 'Perfect Day' is well done by the band while outstanding among the brighter numbers is 'Gypsy Girl'. A fair old try at a variety of material, almost all self-panned, on this disc and most of it comes off, though 'The Prisoner' track which takes up most of side two may be a little over elaborate. Still, as a whole, this is a pretty good showcase for the talents of one of the best larger combos around.'

The Birmingham Evening Mail on the 25th March reviewed the album;
'The Alan Bown – A more progressive sounding Alan Bown group who have switched from the soul department. Good brass work here as always in an acceptable package that includes their last single, Gypsy Girl.'

On the 28th March 1970, my son Julian was born in Amersham Hospital. I was there for the birth. He was my second child and my only son.

Also on 28th March, The Record Mirror published a photo of the band and a review of the album, 'The Alan Bown!' The photo, captioned, 'Alan Bown! Progressive', featured Robert Palmer and the review is reproduced here;
'Another debut LP really isn't a debut. The Alan Bown have been shifting from zone to zone for quite a while, but this LP marks a new route and the appearance of a new member. Robert Palmer now sings lead with meaty zest. A Yorkshireman, Palmer's throaty vocals add much to the brassy sound that has carried Alan this far. The general vein of their music is drifting further from straight, elementary pop and closer to free jazz, marinated with pop progressions. Alan still plays a good trumpet and John Helliwell a fine sax – the whole seven man team approaches orchestral proportions on stage. The Deram LP, The Alan Bown!' should have no trouble, thanks to radio plays, but it's about time some people got off their rear ends to see some bands around here, instead of spouting the usual, 'Oh them...'

On 2nd April, The Radio Times listings included; 'Thursday, Sounds of the 70's (6.0 Radio 1) Timebox – The Alan Bown.'

Also on the 2nd April, The Western Daily Express reviewed the album. The review is reproduced here;
'This band, always a favourite of mine have long been under-rated. There is a heavy, jazzy feeling to their work, which owes a lot to the excellent brass sound that Alan Bown and John Anthony achieve. 'Gipsy Girl' is included and is a good example of their talents.'

The Evening Herald, Dublin on the 8th April 1970 reported;
'Some groups are purely unlucky when it comes (to) getting the breaks and one such case is The Alan Bown! A good live group, they have a fairly distinctive sound, created mainly by leader Alan Bown's trumpet and John Anthony's saxes. Since I last saw them they have had a change of singer, Jess Roden being replaced by Robert Palmer. On The Alan Bown! (Deram) they hit a happy medium between straight pop and heavy progressive. They make very good listening with numbers like Elope, All I Can Do, Kick me Out and Strange Little Friend.'

Disc on the 11th April, in their Tune-In column reported;
'Andy Ferris introduces Clouds and Matthew Southern Comfort in Monday edition of Sounds Of the 70's (Radio 1, 6pm Monday to Friday) Other guests for week: Blodwyn Pig and Alan Bown (Tuesday): Taste and Atomic Rooster (Wednesday): Magna Carta and Slade (Thursday: Sweet Water Canal and Patto (Friday).'

Numerous gigs throughout the following months, took us up to our next recording session at Decca Studios on April the 17th. This was a demo session for songs on the next album but things were getting twitchy with Deram. Their great expectations of taking us into the charts had not materialised. Two singles and an album had failed to impress and the clock was ticking. I had a meeting with Mel Collins and he told me that Chris Blackwell of Island Records was interested in the band! He had seen us play at a London University gig and was very impressed. It was time to move on.

The New Musical Express on 18th April 1970 also reported; 'Radio 1 Latest' and included this mention; 'The Who, Jonathan King and Cats Eyes guest in the Dave Lee Travis Show this Sunday (19) Juicy Lucy and The Alan Bown guest in the Roger Kirk Show, on Saturday; April 25th.'

The Bournemouth Evening Echo on the 7th May reported on 'The Room', a local group. The report mentioned us; 'The Room will be appearing in a two day festival with such famous groups as the Move, the Alan Bown Set*, The Love Affair and East of Eden. In all 30 groups are appearing in the 10,000 seater hall in Lille, playing from 4pm to midnight on Saturday and Sunday. The groups come from all over the Continent.'
*We had dropped the 'Set' as long ago as mid-1967. Three years previously!

We went to France on the 9th May and played in Lille.

Royston Eldridge in The Melody Maker on the 16th May in his 'College Column' reported; ' Isleworth's Borough Road College has Johnny Silvo to-morrow (Friday) and a dance with Alan Bown Set.'

The News, Portsmouth on the 21st May headlined this article; 'Alan Bown back to aid charity' The article began; 'The Alan Bown once commanded loyal support from Portsmouth fans and will be back tonight with an appearance for the Southern Emergency Area Charity Fund at Kimbells, Southsea. Supporting will be the Shocking Dirty Gerty band – well known local outfit disguised in masks.'
(With a name like that, no wonder they wore masks! - Alan).

The West Bromwich Midland Chronicle on the 22nd May in Richard Brookes, 'Variety Round Up' column reported on a proposed festival to be held in the Gornal and Segdley area. 'Booked to appear are local groups, Ket's Rebellion, Galliard and Jack Rat, together with Alan Bown, Clouds, Writing on the Wall, Hard Meat, Principal Edwards Magic Theatre and star attraction, Liverpool Scene.'

The New Musical Express on the 6th June in their 'Sounds Like Radio 1' column, mentioned; 'Andre Pinney Show: Greatest Show on Earth and Almond Marzipan (Saturday June 13th): Alan Bown and Fairfield Parlour (20): Arrival and Trapeze (27).'

Below, is a sample of the band's itinerary at the time (from Jeff's 1970 diary)

June 1970

1st	Nottingham
4th	Potters Bar
6th	Wolverhampton
10th	Birmingham
12th	Southend
13th	Crewe
14th	Bexley
15th	Cambridge University
17th	Barnet
18th	London - John Peel Radio Show
19th	Ormskirk
20th	Durham
28th	Sheffield
29th	London - Island Studio
30th	Coventry

22

ISLAND RECORDS - A NEW ALBUM

After negotiations with Island Records, we had our first recording session in Basing Street Studios, London on the 29th June 1970. The session was from 2pm-midnight. It went well. For Robert Palmer, it was his first opportunity to record an album of songs that he had honed on the road to his own satisfaction. His vocals were strong and authoritative. I was very impressed with his performance. The next session for Island was on 6th July from 10-6pm. The album was entitled 'Listen.' (See discography-albums).

We had a great sleeve designed for us for the album, which was a spoof of the old 'His Masters Voice' logo with the gramophone on the outside and a sitting dog on the inside sleeve so when you pulled the sleeve out the two represented the classic HMV image.

The Lincolnshire Echo on the 30th June, headlined an article with; 'Bown set to liven up Lincoln.' – 'Alan Bown's seven-piece rock band will be livening things up at Lincoln School's Summer Dance on July 11th. Tickets are ten shillings* and everyone is welcome. Go along if you like leaping-and if you want to see big names being continued to be booked for Lincoln dances. Supporting groups will be Virgin Glory and Honeysuckle.'
*(Ten shillings is now the equivalent of 50p).

At the end of June, the band appeared at an open-air festival in Sheffield. The photo of Jeff at The Hammond organ is reproduced opposite. (You can see where Liam Gallagher got his image from!) The front of the organ in the photo is conspicuously minus the original psychedelic artwork and the reason is that this Hammond organ was Jeff's second. The first came to a disastrous end when the roadies literally rolled their van over on the bend of a road and the back doors burst open spewing out the equipment. Fortunately the roadies were not hurt in the accident but the Hammond was smashed to pieces! Also in the photo can be seen the WEM speaker cabinet and amps supplied by that unsung hero Charlie Watkins. There is an amusing sequel to this photo. Jeff recalls;
'The stage had been erected in an open space and was about six feet high but, in the wisdom of the organisers, no one had thought of supplying a ladder or makeshift steps. Consequently, in tight trousers, it was impossible to actually climb onto the stage. Steve heaved me up and, as I stretched my leg to get a

Jeff Bannister 1970

foothold, I felt the seam of my trousers, split at the back from the crotch to the waist! I had to play the whole set with my coat on, to conceal the gaping hole and prevent a serious draft up the Khyber.'

The Sheffield Star, on the 3rd July, headlined this article; 'Plenty For Group Fans' – 'Sheffield Festival has generously satisfied the appetite of group followers in the city. The Festival has attracted some of the country's top groups, Free, Alan Bown, Savoy Brown and Quintessence. It was Savoy Brown and Quintessence who drew the curtain on the Festival's pop concerts at Sheffield University on Tuesday. They followed Free who were at the University on Saturday and Alan Bown and several other groups who appeared in two open air concerts held in Crookes Valley Recreation Ground.'

Also on July 3rd, in The West Bromwich Midland Chronicle ran a further article on the festival at Lower Gornal on the 11th July and gave us a mention.

The Birmingham Evening Mail on the 8th July reported on '...a special pop festival at Lower Gornal Football Club on Saturday (the 11th July)' (We actually played a double on the 11th July, Wolverhampton then Lincoln).

Between recording sessions for the album, we recorded a TV Show called Disco 2 on the 8th July. Also on the show were Justine and Steeleye Span. The show was introduced by Tommy Vance and shown on Saturdays on BBC2. The Producer was Granville Jenkins and the Executive Producer was Michael Appleton.

The Radio Times advertised this for the 9th July 1970 and it's interesting to re-visit the item;
'11.30 Colour – Disco 2, Introduced by Tommy Vance featuring Alan Bown, whose membership remains unchanged, five years after their formation, yet they have the ability to stay ahead of musical trends.'

Tommy really loved the band and knew some of us from the John Barry Seven days. In the same issue of Radio Times we were mentioned again in Dick Lawson's column, 'This Week's Sounds'.

It should be noted that Disco 2 was the forerunner of The Old Grey Whistle Test, which had its first transmission on 21st September 1971.

The Disco 2 appearance of The Alan Bown! on the 9th July 1970 gave our vocalist, Robert Palmer, his first exposure on nationwide television. We performed 'Curfew', a track from our album, and our latest single, 'Pyramid'. Sadly, it now transpires that the recordings of those shows no longer exist due to a BBC policy of deleting selected archives. So Robert Palmer's TV debut is presumably lost forever.

Back at Island Studios, on the 10th July, we had a mixing session from 10-6pm. On the 15th there was another session from 10-6pm.

Disc and Music Echo on the 11th July reported;
'Alan Bown, Justine and Steeleye Span featured in Disco 2 introduced by Tommy Vance on Saturday (BBC 2, 11.35).'

The Evening Standard's Weekend TV and Radio column on the 11th July advertised our Disco 2 appearance.

The New Musical Express, on the 11th July, also mentioned our Disco 2 appearance.

The Barnsley Chronicle on the 11th July ran an article on the

Birdcage in Hoyland, Sheffield;
'A top group to be featured there on July 18th is the Alan Bown. Edison Lighthouse have been booked for later this year.'

The New Musical Express, on the 25th July, mentioned us in their column;
'One-night Stands' – 'Booked for Plymouth's Van Dyke are Alan Bown (tomorrow, Saturday) Yes (July 31) and Van Der Graaf Generator (August 1).'

On the 9th August, we were back in Island Studio from 12-midnight. The next day, we recorded another session from 10-6pm. The album was virtually complete now apart from mixing.

The band went abroad again on the 14th August 1970, this time to Amsterdam for a one-nighter. The 15th and 16th we played in Belgium. This reminded me of an earlier trip we had made there, which had a shock horror element. On that occasions, we checked into our designated guesthouse in a small town and were ushered by the proprietor to the top two floors. He obviously wanted to keep an English band of potential troublemakers away from the other guests. The second floor had a room with about five beds in it so Vic manoeuvred himself into pole position to check out the top floor. Jeff, knowing Vic's instinct for finding the better options, stuck close him as the proprietor ushered the two remaining members of the band to the top floor. In the garret room were two beds. One was a luxurious looking iron framed double bed and the other was a military style bunk bed, the type that Montgomery had probably slept on during the war. As Vic had entered the room first, his case was on the double bed, before a word was spoken. In fairness, he did then offer it to Jeff but the die was cast. Getting close to autumn and realising that the only central heating that this place had ever seen was a candle, Vic produced a hot water bottle and placed in the bed so it would be nice and warm on our return from the gig. As the venue we were playing at was local, it was only a matter of a couple of hours before we were back in the room and Vic, ready for bed, pulled back the covers to get in. What he saw next turned his face to stone. He asked Jeff to come and have a look and they both stood and stared at the sight before them. About two-dozen grubs were surrounding the hot water bottle and moving in a way that was reminiscent of a box of fisherman's bait. It was disgusting and the whole band was summoned to witness the unidentified Belgian life forms clamouring around the source of heat, Vic's hot water bottle. Suddenly, Montgomery's bunk was a delightful option and Jeff couldn't hide a smile. Vic ended up sleeping fully clothed on top of the bed.

Thanks to The Beatles, The Cavern situated in Mathew Street, Liverpool, had become a legendary venue. They are reputed to have played there over 300 times. We played there once on the 29th August 1970.

When we arrived in our American Ford Galaxy saloon and parked on some waste ground opposite The Cavern, two or three scruffy urchins appeared and offered to 'look after the car' for us, for a few shillings. The inference being, that if we didn't agree, we could return to find a few dents in it. It was cheeky but rather than risk damage to the car we paid up.
The interior of The Cavern was, as expected, rough and ready. I recalled old footage of The Beatles on the small stage in the characteristic cellar arch. There was just enough room for a four piece band but with seven in The Alan Bown it was tricky for us to function properly and our usual lively visual routine was severely curbed. The audience could only be described as blasé and it was also painfully obvious that The Cavern's hey day was firmly in the past. We were glad when the gig was over and had no feeling of reverence for the place, only the desire to leave it!

Around this time, to my lasting regret, history was about to repeat itself and Robert broke the news to me that he was leaving the band!

After his move from my mother's house to West Hampstead, Robert had been socialising with Elkie Brooks and Pete Gage who lived in the area and were the catalyst of a nine-piece band with a brass section, called Da Da. They had convinced Robert that he would be a great asset to the band and he agreed to join after seeing them them play several gigs. I couldn't see the advantage for Robert in leaving The Alan Bown! and I felt he had been misguided.

The deciding factor for Robert leaving us had a bizarre twist. He had got into the mystical I-Ching philosophy in a big way and had posed a question regarding his destiny. Practitioners of this art know that one method of doing this is to throw small sticks in the air so that the position, in which they fall, forms a pattern. The significance of these patterns can then be understood using the glossary of examples shown in the I-Ching book, each shape having its own ancient and wise interpretation. Robert told us that he had consulted the I-Ching and had ascertained that an imminent change of direction for him was on the way. This was good enough for Robert who read this as a sign that he should move on. Basically, he gave himself permission to walk away from a band that had nurtured his talent and included him on a crucial forthcoming album. The timing was a disaster for us.

I reflected on my journey up to Scarborough in June last year, which changed the course of Robert's life. Thanks to me, he had become a professional singer of a well-known band with record and television exposure and his new circumstances had even led him to meet his wife.

Da Da eventually shed their brass section and became Vinegar Joe.

I felt for that period of time, Robert's potential lay dormant. I now had a new problem. Robert's vocals were on the album and I had no vocalist!

Once again an album release was put on hold while we invited singers to come along to our rehearsal room in Hanwell to audition. Gary Pickford-Hopkins from the Welsh band, 'The Eyes of Blue', was one of the many that came along. We liked him so much that we arranged to try him out in the studio, as soon as we could. Unfortunately, Robert Palmer had customised the keys of the songs to suit his own voice and some of the top notes proved to be outside of Gary's range. He tried valiantly and the sound of his voice was ideal for the tracks but the keys were beyond him. It was out of the question to record all the tracks again in lower keys and there was no digital technology in those days so I had to tell Gary we couldn't use him. I think we were all as disappointed, because he was obviously a really nice guy and had a good image. But time and money were at stake. We had to keep searching.

On another day, at the rehearsal room, we heard more singers and one guy stood out from the rest. He was Gordon Neville, a Scottish guy, who sang with ease and confidence. Tony, Vic and John were instantly impressed but Jeff, Stan and I were not so convinced he was the right guy. He had a good voice but we had been spoilt by Robert's individuality and charisma. However, with the band moving more toward a 'progressive' style of music, the image side of things was less of an issue now so I went with the flow and we gave Gordon a test run in the studio. Unlike Gary before him, he had no problems with the vocal range of the pre-recorded tracks and therefore, it was decided, he was a suitable replacement for Robert.

On the 20th August 1970, we returned to Island Studios to replace Robert Palmer's vocals on the album with Gordon Neville's. The session was booked from 10am to 6pm. Not long to record an album of vocals but Gordon worked well under pressure and gave a faultless rendition of the songs. Whatever expectations Robert had of hearing his vocals on the album had now been quashed although it was a hollow victory for me. However, many tracks featuring Robert Palmer's vocals survived and were released in 1987 on a vinyl album entitled, 'Robert Palmer – The Early Years'. (See discography - albums).

Robert still had gigs to fulfil with the band and he had agreed to stay on until Gordon had ended a residency at Gullivers, a West End cabaret club.

Robert Palmer's last gig with The Alan Bown! was on October 10th 1970 at The Digby Stuart College, Roehampton.

There was no animosity when he left but it would be sometime before I would see him again.

23

EXIT ROBERT PALMER - ENTER GORDON NEVILLE

Gordon Neville's first gig with The Alan Bown! was at The Black Swan, Sheffield on the 11th October 1970.

We always went down well in Sheffield, a hangover from The Mojo days (now long gone). The Black Swan was a large pub with a music room and the crowd accepted Gordon without reservation. Some long-term fans approached me afterwards and said they had never liked Robert Palmer anyway, because of his blatant posing!

The hardcore supporters seemed happier with the knowledge that the rest of the band was still intact. That was the part of the secret of the band's success in my opinion. There was something for everyone in The Alan Bown! Some people would go for the musicianship of any or all members of the band. Some liked the sparring between John and myself. Female fans had different favourites and so on. It was never just a singer with a backing band and that's why Gordon Neville could fit in comfortably knowing he wasn't following a Joe Cocker or a Rod Stewart. However, as it transpired, Robert Palmer later emerged as a big star in his own right!

The New Musical Express on the 11th October reported; 'Radio 1 Names' – '…and new D.J. Bill Gates introduces his own show on Radio 1 on Sunday the 19th when artists include The Alan Bown and Gulliver's People.'

Three gigs later and on the 18th October, we went to Zele in Belgium for a one-nighter and returned the following day. Gordon settled in quickly and took the lead vocalist role in his stride. He was genuinely thrilled to be in the band and was passionate about doing everything he could to help make it work.

On the 2nd November we played at The Marquee supported by a band called 'Hate'.

We had another photo session with the new line-up, in time for 'Pyramid', our new single, which was released on the 13th of November.

It was our first single for Island Records and featured Gordon's voice.

On the 18th November 1970, Jeff had to attend Sheffield Magistrates Court to answer a summons for careless driving. He had been involved in an accident in Sheffield earlier in the year whilst driving the Ford Galaxy.

We had played a gig in the city at The Black Swan and after checking into the hotel and finding no refreshment, decided to go back into town for something to eat. It was when returning from this trip at around 1am that disaster struck. Not familiar with the area and looking for the right road, Jeff mistook a filter light for an ahead signal and crossed a junction. Some of the band were also in the car and suddenly they saw another car coming down a hill, at speed and on a collision course. Vic said, 'Look out, what's he doing?' Jeff stamped his foot on the accelerator but couldn't get out of the way quick enough. The other car hit the rear side of the Galaxy at an angle which made the other car spin 360 degrees then, as we all watched in horror fascination, it crashed straight through a shop frontage and come to rest inside the shop! We jumped out of the Galaxy and ran over to see if the driver was ok. The front of the shop was completely demolished and shelves had collapsed either side of the car. The roof and bonnet were covered in burst packets of soap powder, tins of pet food and other assorted groceries. The windscreen of the car had shattered and the driver sat there, immobile, still holding the steering wheel and staring straight ahead! Jeff thought he was dead and, after a pause, said, 'Are you alright?' The other band members exchanged nervous glances and the guy suddenly replied, 'I think so.'

The police were called and statements were taken. Jeff was breathalysed but hadn't been drinking. However he was a bit shaken up and at one point inadvertently called the police officer 'Occifer', which didn't gain much sympathy. Jeff wore my pin-striped suit for the court case but it didn't bring him much luck. He had instructed his solicitor to plead not guilty to driving without due care and attention and, after his statement to the bench, the claimant stood in the witness box and was asked his name and profession. He gave his name, and then added, 'retired sergeant of the Sheffield Constabulary'! Jeff's solicitor immediately whispered into Jeff's ear, 'Change your plea to guilty!' Jeff was fined for 'careless driving', had his licence endorsed and ordered to pay for the repairs to the vehicle of the other party.

Having only just got over the trauma of finding a replacement for Robert, I had another personnel change to contemplate but this one was more of a wrench to me. Stan came to me to say that he had decided to leave the band. It was a blow. We went back a long way to my early years in The John Barry Seven and it was Stan who played a part in the formation of The Alan Bown Set. I regarded Stan as more than just a member of the band.

In fact, to me, he was more like a brother. Stan recalls;
'I had become disillusioned with the way the band was going. When I first met Alan back in The John Barry Seven days I always thought he was the epitome of class and showbiz. I always had the greatest respect for him and called him 'guvnor'. To me, he was, but what I was seeing now was a gradual decline in the band's on-stage image. I thought I was alone in having doubts about Gordon Neville's attitude to presentation. On one gig, I was dismayed to see him in an old T-shirt and jeans, drinking a pint on stage and I thought this isn't what represents The Alan Bown! as I knew it. To me, he looked like an ordinary bloke in a pub. Jess Roden may not have been as suave as Robert Palmer but either one of them had enough stage presence to fill The Albert Hall. I felt from the beginning that Gordon was not the right choice but I came to the conclusion that it was me out of step with how everyone felt and the way the band was progressing. On reflection, I should have voiced my concerns with Alan but he seemed to be content with the way things were. I was very depressed after leaving the band and immediately sold my bass guitar. It took me years to regain the enthusiasm to play in a band again.'

'Listen', our first album for Island Records, was released on November the 20th 1970. We had half-page adverts in all the major music papers, displaying the new photos. We also had half-page articles in December issues of 'Disc & Music Echo', 'Sounds' and 'Music Now'. A whole page advert in Melody Maker, November 21st, displayed the sleeve of the album.

The Disc and Music Echo on the 21st November reviewed the new single. In 'Singles Extra', Phil Symes said;
'Alan Bown have a nice heavy sound on 'Pyramid' which simply reeks of Chicago. They've been trying for a hit for a long time. I fear they'll have to keep trying.'

Chris Welch, in The Melody Maker on the 28th November also reviewed the single;
'The introduction reminds me a little of 'Wheels Of Fire' but the feeling is the old brass bite of Bown & Co and maybe their hit at last. Good vocals and a nice sequence.'

In Music Now, on 28th November, Karen de Groot also reviewed 'Pyramid'. The review is reproduced here;
Two tracks from the Alan Bown's forthcoming album, this, the A-side was written by organist Jeff Bannister and illustrates that bands may come and trends may go, the Alan Bown goes on forever perfecting themselves. This is an excellent tight hard rock number with well defined instrumentation, a solid commercial beat and nice things musically from all members of the band. It's a good clean production, with just the right accent on the brass – enough to let

you know it's there and to improve the basic sound, but not overpoweringly so. Naturally the vocals are good and the whole thing adds up to a very pleasing release that should do well.'

In Sounds on the 28th November, Penny Valentine reviewed 'Crash landing', which was the B-side of the single!
'The Alan Bown – Crash Landing' - 'Creeping doom-filled organ heralds a nice set of angry/distressed vocals on this very held-back track. Even the brass lines and guitar solo are really misty and gentle. Very effective.'

We appeared at one of our regular gigs on November 29th at The Torrington in North Finchley. This was handy for Gordon who lived only five minutes away. The Torrington was a large pub with a function room at the rear where all the gigging bands played. The venue was run by George Blevings, who had great respect for the band. We had a good following here right back from when Jess was in the band.

More gigs followed and the itinerary looked like this (from Jeff's 1970 diary);

December 1970

2nd	Birmingham – Mothers Club
3rd	London – rehearsal
4th	Guildford
5th	London – Temple Club
6th	Peterborough
7th	Rehearsal
8th	Birmingham – Henry's Blues House
9th	Hitchin
10th	London College of Printing
11th	Sheffield – Black Swan
12th	Isle of Wight
14th	London – rehearsal
15th	Portsmouth
16th	Cannock
17th	Bristol
18th	Weymouth
19th	Lincoln
20th	Braintree
21st	London – Tooting
22nd	Wisbech
26th	Stoke on Trent – Hanley
27th	Sheffield - Black Swan
29th	Yardley – The Swan

On the 7th December 1970, we rehearsed at Hanwell Community Centre with new bass player, Andy Brown. Andy picked up the songs quickly and his enthusiasm gave us all a lift.

The Disc and Music Echo, on 5th December, published an article and a new photo of the band, which included Gordon Neville. The heading said, 'Alan Bown – or how success has eluded him.' Gordon was mentioned as Jess Roden's replacement!

The Melody Maker, on 12th December, published a photo of me with a letter from A Chambers from Newcastle-on-Tyne. It was headed, 'Bown: our BST?' The letter said;
'Forget the slick, every note contrived cabaret material churned out by Blood Sweat & Tears. Forget the insipid electric ramblings of the very boring, very overrated Chicago. Listen to a British band who write all their own material and 'Listen' is the title of a brilliant funky album by Alan Bown. He is what brass in pop is all about.'

Also on the 12th December, Music Now published a half-page article with photo of the band. The photo was captioned; 'The Alan Bown here for the benefit of their audience'. The article was entitled, 'Freedom after 6 years together.' I was interviewed by Dai Davies and the article was about my career and the band's fortunes.

Sounds, also on 12th December, published a half page article with a band photo. Penny Valentine interviewed me and the article was headlined, 'Alan Bown – The Seven Year Slog.' I wasn't pleased with this. It sounded like we had been on the treadmill forever. Far from it! The gist of the interview was my origins and the career of the band. The new album 'Listen' was given a positive plug.

Stan Haldane, long term friend and bass player, played his last gig with the band on the 15th December in Portsmouth. Now only Jeff and I remained from the origins of The John Barry Seven.

The following day we travelled to Cannock for our first gig with bass player, Andy Brown. He had no problem with the repertoire and his playing was inspirational.

Penny Valentine of Sounds reviewed the new album, 'Listen' on the 19th December;
'This is one of those tight compact little albums that bears the rare distinction of fine musicianship and a gelling of musicians heads so that nobody sounds like they're fighting to get the upper hand. Gordon Neville's unflashy vocals, Bown's flugel horn, marracas and trumpet work, Jeff Bannister's fine organ are

all worthy of mention and it's a pleasure for once to hear a brass line-up that doesn't go all out to copy Chicago. In a way, the carefully held-back quality on the tracks reminded me of Traffic and at times, Procol Harum.

The Alan Bown! Autumn 1970
Back row left to right: Tony Catchpole, Vic Sweeney, Jeff Bannister, Andy Brown
Front row left to right: John Anthony Helliwell, Alan Bown and Gordon Neville

187

Their single 'Crash Landing' is included – and a fine track it is too – and it's nice to hear a set that sounds as though everyone had an interesting time in the studio and there were no egos to deal with.' As previously mentioned, 'Crash Landing' was the B-side. 'Pyramid' was the A-side.

It wasn't common knowledge either that Gordon had replaced Robert Palmer's voice on all the album tracks, which was no mean feat.

Also in the 19th December issue of Sounds, The Torrington in Finchley was featured in their 'Sounds Around' column. Being one of our regular gigs, the band also had a mention.

As the year came to a close, I reflected on the changes and how they would affect our future prospects. I was sorry to see Robert go but more sorry to lose Stan. As a result of these changes there was a shift of emphasis in the music. Gordon's vocals had certain maturity to them but I still wondered if his voice was distinctive enough. However, Andy's bass playing gave all the songs a refreshing makeover with his very musical approach and he also had a good voice. I felt the band was safe in these guy's hands but was it a winning formula for the record buying public? Only time would tell as we embarked into 1971.

On the 3rd January 1971, we appeared at the Roundhouse, Chalk Farm, London. Also on the bill was The Brian Auger Trinity. The Roundhouse was a huge old shed originally built to house a giant turntable for steam locomotives on the railway. Long since redundant and the turntable removed, it had become a primitive venue for budget concerts. However, it was popular with audiences who enjoyed plenty of space in the vast auditorium. I wouldn't say it was a joy to play there but we had a good reception.

In the 19th January edition of Sounds, I was interviewed and given a half page article with a photo. The headline was 'Alan Bown working for the big time'. The forthcoming album, 'Stretching Out' was mentioned.

On the 21st January and after a series of gigs in the provinces, we played at Ronnie Scott's Upstairs. This was a venture of Ronnie Scott to feature bands that would not fit into the jazz category but nevertheless had a certain pedigree. The room designated for such bands was literally upstairs and Ronnie would joke that he never actually ventured up there, which amused the ardent jazz clientele. I got on well with Ronnie Scott and his business partner, Pete King. Ronnie encouraged all types of musicians. He never held non-jazzers with contempt, unlike some of his contemporaries. In a way it was an honour to step over the threshold of such a prestigious club as a musician, although, over the years, I had been there many times as a customer. I was one of the many that were sad to hear the news of Ronnie Scott's death in 1996.

We had a rehearsal on the 8th February and a photo session on the following day.

On the 11th February, it was back into Island Studio to record two tracks; 'Find a Melody' and 'Thru the Night'. Both songs were written by Jeff and myself. The Catchpole/Roden team was now dissolved and Gordon didn't appear to be a contender for any song-writing input.

The band went to France on the 20th February 1971 and we played at The Paris Olympia, supporting Cat Stevens. A lot had happened in my career since I first played here with The John Barry Seven in 1964! The next night, we travelled to Lens in France, for a gig at The Eden Ranch. We first played here in 1967 when Jess was in the band. This trip certainly gave me my share of déjà vu. We returned to England on the 22nd.

During March, Jean and I moved from Penn to Hitchin in Hertfordshire. We had found a nice family house and this time it had no ghost!

On the 7th March, The Alan Bown! appeared at The Lyceum in London. Also on the bill was Free.

The 18th of March 1971 saw us back in the BBC Studios to record another Disco 2, TV Show. On our previous appearance, Robert Palmer was in the band whereas this time Gordon Neville took the vocal honours. We recorded two numbers for the show, 'Wanted Man' from our 'Listen' album and 'Thru' the Night' from the new sampler album 'El Pea', soon to be released by Island records.

April the 5th and 6th saw us back in Island Studio for overdubs and mixing sessions.

On the 30th April we went abroad once again. This time to Holland, then to France for the 1st and 2nd of May.

Island records placed a full-page ad with the May 1st 1971 issue of Melody Maker, for their sampler double album entitled, 'El Pea'. It cost £1-99! We had one track on it, which was 'Thru' the Night'. Also featured on the two albums were, Quintessence, Amazing Blondel, Mick Abrahams, Cat Stevens, Bronco (Jess Roden's new band), Mott the Hoople, Nick Drake, Free, Mike Heron, The Incredible String Band, Sandy Denny, Jimmy Cliff, Tir Na Nog, Fairport Convention, Emerson Lake and Palmer, Mountain, Head Hands & Feat, Traffic, Jethro Tull and McDonald & Giles.

I was starting to feel around this time that there was an air of dissatisfaction in the ranks, possibly with the musical direction of the band. I couldn't put my finger on it but I seemed to walk in on conversations that abruptly ceased or changed direction. The one person who always seemed to be involved in these conversations was Gordon Neville. I know that Andy Brown didn't want to know about politics. He actually said that his loyalty was with the guy that gave him the gig and he refused to be drawn into any collusion. A few gigs later, I chewed it over with Jeff Bannister. He had picked up the same vibe and was aware of the rumblings that were going on although he had not overheard anything tangible. Jeff suggested that if Gordon was really not satisfied with the band we should consider going out as a five piece without him and shedding either Tony or John, depending on who was keen to stay. Jeff thought that he and Andy were capable of handling the vocals. I thought such a change would be too drastic and decided to ignore the discontent, although the resonance of a conspiracy lingered on. In retrospect, I should have nipped this in the bud but didn't think it was that serious.

Sessions for our next album, 'Stretching Out' began in May. These were booked for the 25th, 26th, 27th and 28th at Island Studio, Basing Street, London. We went back in on June 2nd for the final session. The recordings went well and for a while the sessions appeared to have shored up the differences in the band. However, the politics in the band finally got to Jeff and at the end of the sessions he told me that he had decided to leave! He still felt radical changes were needed and couldn't see any other solution.

On 12th July 1971 The Alan Bown! recorded at the BBC Studios for the Radio 1 show, 'The Sound of the 70's'. The songs performed were, 'Stretching Out', 'Find a Melody' and 'Up Above my Hobby Horses Head'. The show was transmitted on August 3rd.

On July 16th we went to Cornwall for two days, playing in Truro on the first night. The following day, on 17th July 1971 in St Ives, Jeff Bannister played his last gig with The Alan Bown!

Our long journey together of seven years on the road had come to an end. Jeff said his heart was no longer in the band, which he felt had lost its magic. I couldn't deny that I shared the same feeling. The constant touring was an added factor and Jeff felt it was time to try a new path with song writing and perhaps a solo career. Over the years he had developed a good relationship with the publishers, Robbins Music and many singer/song-writers were now emerging, signifying more opportunities in that field than ever before. The band decided collectively not to replace Jeff with another keyboard player.

24

STRETCHING OUT

On August 7th 1971, our new album 'Stretching Out' was released on Island Records. (See discography-albums).

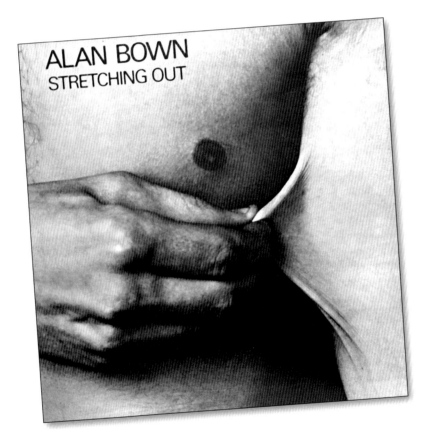

Preceding the album release, a full-page advert featuring a bare torso with the skin being stretched, appeared in Sounds and Time Out.

Mel Collins, our Manager, had an anxiety attack during the recording of the title track. He was in the studio listening to Gordon Neville overdubbing the vocals with the opening lyrics of the song; 'Listening is sometimes boring – taking part is much more fun'. Mel turned to me and said abruptly, 'You'll have to change that!' I was puzzled and replied, 'Change what, Mel?' 'We can't have that,' he said emphatically, shaking his head, 'It's not acceptable.' 'What isn't?' I queried. Mel said, 'You can't have, taking pot is much more fun.' We all fell about and explained that it was 'Taking part…' but Mel wasn't convinced, 'You won't get radio plays with those lyrics,' he said. In reality, it was probably Gordon Neville's Scottish accent that had changed the sound of the word, 'part' but Mel felt it was an issue and to dispel any doubt, he had the first two lines of the song printed on the album's promotional material.

Full-page adverts for the new release, featuring the album cover, appeared in Melody Maker on the 7th and 14th August 1971.

The album was given a positive review by Chris Welch in the Melody Maker on 7th August but it is interesting to note that he failed to mention Gordon Neville's vocal contribution.

This was also true of the next review, confirming my fears that Gordon was not making an impact or receiving the praise that had been given to his predecessors, Jess Roden and Robert Palmer.

Disc and Music Echo gave the album a good review on August 21st, mentioning that Jeff had left the band. The review is reproduced here; 'Alan Bown's Stretching Out (Island ILPS9163 £2.19) has an unpleasant cover but sounds pleasant. There are many different moods on the six tracks and this band has really developed an individual style. All the capabilities of the brass-organ-guitar-bass-drums line-up are exploited. Some numbers are pretty strange, with a lot of unexpected happening but Ritchie Haven's 'Up Above my Hobby Horses Head' is treated with respect. Organist Jeff Bannister has since left the group and you'd think from his contribution that he would be seriously missed but having seen the band 'live' without him, it's not the case. He and trumpeter Bown wrote four of the tracks and the best is 'Build Me a Stage'. The album hasn't the initial impact of their previous one but it's the sort that you will get more from with each listen. Pity that guitarist Tony Catchpole isn't featured more. It's difficult these days for a rock band with brass to have its own identity but this one has. Quality - Good Value – Good.'

A series of gigs to promote the album, were advertised in the press;

August 1971

10th	Barry - Memorial Hall
12th	Bristol – Old Granary*
14th	Bath - Pavilion
15th	Corby - Festival Hall
16th	Guildford - Civic Hall
17th	Southampton - Guildhall
19th	Cornwall – Redruth
20th	Plymouth – Guildhall
21st	Torquay – Town Hall
23rd	Chelmsford - Civic Theatre
26th	Chatham – Central hall
28th	East Kilbride – Olympia

* I appeared at this venue and was supported by Crimson Earth. By co-incidence, my old friend and mentor Hank Shaw appeared at this venue the night before as a special guest with The John Critchinson Trio.

Hank was also in a band called The Bebop Preservation Society at the time and they released an album in 1971, which also featured Pete King/sax, Brian Spring/drums, Spike Heatley/bass and Bill Le Sage/piano and vibes.

I dropped in to the studio in London when this album was being recorded and was very impressed with the performances of all the musicians. I had to own up to myself that this 'higher plane' of music was attainable only by the privileged few. However, as any jazz musician will tell you, being a purist and keeping ahead of the bills is not the easiest path to follow.

After this series of gigs, Andy Brown decided to leave the band and on Gordon Neville's recommendation, was replaced by Dougie Thompson on bass guitar. Gordon and Dougie already knew each other from their roots in Scotland and after joining the band, Dougie stayed at Gordon's flat.

In New Musical Express, also on the 23rd October, a letter was published from a reader; 'Since organist Jeff Bannister left The Alan Bown, nothing has been heard of him. I hope he doesn't fade into obscurity, his talent is too good to be wasted. Why don't we hear more of this hard-working underrated group.'

The atmosphere in the band had not improved since Jeff and Andy had left and Tony Catchpole now decided to leave.

Tony placed an advert in The Melody Maker on the 23rd October 1971, which announced his departure and invited offers of work. It said, rather disparagingly I thought;
'Tony Catchpole has just left The Alan Bown. Following their extensive 5-year whistlestop tour of Britain and would like to hear from anyone who could use his ability on 8 and 12 string electric guitar.'

Now the only surviving original member of The Alan Bown Set still in the band, apart from myself, was Vic Sweeney.

The Melody Maker on the 4th December 1971, in their 'Making Music' column, published an article, which was headed, 'To bug or not to bug'. This was accompanied by a photo of myself, which was captioned, 'Alan Bown: pick-up in his trumpet mouthpiece' The interview and article began; 'Whether or not to use a pick up has become a heated controversy among brass and reed players who differ considerably in their views of the advantages and disadvantages technically and tonally.'

The article went into some depth on various 'bugs' then continued, 'Two band colleagues with opposite opinions of pick-ups are trumpet leader Alan Bown, who firmly favours them and his sax-clarinettist John Anthony, who definitely doesn't. Alan, who plays a Super Olds trumpet with a Giardinelli mouthpiece, uses a King pick-up, which he bought at London's Drum City. A plug is fitted into a hole bored in his mouthpiece and a mike clips onto the plug. The mike goes through an octave divider, into a wah wah and through the 400 watt WEM PA. The octave divider, a box clipped to his belt, has little switches on top of it to provide different sounds. 'I get various effects with it,' said Alan. 'I can get all the octaves. For instance, if I'm playing in F sharp it gives me the octave below the bass note. It also gives me an oboe and clarinet sound and when I'm using the wah wah I get a fuzz sound. There are lots of ways I can use it, so I can interchange it. I use it at different times in various tunes but I feature it especially all the way through 'Stretching Out' the title track of our last album.'

This article does more than inform the reader about bugs. For me it showed how diametrically opposed John and I was when it came to embracing electronics. It was another factor that would add to a widening gap between us.

I held auditions for a replacement guitarist at G.C.D. rehearsal rooms in Lillie Road, Fulham on the 20th December 1971. I decided to offer the gig to Derek Griffiths who was a very accomplished guitarist and his style had an empathy with mine.

With two new members, I now felt that the band could progress into a more jazz/rock field. The old repertoire was sounding stale to me and I wanted to inject some musical excitement into the act. I talked the idea over with the band but met with some unexpected resistance from the old regime and concluded that they didn't even want to give it a try. I have to concede that Gordon Neville in particular must have seen this as a threat to his status, as more emphasis on instrumentals would have left him without much to do. I had always been a democratic bandleader and accepted the majority vote but the unwillingness to change left me feeling unfulfilled and isolated.

With the new line-up we embarked on a series of gigs with road manager, Ian Fieldsend, who had replaced our long serving roadie, Steve Hackett.

Dates by courtesy of Derek Griffiths;

December 1971

21st   Sheffield - Penthouse
27th   Crewe – Up The Junction

January 1972

11th   Northampton – Fantasia
15th   Reading – Bulmershe College
21st   Leicester – Teachers training College
22nd   Cranfield – College of Technology
23rd   Torrington – Finchley

February 1972

5th   Farnborough – Technical College
9th   London - Greyhound

One evening, a few weeks after this series of gigs, I had a call from George Blevings, the promoter at the Torrington. The Torrington was still a popular music venue, which had hosted The Alan Bown on many memorable gigs. He rang me about 7pm to tell me that a band called Wizard* was at the venue and he said that it was my band with a different name! George rightly surmised that I knew nothing about this and because we had known each other for years, he had felt he should give me a call. I was dumbfounded and promptly decided to go to Finchley to check this out. When I arrived at The Torrington and went in, my heart sank. All the guys were there and I couldn't conceal my anger and disgust. I just confronted them and said, 'That's it. It's all over.' Then I walked out.

I have since learned that Wizard was evolved out of frustration mainly because of my proposal to move into the jazz/rock field. Whether or not my desire to change had been regarded as uncompromising, nothing had been said to me and I felt betrayed by these guys, some of whom I had known for years.

Wizard continued under that name (without me) but it all came to an end when my manager, Mel Collins, repossessed the equipment and the van.

*Wizard was not associated in any way with Roy Wood's Wizzard.

25

THE ALAN BOWN! - ONE MORE TIME

Because of recent developments, I decided to cut my ties with the old band and form a new ensemble with guys I had either known or heard of.

With this in mind, I rang keyboardist Dave Lawson and on February the 7th 1972, he met me at Mel Collin's office where we discussed the prospects of forming a new band. Dave suggested that Alan Coulter and Tony Dangerfield might be interested so I also got in touch with them. Dave Lawson had been an RAF bandsman all those years ago when I was in the service and I remember him playing clarinet at the time. We didn't really get to know each other then but I soon discovered he was not only a very accomplished musician but a genuinely nice guy.

The line up of this new incarnation of The Alan Bown! was; Alan Bown/electric trumpet, Tony Dangerfield/lead vocals/bass, Dave Lawson/ B3 Hammond organ /vocals, Frank White/guitar and Alan Coulter/drums. Dave Green/bass played on some gigs as did Gaspar Lawal/ percussionist. John Goodsall/guitar later replaced Frank White and Kenny Slade/drums later replaced Alan Coulter.

We rehearsed at my house in Hitchin during February. The house was detached and there was plenty of room and no problems with noise. More rehearsals followed throughout March and during April. Mel Collins, our manager, came along for a listen on 6th April.

Dates by courtesy of Dave Lawson;

April 1972

21st   Stevenage – College
28th   Burton on Trent – 76 Club
29th   Sheffield

May 1972

5th   Manchester University
6th   Lincoln – Aquarius

May 1972 continued

11th	Northampton – Fantasia
12th	High Wycombe – Nags Head
13th	Bradford University
20th	York Agricultural College
21st	Stoke on Trent

June 1972

8th	Northampton – Fantasia
16th	Oxford
24th	Crewe – Up the Junction

July 1972

1st	Kingston Polytechnic
3-6th	Birmingham
7th	Weymouth

On the 19th July Alan Coulter left and Kenny Slade replaced him.

Dave Lawson recalls; 'One day we were in a transport café just outside Sheffield's 'shitty shenter' as one of the locals called it. An old boy in the café said to Kenny, 'Are you in a band?' to which Kenny replied, 'Yeah, that's right.' The man said, 'Thought yer were, clothes an' that. What d'yer play?' Kenny replied, 'I'm a drummer.' The old boy said, 'Hmph! moony fur nowt!' We all cracked up and Kenny was in his home town!'

This was the last line-up of The Alan Bown! It was the most musically satisfying since the early days of the band with Jess Roden and Robert Palmer, but financially it proved too difficult to sustain.

In Melody Maker on 18th November 1972, I was featured in their column, 'Rock 'n' Roll Star?' with the heading 'Bown : My trumpet is part of me.' The feature was a potted history of my career and also included a photo of me blowing the trumpet. I was wearing the famous 'Mr Freedom' Ice-Cream motif T-shirt (for those that remember it).

The 1973 publication of 'The NME Book of Rock 2' stated; 'Alan Bown best known for his jazz-rock outfit, Alan Bown Set which at various times included such luminaries as Robert Palmer, Jess Roden, John Helliwell, (Supertramp) Dave Lawson/keyboards (Greenslade) and Terry Stannard/drums* (Kokomo).'
* Terry Stannard worked with Andy Bown and not with my band.

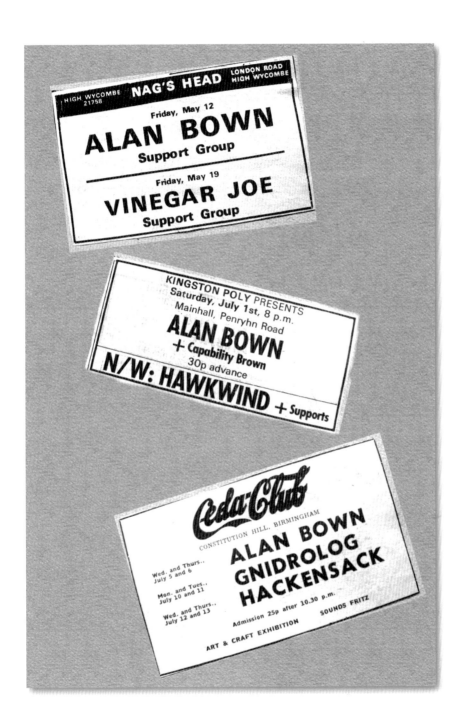

26

JONESY

Turning the clock back a couple of years to when The Alan Bown! made regular appearances at Dreamland, Margate, the audience then included two guys who were eventually to play a major role in the next phase of my career. They were John Jones and his brother, Trevor. They both made a point of coming over to say how much they loved watching the band. It turned out they were also keen musicians and after my band broke up they contacted me with a view to joining Jonesy, a band they had formed in 1971.

They were particularly keen on the electronic sounds I had been producing using my pedals and octivider so I went along to a rehearsal room in Putney for a blow with them and it worked out really well.

Jonesy 1973
Standing left to right: Trevor Jones, Richard 'Plug' Thomas
Seated left to right: John Jones, Jimmy Kaleth and Alan Bown

In February 1973, I joined Jonesy and played at The Marquee, London on the 16th February. The band had already gained a following here, having played at The Marquee many times since their first appearance in April 1972. It was a buzz playing at the club, which had inspired me on so many Alan Bown Set gigs. My mind went back to September 1966 and the live album recording of 'London Swings Live at The Marquee Club.' Seven years had passed but once again I was on the stage of this famous club with an exciting band. The mutual respect with these guys was a refreshing change from the regretful demise of my penultimate band.

In March 1973, I went into Escape Studios to record 'Keeping Up', my first album with Jonesy. (The band had already recorded an album entitled, 'No Alternative'). The band now comprised of, John Evan-Jones/ guitars, vocals, Trevor 'Gypsy' Jones/electric bass, recorders, lead vocals, Jamie Kaleth/keyboards, lead vocals, Alan Bown/electric trumpet, electric flugelhorn, percussion and Richard 'Plug' Thomas/drums, percussion, vocals. The album was produced by John Evan-Jones and Jonesy and released on The Dawn label, a subsidiary of Pye Records.

The March 1973 edition of Beat Instrumental included an article headed, 'Quad – can this be the real thing?'

Three consecutive full pages were devoted to Jonesy. The first page featured a photo of the band, the second page, carried an advert placed by Pye records for the new quadraphonic single, 'Ricochet' and the third page was a profile of the new introduction into the market of quad equipment, nominating Jonesy as the pioneers, sponsored by the Japanese electronic giant, Sansui. The third page also gave the band a full name-check, noting that I had recently joined. '....and as of February this year one of the most respected musicians on the scene – Alan Bown.' The back page of the same edition of Beat Instrumental carried a full page advert placed by 'Olds-the top brass' and is reproduced on page 202.

Jonesy was very much a gigging band and an itinerary is reproduced here, thanks to documentation from Trevor Jones;

March 1973

17th	Nottingham - Boat Club
18th	Loughborough – University
19th	London – Goldsmith College
20th	Portsmouth – Tricorn Club
23rd	Sunderland – Locarno
25th	Rugby – St Pauls College
26th	Nottingham – Shipley Boat Inn

Beat Instrumental March 1973

March 1973 continued

27th   Birmingham – Crown hotel
29th   Newport – Kensington Court Club
30th   London – Marquee Club*
31st   Canterbury – Christchurch College

*On 30th March, I appeared again at The Marquee with Jonesy. We were headlining with no support band.

April 1973

1st   Manchester – Stoneground
2nd   Doncaster - Top Rank
3rd   London - City University
6th   Southgate - Badgers Club
8th   Wolverhampton – Catacoombs
9th   Cleethorpes
10th   Southampton - Coach House Club
13th   Burton-on-Trent - 76 Club
14th   Wallasey – Town Hall
15th   Stoke-on Trent – George Hotel, Burslem
17th   Northampton – Fantasia
19th   Liverpool - Cavern Club
21st   Germany – Keil Music Festival
22nd   Germany – Kassel Rock Club
23rd   Germany – Tubingen University
27th   Scarborough – Penthouse
28th   Rotherham – Rawmarsh Leisure Centre
30th   London – Marquee Club*

*On 30th April, I appeared with Jonesy at The Marquee, headlining with no support band.

In April 1973, Jean and I moved from Hitchin back to Slough.

The album received good reviews as we toured UK and Europe. On the 5th June 1973, I travelled to Belgium with Jonesy, then on to Germany. During the trip, we were booked for a gig at The Beat Club in Langelsheim and stayed in a nearby hotel in Goslar. Vinegar Joe appeared on the Friday night and we were due to play on the Saturday. We went to see Vinegar Joe to cheer them on but having a night off in a foreign town was always fatal and, apart from myself the other members of Jonesy got seriously wrecked. It was weird watching Robert Palmer, my former vocalist, on stage with another band. What struck me was that Elkie Brooks took most of the vocal honours so she was consequently the focal point of the band. I found this difficult to comprehend and felt that Robert would have reached greater heights with The Alan Bown! In Vinegar Joe, he appeared to be neither the front man nor lead vocalist. His prestige seemed to have gone down instead of up. I have since wondered if the I-Ching had revealed to Robert that Vinegar Joe would split up before the end of that same year.

I spoke to Robert briefly that evening but he came across as distant. I never met him again after this.

In August 1973, Wilf Pine took over management from Eddie Kennedy and thanks to Wilf, Jonesy played a prestigious gig at the Alexandra Palace on the 2nd August, supporting Black Sabbath. It had been a long time since the early days when The Alan Bown Set had appeared on the same bill as this band.

In September, I went back into the studio with Jonesy to record their third album, 'Growing'. We recorded this at Escape Studio and Air Studios and the album was produced by Rupert Hine. I had met Rupert sometime previously through Martin Hall who used to come to see The Alan Bown Set at the Lafayette Club in Wolverhampton. I was much happier with this album and working with Rupert was inspirational.

The line up in the band had not changed since the previous album except, Bernard Hagley from the original band, added electric saxes and Ken Elliot added clavinet/ARP synth. Extra percussion was provided by Maurice Pert. The writing of all the compositions was credited to Jonesy, ie equally among all the band members (see discography-albums).

More itinerary dates, courtesy of Trevor Jones;

<u>November 1973</u>

5th	Portsmouth - Guildhall
7th	Bournemouth – Winter Gardens
13th	Glasgow – Apollo
14th	Aberdeen – Music Hall
15th	Edinburgh – Caley Cinema
18th	Oxford – New Theatre
20th	Guildford – Civic Hall
21st	Birmingham – Town Hall
22nd	Barrow in Furness – Civic Hall
23rd	Newcastle – City Hall
24th	St Albans – City Hall
25th	Liverpool – Royal Court Theatre
26th	Brighton – The Dome
27th	Leeds – Town Hall
29th	Preston – Guildhall
30th	Sheffield - City Hall

In 1974, the album 'Growing', received The Montreux Diamond Award as the top rock/pop album of the year, beating Bob Dylan, Stevie Wonder and King Crimson among others.

Soon after this period, Jonesy dissolved partly through internal squabbles but, from the ashes, a new band was formed with Martin Lawrence/guitar, Mike O'Donnel/bass, Jimmy Kaleth/keyboards, Richard 'Plug' Thomas/drums and Alan Bown/electric trumpet. We rehearsed in the air raid shelter in my garden. Plug helped me to turn it into a suitable rehearsal room but it was hell for me as everyone smoked and I didn't. As you can imagine, it used to get very stuffy but I became more concerned about the musical direction that the band was taking than the passive smoking. As much as I liked the guys, I felt that my style no longer suited what I was hearing, so when I was offered a job at CBS I had to give it serious consideration.

Plug Thomas, Jonesy's drummer, has his own recollections;
'Even before I turned pro as a musician I was always hearing about how

great 'The Alan Bown Set' were. I lived in Birmingham and one time I travelled with mates to a club in Hanley, near Stoke to see them but the place was full and they wouldn't let us in! So when I got to meet Alan, when he joined Jonesy those years later, I was a bit in awe of him. I had expected a hard bitten pro and he was anything but. I couldn't believe what a lovely and gentle guy he was. Always positive and happy, very clean living and a complete family man. I had never worked with a trumpet (or any brass) player in a band before. Alan was always trying to get me to listen to Miles Davis but I must admit at that time, I didn't really get it. (Years later when I finally bought 'A Kind of Blue' I realised what he was on about). But it was a joy working with him in Jonesy and hearing him play. He turned the band on to a few other jazzy type bands. One thing, which always used to amaze me about Alan, was how well known and liked he was. Whenever we would get to a gig early, in any town in the UK and so we would have time to wander around that town, someone would always come up smiling and say, 'Hello Alan, how are you?' It was like he knew someone everywhere, quite incredible. It happened just about every time. Alan is one of those people who everybody loves and you never forget. I think when we worked together he and I became good friends and it was a great pleasure getting to know him and his family.'

Trevor Jones recalls; 'Alan was always a great guy to work with, dedicated, positive, entertaining, inspirational and just plain good fun. I've always been focused on the importance of teamwork and Alan is exactly the same. In so many ways he was pivotal to the team spirit.'

John Jones, recalls; 'My fondest memories of Alan all focus on his humour and chronic self-depreciation. The funniest story was 'recorded' and was responsible for the title of 'Can you get that together?' on the album 'Growing'. His famous line is 'inserted' into a brief pause in the track. I also remember his strong love for his wife and kids. Musically, he was responsible for introducing me to Miles Davis & Don Ellis in a different way.'

When I left the band and joined the A&R department at CBS, the band continued as a four piece, under the name 'Gold'. I kept in touch with the guys and became their manager, eventually securing them a deal with CBS.

On the 14th April 1974, at Ramport Studio, I played trumpet on Roger Daltrey's second solo album entitled, 'Ride a Rock Horse' The track was called 'Proud' and was written and produced by Russ Ballard for Goldhawke Productions. Musicians playing on the track were Russ Ballard/piano and brass arrangement, Dave Wintour/bass, Henry Spinetti/drums, Tony Meehan/conga, Alan Bown/trumpet, Sweedies/backing vocals. The album was released in 1975 on the Polydor label.

27

CBS AND SOLO SINGLES

I joined the A&R department at CBS in mid 1974, after being headhunted by Dan Loggins, who had been a big fan of The Alan Bown Set and later incarnations of the band. He thought Jess Roden was an exceptional vocalist. He already had two of our albums, 'London Swings Live at The Marquee Club' and 'Outward Bown' and he thought the band was highly individual. As Americans, he and his brother, recording artist Kenny Loggins, were convinced we could have made a big impression in the USA.

Dan was my immediate boss and was more relaxed than most people in these executive positions. I got on with him extremely well and he had a very good ear for music. He understood why I had taken the job, basically to pay the bills and instinctively knew that my heart wasn't really in the administration side of the music business. Paul Russell, head of CBS Legal Affairs welcomed me into the company and revealed that he had been a fan of The Alan Bown! He had seen us many times at London colleges and universities and also, at The Marquee. Dick Asher was the MD at CBS and I got on so well with him that he offered to put me in to the studio to record some tracks. He was so enthusiastic that, with his blessing, I could have recorded an album! So, I felt that I had walked into an appreciation society! The salary was even more welcome, after years of being on the road.

I got on with everyone well at CBS but soon found that 'the other side of the coin' of the music business had its own frustrations. Now I was witnessing first hand how record company boardroom decisions could affect the destiny of bands without their knowledge or consultation. With my band, I used to be travelling up and down the motorway thinking that the management and record companies were 100% behind us. Now the stark reality began to reveal itself. This rankled me but in a new job I had to bite my lip, to begin with anyway.

When I did go along to see bands at gigs, if it was exciting, I would shout my approval. This startled other CBS people who had also come along to the gig. They were inclined to be more reserved and perhaps thought that such behaviour was unbecoming of a record company representative. I could never conceal my enthusiasm for good music and that seemed to be frowned upon.

Even though I championed musicians in this way, I could still be unbelievably maltreated by them. Many of them couldn't understand why I took this job and one day members of Kokomo, who were signed to CBS, came into the office and gave me a hard time, taunting me with remarks like 'What's the great Alan Bown doing here then?' I think my answer was something along the lines of, 'Earning a living' but I thought their attitude was unnecessarily churlish. Let's put it this way, it didn't endear me to them. They were under the impression that a fellow musician had 'sold out' but in truth, I felt that being in the administration could only be good news for artists and bands, now having someone with my experience and empathy to represent them.

When I first joined CBS, their offices were located at Theobalds Road, London but they moved to Soho Square on April 1st 1975. By coincidence, this was also the first day that Hugh Attwooll joined the company as International A&R Advisor (Hugh became head of International A&R years later, finally leaving in 1987). He and I had not met before but would become good friends. It emerged that Hugh had been the drummer in a band called The End from 1966 to 1968, which was managed by Bill Wyman. I also met Nicky Graham here and he had been in The End with Hugh. This gave us common ground with first hand experience of bands on the road and all the problems they encounter.

Soon after the company moved to Soho Square, Dick Asher went to New York and Maurice Oberstein took over. Maurice was a very congenial person. An American with a great sense of humour, he had a softer touch than Dick Asher and I never saw him lose his temper. Everyone called him Obie. Also in the CBS team was Robin Blanchflower who I knew from my old days at Pye, so we had an instant rapport.

During my time with CBS, I was instrumental in discovering and signing to the label, The Dead End Kids, The Sutherland Brothers and Café Jacques. I also pursued Sailor and Mott the Hoople, who eventually signed to CBS. I already personally knew Ian Hunter and some of the members of Sailor, George Kajanus and Phil Pickett. I also attempted to sign Generation X and The Stranglers to CBS. I went along to see these bands many times and thought Billy Idol was a great performer. The Stranglers also appealed to me because of their hard uncompromising image. Frustratingly, CBS as a company didn't share my enthusiasm for these artists and rival labels soon snapped them up.

As mentioned, I also secured a deal for 'Gold' the band that followed on from Jonesy. I hadn't abandoned my musical aspirations and I was invited to join former Free bassist, Andy Fraser for some studio sessions that led to his solo album

In January 1975, I had a call from Tommy Vance's office to record some tracks for Capital Radio. Tommy remembered The Alan Bown Set with reverence and was keen to have me on his show. It was a great opportunity for me to have a blow so I invited Robin Lumley/keyboards and Jack Lancaster/sax & flute to join me, knowing they would be ideal. I also pulled in Mark Allen/guitar and Mac Poole/drums. Mac recommended Keith "Smoke" Abingdon on guitar and Colin Williams on bass. Also, as I wanted to air some tracks from the old Alan Bown catalogue, I asked Jeff Bannister if he could provide lead vocals on these and he was only too pleased to be involved.

I then put the band together under the name 'Alan Bown – No Surrender' and we rehearsed in PSL Studios in Wandsworth on the 6th, 10th, 14th and the 16th of January.

The Capital Radio session was on the 18th January from 10-11am and 12-1pm. The six tracks we played were, 'Scaramouche', 'It's Not Funny', 'Stretching Out', 'Build Me Up', 'Forever' and 'Perfect Day'. It went very well and was transmitted live. Tommy Vance was very congenial and chatted to me freely on air between numbers.

During 1975, I recorded two singles. The first was 'Moanin'' an old Jazz classic with a modern interpretation. The second was a version of the theme from the TV series, 'The Rockford Files'. It was Dan Loggins who was enthusiastic about getting me into the recording studio. Thanks to him I had more than one string to my bow at CBS.

'Moanin' was recorded at CBS Studios on the 2nd March 1975. It was produced by Dan Loggins and arranged by Bruce Baxter.
The musicians on the session were, Bruce Baxter/guitar/synthesizer John C Perry/bass guitar - Jeff Bannister/keyboards/vocals - Eric Dillon/ drums and myself, playing electric trumpet and flugelhorn. Tony Rivers added harmony vocals.

The B-side of Moanin', entitled 'Time to Change', was co-written by Jeff and myself. This was recorded at CBS Studios, on 12th March, with the same line up of musicians. It was produced by Dan Loggins and myself.

One of the CBS bands at the time, 'Starry Eyed and Laughing' had a session booked and needed a keyboard player. I gave Jeff Bannister a call and he joined them at Sarm Studios on 3rd June. Dan Loggins produced the tracks.

The single, 'Moanin' was released on the CBS label 20th June 1975.

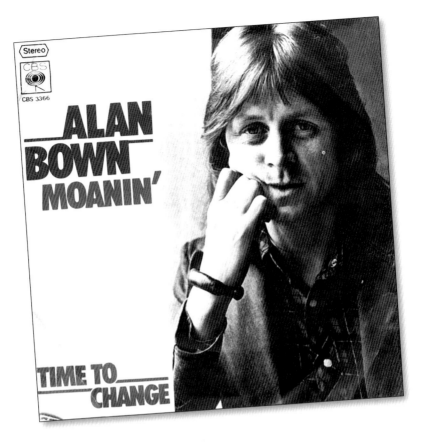

The Melody Maker on 21st June, in their 'What's New' column announced, 'Major new records in the shops this week include:- Alan Bown 'Moanin' (CBS 3366)'

On the 28th June, thanks to Tommy Vance, I guested on Capital Radio for an interview with Sarah Ward.

The July 1975 edition of Beat Instrumental magazine now coupled with International Recording Studio, published an article about me. A photo accompanied the article and was captioned 'Electric Horns'. The article is reproduced here;
'Thinking of taking up trumpet to avoid heavy outlay on amplification? If you are, perhaps you'd be well advised to look at what Alan Bown is using to get his own sound to fit in with the current craze for electronic supremacy. Starting from the top, with his music-goes-round-and-round Super Olds trumpet Alan gets it to 'come out here' with a choice of two bugs and octave dividers made by King and Tootle, an Echoplex, a Gibson Maestro, a Cry-Baby wah-

wah, De Armond volume pedal, Maestro phaser, Hi-Fi sound modulator and a Fender Twin Reverb. And we always thought a trumpet was as 'acoustic' instrument! Alan, since the disbandment of The Alan Bown! and his split with Jonesy, has been working as A&R man for CBS for several months now, but he has not been idle. Practising, producing artists and sitting in on sessions has encouraged Alan to perfect his recording technique and the result of this new single -an electronic updated version of the jazz classic Moanin', b/w Time to Change produced by Dan Loggins. Appearing on the record with Alan are Jeff Bannister, keyboards, Bruce Baxter, guitar and synthesizers, John C Perry, bass guitar and Eric Dillon, drums.'

Around this time I played in the brass section on the sound track of a movie, which was called 'Jersey Contrasts'. This was a Rank documentary about the Channel Islands and was shown in cinemas before the big movie. The music was written by Jack Lancaster and Robin Lumley. Thanks to these guys, I also played on 'The Rock Peter and the Wolf' album, which was recorded at Trident Studios and is still available on Verdant Records.

My next single, 'The Rockford Files' was recorded at CBS Studio. The B-side entitled, 'I Don't Know' was co-written by Rupert Hine and myself. Rupert produced and arranged both sides. It was released on the CBS label, 31st October 1975.

The New Musical Express 15th November 1975, published an article headed, 'Playing in the Band' and sub-headed;
'It happened to Alan Bown and for a trumpeter, that's a serious thing. He had to have his teeth re-set in concrete…Rex Anderson hears the story and gives a run down of Bown's special effects repertoire'

The article was accompanied by two different photos of me, both blowing the trumpet and it began with a tribute to Fred Della-Porta who was one of the founders of The Premier Drum Company in 1922. The main part of the article, concerning me, is reproduced here;
'Now, on to trumpet. More specifically, electric trumpet. I've been trying to get Alan Bown to demonstrate his setup for some weeks now, but he won't because regrettably he is not blowing at this moment in time. Sometime ago John Helliwell, now sax man in Supertramp, accidentally socked him in the gob with a microphone. The idea was that during a set the two would swap vocals and the mike was supposed to be passed across. That was when it happened.
A mike in the mush is not generally prescribed for trumpet players, especially when it results in loose teeth that subsequently turn black. Alan finally had to have the roots removed and replaced with Grade A industrial concrete. This takes about six weeks to set, during which time he has been warned off blowing. Further, it has been suggested that when he does blow again he should use the right side of his mouth instead of the left. Interestingly, Alan is not perturbed at having to change his embouchure. He pointed out that after six weeks he would have lost all his embouchure anyway. The muscles used to create the correct lip shape need to be used every day for an hour or so or they just stop working. Alan reckons it will take him a month to get back up to standard, practising two hours a day. Now, people informed on this sort of thing tell me that Alan Bown – formerly of the Alan Bown Set and Jonesy, and now working in A&R for CBS – is a very good trumpet player. He has a single out at the moment, which gives you some idea of where he was at before the operation. It's a disco version of the 'Rockford Files' TV theme music. Apparently he was just a boring, straight trumpet player until he heard Don Ellis at Ronnie Scott's club one evening and now he produces some amazing sounds just by the addition of a few electronic effects. He blows a Super Olds trumpet he's had for ten years and to electrify it he has a mouth-piece fitted with a bug – a little pickup mike. Actually he has three different bugs, because after blowing for a while they get clogged up with water or to use the correct technical term, spittle.
The bugs are (1) an RB (2) a King and (3) a bug made by a man with the

unlikely name of Ken Tootle. This last not surprisingly, he called a Tootlebug. And Tootle also makes an octave divider that Alan uses along with a Gibson Maestro, wah wah, phase unit and an Echoplex. The octave divider gives small intervals like fifths and an octave while the Maestro enables a trumpet to sound like a clarinet, sax or oboe. He also has a machine for which he cannot remember the name, which is used on the B-side of the single. He says it sounds like blowing a trumpet in a bucket of water. Onstage he tends to use all the effects, switching from one to another. It is arguable that a good trumpet player should be satisfied with one type of sound at a time and use his technique, but Alan is kind of obsessed by the possibilities of electronics.

He can even create an electric guitar sound most guitarists would be jealous of. Acoustic trumpet on its own is capable of a lot of expression and it's a neat, handy instrument for a front man. Bown's personal dream is to lead a band again – this time with greater freedom and a firm financial footing, because an experienced musician with a wife and family needs security as well.

Putting a band together and carting round a lot of electronics is an expensive business if it's to be done properly and successfully. So Bown had the idea of attempting to make a hit single first, which would give him the financial backing he needs. He's trying to be a sort of funky Eddie Calvert and the formula is about right. An electric trumpet player must be good television and it's the TV pop shows that make the stars.'

In Sounds on 29th November 1975, an article about trumpets appeared on 'Blowin' – The page for musicians by James Wynn'. The article, headed, 'They huffed and puffed' featured a photo of Ian Carr, captioned, 'Ian Carr: technology a boost to his career.' After the opening paragraphs, in which Ian Carr recalls when he first heard Don Ellis in 1968, I was introduced into the article;

'Alan Bown, leader of several fine bands over the past 10 years, heard Ellis at London's Ronnie Scott's Club the same year. 'What I heard changed my whole concept of musical thinking. Ellis' use of electronic devices opened up a whole new world of trumpet playing and for the first time in years, I could see a future for the instrument. – and myself – in amplified rock music.'

Bown pinpoints some of the problems that beset trumpet players in the early days of rock. 'For a start the sound was all wrong. It just didn't fit. I mean, it was fine for thickening out the ensemble figures and adding a bit of bite and edge to the riffs, but as a solo horn – forget it! There were times when I felt like a passenger in my own band.' Once into electronics, Bown made effective use of wah-wah devices and then got to grips with octividers and multividers. His work was initially influenced by Ellis and Miles and later by Randy Brecker and ex-Woody Herman soloist, Bill Chase, who did so much to advance electric trumpet techniques in the early seventies.

But although exhilarated by his new-found freedom of expression as an instrumentalist, Bown sounds a warning note concerning possible over use of electronic aids. 'It's a question of perspective.

The electronic devices are an extra and you have to keep them under control. You can't use them all the time. I really do believe that there's a real danger of misuse, even abuse and I would hate for people to forget how a trumpet sounds without amplification.'

It's easy to see from these interviews, that I was still passionate about being a musician and this was to lead to a serious conflict of interest in my job.

One fateful afternoon in the boardroom at CBS, I was involved in a heated dispute with members of the A&R department. During that meeting, the roster of artists had come on to the agenda and the prospects of each artist or band were discussed in turn. It was decided that certain artists were no longer considered a viable proposition and were consequently taken off the list for further promotion. Although I didn't oppose this in principal, I thought the artists should be informed that the record company no longer planned to promote them. This, I pointed out, would give the artists the chance to shop around for another deal. I was told that this was not company policy and contracts had to run their course. Quiet frankly, I thought this stank. Having been on the road with my band I would have been mortified if I thought I had been abandoned by the record company but not told about it. It seemed a cruel injustice. I voiced my opinion a little too loudly and it was suggested that if I couldn't accept company policy, I shouldn't be in the job! After giving this issue serious consideration, I came to the conclusion that I couldn't justify doing a job that was in conflict with my principles.

A month later, I left CBS.

28

FUSE MUSIC
PARIS, NEW YORK AND MEMPHIS

I joined Fuse Music/Black Neon group of companies in 1976, soon after leaving CBS. Rupert Hine introduced me to the company.

This group was first and foremost, a music publishing company. Already signed to the company, was Brand X, which featured Phil Collins on drums. He and I got on well having met many times before on the gig circuit when he was with Genesis. (See the quote from Phil Collins on the back cover of this book).

Fuse Music was owned by Francis Dreyfus and Nigel Haines was the MD. Francis Dreyfus was French and had seen The Alan Bown! in Paris at The Locomotive Club. Robert Palmer was with the band at the time and Francis thought he had superstar qualities. I first met Nigel Haines when he was working for Chrysalis Publishing Company. I was talent spotting on gigs at the time for CBS and Nigel was doing the same for Chrysalis. He recognised me, then introduced himself and asked me where my blue trumpet was! It was Nigel who had introduced me to producer Rupert Hine who was involved with Jonesy. Now we were to form a good working relationship at Fuse. Also at Fuse was Martin Hall who, like myself, would play a role in the publishing of 'Oxygene' by Jean Michel Jarre.

Soon after I joined Fuse Music, I was reunited with old friends Trevor Morais, Rupert Hine, John Perry and Mark Warner who had formed a band called Quantum Jump. Together, with other musicians, they recorded enough tracks for two albums at Trevor's Farmyard Studios. I went to the studio this time on behalf of Fuse Music who were to publish one track on one album and three tracks on the other. Elkie Brooks was on some of the sessions but Vinegar Joe had long since disbanded.

Nigel Haines and I were invited to meet up with Francis Dreyfus at his office in central Paris. On the 13th December 1977, we flew to France and were met at the airport by Stan Whittold, the assistant to Francis Dreyfus. He drove us into the city and our first stop was at the company office where Francis was waiting to greet us.

Fuse Music colleagues circa 1976
From left to right: Nigel Haines, Martin Hall, Alan Bown and Roland Rogers

He had booked a hotel for Nigel and me then later, after checking in and freshening up, we went out to dinner with Jean Michel Jarre. He was quite young at the time and was still bathing in the glory of his mega hit record, 'Oxygene', released earlier in the year.

Around March 1978, a trip to America was presented to me. In collaboration with Nigel Grange, the MD of Ensign records, Nigel Haines arranged for me and other company representatives to go to Memphis to meet Robert Johnson, who was a Fuse Music and Ensign Records artist. (Obviously, this wasn't the legendary black bluesman Robert Johnson who wrote 'Crossroads' and died in 1938!) I was accompanied on this trip by Nigel Haines and his assistant Martin Hall plus Roland Rogers and Mike Turnball who was a freelance management consultant. I got on well with Mike, an easy going and amusing character. Not your typical corporate animal. He remembered seeing The Alan Bown Set on 'Ready Steady Go' and several of our live performances and he had a great respect for the band.

On 10th April 1978, we arrived at the airport of Boston Massachusetts, USA. I stayed in a hotel with Nigel, Martin, Roland and Mike in New York for four days. It was close to Greenwich Village so we could check out the local music venues.

From there we flew down to Memphis and booked into a motel for a couple of weeks, during which time we saw Robert Johnson perform live at several clubs with his bass player, Dave Cochran and drummer, Blair Cunningham. The band was hot and there was no doubt that Robert Johnson was a superb blues guitarist. Unlike his namesake, Robert was white and in his late twenties. He was very popular with audiences and undoubtedly had commercial appeal.

Alan Bown
with
Vernon Presley

———

Gracelands
1978

During our trip to Memphis, we took the opportunity to visit Gracelands. I met Elvis Presley's father, Vernon and had my photo taken with him just inside the gates of Gracelands. This was just after my official tour of the house, which was a wonderful experience.

The primary reason for our visit to Memphis was to confirm that Robert Johnson and his band would be willing to come to England. He agreed and a few weeks later, he came over and played several London venues.

The album 'Close Personal Friend' by Robert Johnson was released on the Ensign label in 1978. All tracks were written and produced by Robert Johnson and published by Fuse Music.

Later, in 1978 I went into the studios with Sean Byrne to record an album of his songs to be released on The Smack label. Sean had decided to use a collective band name, 'Legover'. The album was called 'Wait Til Nighttime'* and the tracks were recorded at four studios, Olympic, Eden, Trident and Moulinex Studios. It was produced by Pierre Tubbs, for Fuse Music. Because of my close friendship and long association with Sean, I was invited to play trumpet on several of the tracks and have a credit on the album sleeve. Apart from Sean Byrne/lead vocals/lead guitar, the other musicians were; Keyboards -Dave Rose and Derek Austin. Bass - Micky Feat, Delisle Harper, Philip Chen. Drums – Theodore Thunder, John Dentith and Glen LeFleur. Blowers – Bill Skeat/saxes/clarinet and Alan Bown/trumpet, George Howden/trombone, Mick Pace/harmonica, Raphael Ravenscroft/saxes/flute/cello. David Ulm/percussion/flute/vocals. Lindsay Scott/electric violin/vocals. All titles published by Fuse Music/Charly* Music. *(Spelling on the label).

In 1979 I was back in the studio to record trumpet on a 'disco-slanted' 45rpm single with Sean Byrne entitled, 'Dancing at the Rubber Ring' by Byrne and Bown for Acrobat Records, marketed and distributed by Arista Records. Sean and I shared the writing honours for the A-side and the B-side, 'Because of You', was written by Sean and produced by Christopher Neil. The single was published by OK Music/Black Neon Ltd and financed by Francis Dreyfus of Fuse Music (See discography - singles).

Soon after this, Francis Dreyfus decided to wind up the company and my association with Fuse Music came to a close. It was a disappointment for all concerned that the company had to be dissolved.

29

ALAN BOWN MANAGEMENT

In 1979, I formed my own company, Alan Bown Management.

Over the next few years I had a full roster, including the following artists and bands:-
John Butler and the band Flicks, Sean Byrne, Jerri Woolfe, whom I signed to Polydor Records in 1982, The Masked Orchestra featuring Kevin McCrea and Mark Fischman, The Outboys, Tim Cody, Billy April and Funkrew, which evolved into the band Strength. In between times I also worked for publishing companies, Calvalcade Music and Minder Music.

The Windsor Press newspaper interviewed me on 20th October 1980. The interview, written by R. S. Webb-Taylor, profiled my career for the last 20 years.

In 1981, Keith Mansfield, my old friend whom I had first met all those years ago in The Slough Boys Club, asked me to work for him at his Warfield Studio in Ascot. I agreed, on the understanding that I could continue my management pursuits. In the same year, Keith arranged and recorded the traditional song, 'The Best of Christmas' released as a 45rpm vinyl single on EMI under the name 'The Nuptown Keys'. It was produced by Keith Mansfield and Peter Cox for KPM Music Ltd and was published by Keith and myself through ManBown/KPM Music Ltd. The single was given wide coverage on Radio Two and BBC Television.

In the New Musical Express on the 26th October 1984, a whole page was devoted to charts showing lists of the latest records being played in various clubs. A chart compiled by Slack and Brian Gardner of The Wag Club, Wardour Street, London showed their number 23 position held by 'Emergency 999 by The Alan Brown (sic) Set (Soul Supply)'. Who Soul Supply were and where the performing rights royalties went, remains a mystery.

In 1985 a vinyl compilation album entitled 'The Alan Bown! Kick Me Out' was released on See For Miles Records. The title was taken from one of the tracks and featured Robert Palmer on vocals.
(See discography - albums).

A compilation album called 'The Early Years'- Robert Palmer with The Alan Bown was released on C5 records in 1987 on 12" vinyl. (The compilation was originally put together by Colin Miles in 1985).
The sleeve notes are reproduced here;
'Following Robert Palmer's phenomenal impact on the World's Hit Parades during 1986 there has been an extraordinary interest shown in his early recordings – and we are delighted to be able to present his very earliest known commercially released records here in their entirety, made when he was the lead singer with The Alan Bown Set – a London based Soul Band in the late 1960's.

Born in Batley, Yorkshire, but raised in Malta, Palmer's infatuation with R&B and Soul Music began as a youngster listening to AFN. As a teenager, he formed a semi-pro group The Mandrakes whose repertoire comprised covers of contemporary American R&B material and at 19 he packed in his day job as a graphic designer and moved down to London to front Alan Bown's band – at that time one of the few brass-equipped Rock bands in the UK.

The Alan Bown! - as they were later billed – were a large Soul Revue band who spent their lives on the road, gigging relentlessly, taking their unique good-time party atmosphere to tiny clubs the length and breadth of the UK. They enjoyed enormous grass-roots following and provided Robert Palmer (who had taken over as lead vocalist from the powerfully-voiced Jess Roden) with the perfect platform to learn his trade. Although he only stayed with the band for little over a year he appeared on their first album* (originally released in 1969 and reissued here in its entirety) which is remarkable in that it doesn't sound in the least bit dated – these tracks, and specifically Palmer's vocals – sound as great as they did when they were first laid down, nearly twenty years ago. As a bonus, two further tracks are included here which feature Palmer's predecessor Jess Roden on lead vocals, which were released on a single at the time Palmer joined the band.

The following year he joined DaDa, an ambitious and experimental 12 piece outfit in which he shared vocals with Elkie Brooks, which evolved into the raunchier Vinegar Joe in 1971 – where Palmer really started to attract attention and create something of a reputation for himself. He quit to pursue a solo career in 1973 – and the rest is history. Since the mid-seventies he has been enormously successful, all his albums being massive sellers, yielding numerous hit singles. His crowning achievements came in 1986 with 'Addicted To Love', which gave him his first No.1 record and won countless awards and accolades.

This album allows a unique opportunity to hear Robert Palmer at the outset of his long and illustrious career, at a time when his vocal style was a lot rawer, less polished – and in many ways a lot more exciting than it is today. Nearly twenty years on, Robert Palmer need not be ashamed of his musical roots, as these timeless recordings demonstrate.'

*This wasn't the first album from The Alan Bown! There were two previous albums both featuring Jess Roden on vocals; 'London Swings - Live at The

Marquee Club' and 'Outward Bown'. (See discography - albums).

I secured a deal for Peter Goalby in 1990 with Rondor Music. Music Week magazine on the 19th May 1990 published a photo with the following caption and report, 'Former Uriah Heap and Trapeze vocalist, Peter Goalby has signed to Rondor Music.' The photo featured myself, Peter Goalby and Rondor General Manager, Alan Jones.

In 1993, Edsel Records, a division of Demon Records released a CD entitled The Alan Bown – Listen & Stretching Out. (See discography - albums).

In 1995, EMI released a CD entitled 'John Barry The EMI Years Volume Three 1962-1964'. Included in the 27 tracks were 'Twenty Four Hours Ago' and 'Seven Faces' both recorded by The John Barry Seven when I was the leader. (I co-wrote 'Seven Faces' with Keith Mansfield).

In 1997, 'Outward Bown' was reissued by Tenth Planet TP027. Limited to 1,000 copies, it was originally released on Deram in 1968.

In 1998, a new CD entitled 'The Alan Bown! – Outward Bown... plus' was released by Colin Miles on his See For Miles Records label. (See discography - ablums).

The November 1998 edition of Record Collector magazine included The Alan Bown in a feature headed; 'The British Psychedelic Trip' and sub headed; 'Nigel Lees begins a major new series. Part 1 : Accent to Dantalion's Chariot'.
A photo of the band was included, which was first published during the band's hey day of 1968. A review accompanied the photo and is reproduced here;
'The Alan Bown : Sandwiched between a string of blue-eyed soul 45s on Pye and some average pop singles for Deram, the Alan Bown's flirtation with psychedelia is best exemplified by 'Story Book', which displayed a harder-edged sound than the 'Toyland' 45s which preceded it. 'Toyland/Technicolour Dream' is still worth seeking out, though the A-side is very twee indeed and slots alongside some of Rupert's People & The Wolves records from the same period. The bands output for Music Factory also warrants investigation.'

In July 1999, I made an appearance on a chat show for Thames Valley TV. The show, called Face to Face, was hosted by Raymond Burton and he interviewed me recalling certain events in my career. During the show, extracts of records I had made with The John Barry Seven and The Alan Bown Set were played and photos of the bands were shown. The highlight of the show was the screening of a video featuring Robert Palmer with The Alan Bown! during an appearance on BBC's Disco 2 (recorded on 11th July 1970). This video was a copy of a Super 8 film, which was shot by Jeff Bannister's father, straight from the television! The quality was not very good, being black and white and the sound track, which had later been dubbed on, was out of sync here and there but nonetheless the footage was quite remarkable. The band played 'Curfew', one of its current songs at the time and Robert sang lead vocals. (Unfortunately home video recorders were not available to consumers until 1972 so consequently none of our television appearances were recorded using that format). At the end of the interview with Raymond Burton, the show faded out to The Alan Bown! single, 'We Can Help You'.

The Alan Bown!
Photo featured in Record Collector Magazine November 1998

The December 2000 issue of Record Collector included an album review of a new CD release. The review, was entitled; 'The Alan Bown Set – Emergency 999 : Sequel/Sanctuary KEMCD 483'. It was accompanied by a photo of the new CD sleeve, which was a composite of previous album covers. The review is reproduced here;

'Never Top 50 stars, but appreciated by the more sophisticated mods for their stylistic tenacity and exacting standards, their 'Headline News' was forever on pirate radio. And it was the Edwin Starr template that snatched slight UK chart honours in 1966, when the Set were in the same bag as luckier outfits led by Georgie Fame, Cliff Bennet and Zoot Money.

Rather than the better-known James Browns and Wilson Picketts, trumpeter Bown drove his septet through works by the then more erudite likes of Starr, The Temptations, Solomon Burke, Don Covay and Little Anthony. There were stylised originals too – a gathering of 45's, previously remaindered items and excerpts from both a show at The Marquee and a French film soundtrack that, with singer Jess Roden and guest pianist Jacques Loussier's awful lyrics, provides a link between the soul band and Bown 'going psychedelic' in 1967, without quite getting the point.'

Towards the end of 2005, my long-term administrative job for Keith Mansfield came to an amicable close. Over the years, I had been a friend and advisor to all the members of the family and Keith still regards me as an uncle to his children, who have now all grown up.

On 19th April 2006, Julian accompanied Jean and me to Monkton near Ramsgate to visit Hank Shaw and his wife Jenny. We were all very pleased to see each other. Recapturing our early years together was priceless.

On 20th August 2006 at Cantley House Hotel, Wokingham, I was delighted to witness my only son Julian, marry his fiancée, Catherine. It was a beautiful ceremony and superb reception. All my family were there; Jean, my wife, Ted my brother and Marion my sister. Nicole my daughter and her husband Nick with their children, Lauren and James. Many of the guests were old friends of mine, including Keith Mansfield and his daughter Helen, Hugh Attwooll, John Adams, Dave Martin, Pat Kelly and Jeff Bannister with his wife, Jules. Julian had booked a jazz trio for the wedding breakfast and the bass player was Dave Richmond who was in The John Barry Seven when I first joined, 43 years ago!

In the closing stages of 2006, Nigel Lees, the Director of Top Sounds approached me with a proposition to release vintage BBC radio recordings of The Alan Bown! He had negotiated a deal with the BBC to lease out recordings from various radio shows of the 60's and had already released a compilation album of other bands. Nigel sent me a tape of the BBC recordings he had of The Alan Bown! featuring Jess Roden and Robert Palmer.

I have to say that I was pleasantly surprised with the sound quality and the performances of the band on these recordings. In fact, they captured the live sound of the band better than some of the albums we made!

I agreed that these tracks should be heard and the wheels have now been put in motion for Top Sounds to include three tracks of ours, for a release on CD in 2007. These will be;

1   'Pandora's Golden Heebie Jeebies'
        Top Gear, recorded 29th November 1967

2   'Magic Handkerchief'
        Saturday Club, recorded 2nd July 1968

3   'Movie Star baby'
        Radio One Club, recorded 30th June 1969

(Top Sounds can be contacted by e-mail at Virginsleep@aol.com).

30

ENCORE

As a performing musician, I have long since passed the baton to my son Julian. He is now an accomplished professional drummer and a qualified music teacher.

To keep the embouchure in shape, a brass player has to play everyday. Since I turned my attention to the management of artists and other pursuits, I have not maintained my 'chops' but I still have the blue trumpet. So who knows, one day I may pick it up and blow some of the riffs from The Alan Bown Set that can still be heard today on I-Tunes®!

To those of you who used to come and see the band, once again I say a sincere 'Thank you.' It was always the excitement of live audiences that kept my batteries charged. To those of you who never saw the band, I hope that this book recreates the magic of those times as much as it has for me.

DISCOGRAPHY
SINGLES

THE JOHN BARRY SEVEN

Twenty Four Hours Ago (Suede) Active Music

Seven Faces (Bown, Mansfield) EMI Music Ltd

Released 1964 on Columbia DB7414

THE ALAN BOWN SET

Can't Let Her Go (Leese) Anim Music

I'm The One (Curtis Mayfield) Ivan Mogull Music

Released 1965 on Pye 7N15934

Baby Don't Push Me (Townsrow) Pall Mall Music

Everything's Gonna Be Alright (Mitchell) Burlington Music

Released 1966 on Pye 7N 17084

Headline News (Hamilton, Morris, Hatcher) Essex Music

Mr Pleasure (Creighton, Stafford)* Pall Mall Music

Released 1966 on Pye 7N17148

*The names Creighton and Stafford were pseudonyms for Bannister and Bown. Jeff Bannister lived in Creighton Road and Alan Bown lived in Stafford Avenue. The writers had to use this tactic because Alan was still signed to EMI publishers at the time, a legacy of The John Barry Seven. A bona fide publishing agreement was secured soon after the release of 'Headline News'.

Emergency 999 (Korda) Welbeck Music

Settle Down (Bown, Bannister) Pall Mall

Released 1966 on Pye 7N17192

Gonna Fix You Good (Randazzo, Pike) Carlin Music

I Really Really Care (Bown, Bannister) Pall Mall

Released 1967 on Pye 7N17256

THE ALAN BOWN!

Toyland (Catchpole, Roden) Campbell Connelly

Technicolour Dream (Bown, Bannister) King Publishing Co

Released 1967 on MGM 1355

Story Book (Bown, Bannister) Campbell Connelly

Little Lesley (Catchpole, Roden) Campbell Connelly

Released 1968 on MGM 1387

We Can Help You (Patrick Campbell-Lyons, Alex Spyropoulos) MCPS

Magic Handkerchief (Bown, Bannister, Catchpole, Roden)
                    Campbell Connelly

Released 1968 on Music Factory* CUB 1   *A subsidiary of MGM

Still as Stone (Roden, Catchpole, Bannister Bown) Robbins Music/EMI

Wrong Idea (Roden, Catchpole, Bannister, Bown) Robbins Music/EMI

Released June 1969 on Deram DM 259

Gypsy Girl (Bown, Bannister) Robbins Music/EMI

All I Can (Catchpole) Robbins Music/EMI

Released October 1969 on Deram DM 278

ALAN BOWN – SOLO PROJECTS

Moanin' (J Hendricks/B Timmons) Key Music.

Time to Change (Bown, Bannister) April Music

Released 20th June 1975 on CBS 3366

Rockford Files (Post, Carpenter) Leeds Music.

I Don't Know (Bown, Hine) April Music/McIver Hine Music.

Released 31st October 1975 on CBS 3721

BYRNE AND BOWN:

Dancing at the Rubber Ring (Byrne and Bown) OK Music/Black Neon Ltd

Because of You (S, Byrne) OK Music/Black Neon Ltd

Released 1979 on Acrobat Records 144.678

———————

DISCOGRAPHY
ALBUMS

LONDON SWINGS LIVE AT THE MARQUEE CLUB

Side One : Jimmy James & The Vagabonds

Side Two : The Alan Bown Set - featuring the following;

It's Growing (Robinson – Moore) Jobette Music UK

Emergency 999 (Korda) Welbeck Music

I Need You (Mayfield) EMI Music

Sunny (Hebb) Campbell Connelly

Headline News (Hamilton, Morris, Hatcher) Essex Music

Down in the Valley (Burke, Berns) Carlin Music

The Boomerang (Ott/Covey/Randolph) Carlin Music

Recorded Live at The Marquee Club Sunday, 25th September 1966

Released on Pye NPL 18156 Mono

OUTWARD BOWN

Side One

Toyland	(Catchpole, Roden) Campbell Connelly
Magic Handkerchief	(Bown, Bannister, Catchpole, Roden) Robbins Music Corp
Mutiny	(Catchpole, Roden, Bown, Bannister) Robbins Music Corp
All Along the Watchtower	(Dylan) Feldman & Co Ltd
Sally Green	(Bown, Bannister) Robbins Music Corp
Penny for your Thoughts	(Bown, Bannister) Robbins Music Corp

Side Two

Story Book   (Bown, Bannister) Campbell Connelly
Technicolour Dream   (Bown, Bannister) King Music Ltd
Love is a Beautiful Thing (Pearl) Yale Music Corp
Violin Shop   (Catchpole) Robbins Music Corp
You're Not in My Class (Bown, Bannister) Forecast Music Ltd
My Girl the Month of May (Dion Dimucci) Copyright Control

Produced by Mike Hurst

Released 1968 on MGM Records CUBLS 1 Stereo

THE ALAN BOWN!

Side One

My Friend   (Davis, Scaggs)
Strange Little Friend   (Bown, Bannister)
Elope   (Roden, Catchpole)
Perfect Day   (Bown, Bannister)
All I Can   (Catchpole)
Friends in St Louis   (Bown, Bannister)

Side Two

The Prisoner   (The Alan Bown)
Kick me out   (Catchpole, Anthony)
Children of the Night   (Bown, Bannister)
Gypsy Girl   (Bown, Bannister)

Released 1969 on Deram SML 1049 Stereo
Robert Palmer sang lead vocals except on 'All I Can', which featured Tony and
Vic and sections of 'The Prisoner', which featured Jeff and Tony.
John Hemmings : Trombone
Produced by Mike Hurst.
String Arrangements by Phil Dennys
All songs published by Robbins Music Corporation except 'My Friend'
(Apple Publications)

The Alan Bown! album was also released in USA 1969 DES 18032 through A
Gallico Music Corp (BMI) 101 West 55th Street New York. ('My Friend' was
substituted with 'Still as Stone'). Jess Roden sang lead vocals, with above

exceptions. The double sleeve portrayed individual photos of the band and also included an image of Robert Palmer. However, Robert's voice was not featured on the album. It was a ploy to introduce his name and image into the American market. Under Jess's image was the name Jeremey Roden!

LISTEN

Side One

Wanted Man	(Bown, Bannister, Catchpole)
Crash Landing	(Bown, Bannister, Catchpole)
Loosen Up	(The Alan Bown)
Pyramid	(Bannister)
Forever	(The Alan Bown)

Side Two

Curfew	(The Alan Bown – lyric Bannister)
Make us all Believe	(Bown, Bannister Catchpole)
Make up your Mind	(The Alan Bown)
Get Myself Straight	(Bown, Bannister, Palmer)

(Robert Palmer's lead vocals replaced by Gordon Neville, prior to release).

Released 1970 on Island ILPS 9131 Stereo
Produced by Mel Collins for Active Records and Tapes Ltd
All songs published by Robbins Music Corporation

ALAN BOWN – STRETCHING OUT

Side One

The Messenger (Bown, Bannister)
Find a Melody   (Bown, Bannister)
Up Above my Hobby Horses Head* (Havens)

Side Two

Turning Point   (Anthony)
Build me a Stage (Bown, Bannister)
Stretching Out   (Bown, Bannister)

Released 1971 on Island ILPS 9163 Stereo

Produced by Mel Collins for Active Records and Tapes Ltd
All songs published by Robbins Music Corporation except * (Feldman's Music)
Recorded at Island Studios 11 Basing St London in May and June 1971

EL PEA

Double Album compilation featuring all Island recording artists

Side One : Track 3

Thru the Night (The Alan Bown –lyric Bown, Bannister)
               Robbins Music Corp

Released on Island 1971 IDLP-2-1

JONESY – KEEPING UP

Side One

Masquerade   (J. Kaleth)
Sunset and Evening Star (J. Evan-Jones)
Preview   (J. Kaleth)
Questions and Answers   (J. Kaleth)

Side Two

Critique   (J. Evan-Jones)
Duet   (J. Evan-Jones)
Song   (J. Kaleth)
Children   (J. Evan-Jones)

John Evan-Jones : Guitars Vocals
Jamie Kaleth : Keyboards, lead vocals
Alan Bown : Electric trumpet, electric flugelhorn, percussion
Gypsy Jones : Electric bass, recorders, lead vocals
Plug Thomas : Drums, percussion, vocals
Released 1973 on Dawn* DNLS 3048   *A subsidiary of PYE records
Produced by John Evan-Jones and Jonesy.
Recorded at Escape Studios, March 1973. All songs published by Bruno Music

JONESY – GROWING

Side One

Can You Get That Together   (Jonesy)
Waltz for Yesterday   (Jonesy)
Know Who Your Friends Are (Jonesy)

Side Two

Growing   (Jonesy)
Hard Road (Jonesy)
Jonesy   (Jonesy)

Released on Dawn DNLS 3055
Produced by Rupert Hine.
All songs written by Jonesy and published by Heat Music
Recorded at Escape Studios and Air Studios September and October 1973

THE ALAN BOWN! - KICK ME OUT

Side One

My Friend
Strange Little Friend
Elope
Perfect Day
All I Can
Friends in St Louis,
Still as Stone

Side Two

The Prisoner
Kick Me Out
Children of the Night
Gypsy Girl
Wrong Idea

Kick Me Out was a vinyl compilation album released in 1985 on See For
Miles Records The title was taken from one of the tracks. All the vocals were
by Robert Palmer. The sleeve notes were written by Chris Welch.

**THE EARLY YEARS – ROBERT PALMER with THE ALAN BOWN!**

Side One

My Friend
Strange Little Friend
Elope
Perfect Day
All I Can
Friends In St Louis
Still As Stone

Side Two

The Prisoner
Kick Me Out
Children Of The Night
Gypsy Girl
Wrong Idea

Released in 1987 on C5 Records (C5 501) 12 inch Vinyl
All titles under copyright with original publishers

CD RE-RELEASES :

THE ALAN BOWN! – OUTWARD BOWN Plus

Re-issued 1988 by See For Miles Records Ltd : SEECD 490
The compilation CD included all the tracks from Outward Bown plus extra tracks;
'Little Lesley', 'We Can Help You', 'Technicolour Dream' and 'Toyland'.

THE ALAN BOWN! – LISTEN & STRETCHING OUT

Re-issued 1993 by Edsel Records, a division of Demon Records : EDCD 362
The compilation CD included all tracks from both entitled albums

THE ALAN BOWN! - OUTWARD BOWN

Re-issued 1998 by Tenth Planet Records : TP027. Limited to 1,000 copies

THE ALAN BOWN SET – EMERGENCY 999

Re-issued 2000 by Sanctuary Records Group : NEMCD 483
The compilation CD included all the early Alan Bown Set PYE singles plus 'Jeu De Massacre' EP tracks and 'London Swings Live at The Marquee Club'.

Further publications from Banland Publishing Ltd.

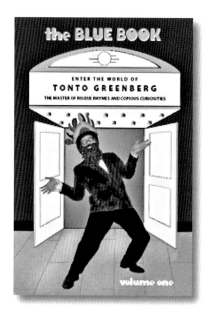

The first in a series of books which takes a darker look at contemporary life from an adult perspective.

Witty and humorous, with spoof adverts, stories and rhymes.

Richly illustrated.

ISBN: 978-0-9551513-0-9

A glossary of over 200 fully illustrated chords, easily played using this unique method.

Suitable for beginners, intermediates and professionals alike.

Available in the USA for over a decade, now available in the UK.

ISBN: 978-0-9551513-1-6

Forthcoming publications from Banland Publishing Ltd.

An isolated country cottage
hides a sinister secret, which
engulfs an unsuspecting
married couple.

ISBN: 978-0-9551513-3-0

A clandestine organisation
is using an ancient arcane
process to infiltrate and
control the higher realms of
global society.

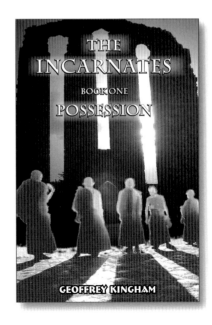

ISBN: 978-0-9551513-4-7

www.banlandpublishing.com